PEDRO LASCH

20 22

ART BIENNIALS AND OTHER GLOBAL DISASTERS

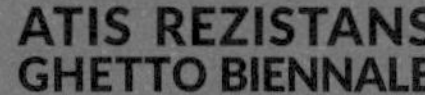

ATIS REZISTANS
GHETTO BIENNALE

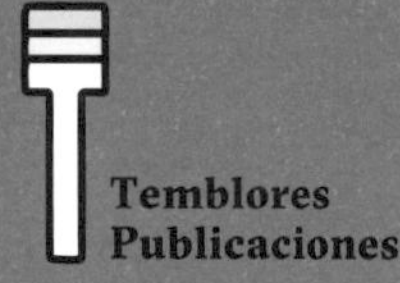

Contents

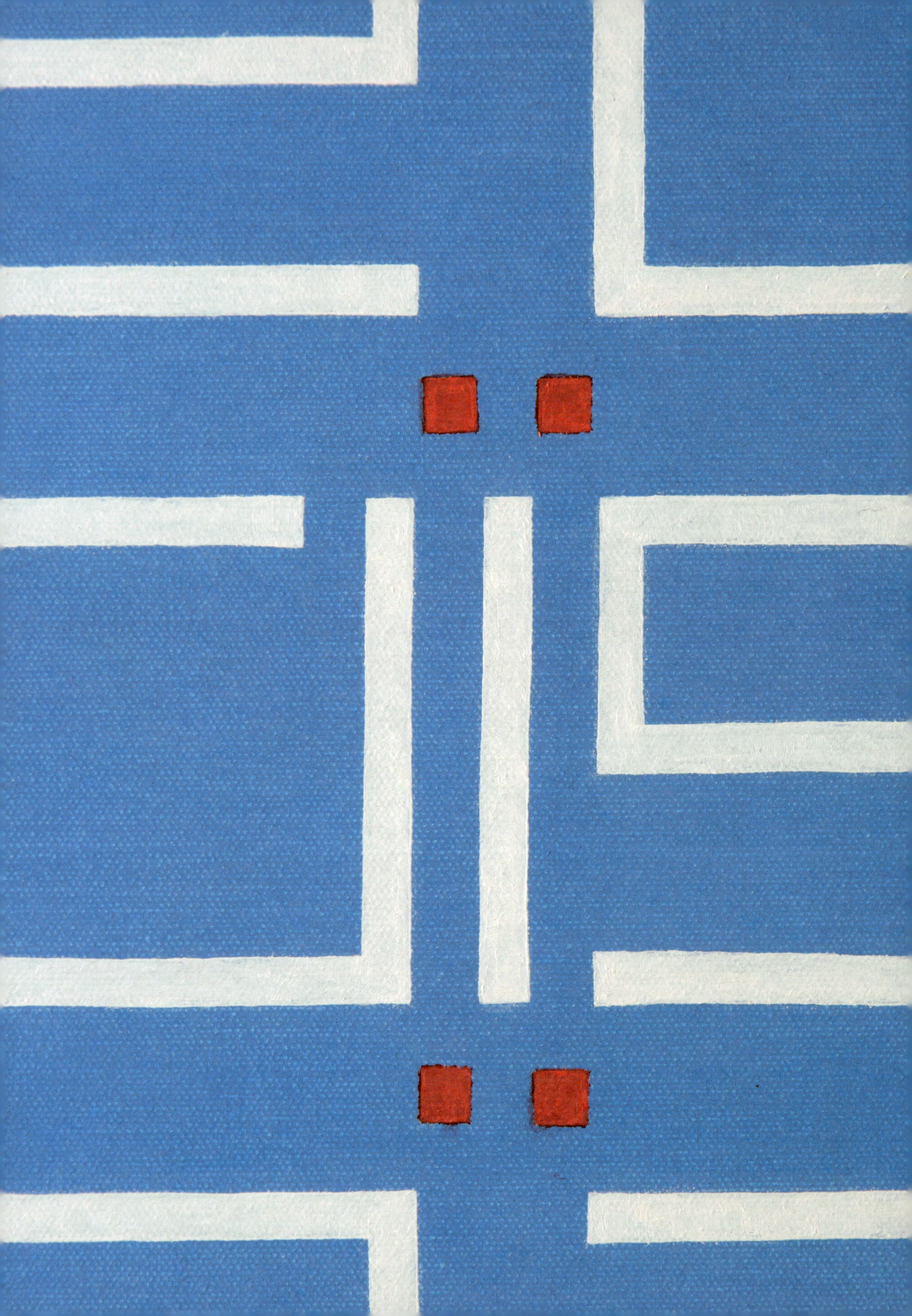

20 22: Introduction and Artist Statement

At the end of 2009, I was working with Leah Gordon, Andre Eugène, and Port-au-Prince collective Atis Rezistans on the first edition of the Ghetto Biennale (2009). I produced two projects in Haiti at the time, one in collaboration with Miguel Rojas-Sotelo and the other with Esther Gabara, both documented later in this book. The event was truly memorable and successful in many ways, but despite our numerous efforts to bring the relevance of the Biennale and Haiti to international attention, there was little to no art or political media engagement with the event. In early January 2010, only a few days after I had left Port-au-Prince and the Ghetto Biennale had ended, Haiti was shaken by one of the most tragic earthquakes in human history.[1] Many thousands died or disappeared, including collaborators with whom we had worked at the Biennale. The same international media that had consistently neglected this land had now suddenly descended upon it, turning it into a global

—

1   The earthquake that struck Port-au-Prince, Haiti, on January 12, 2010, registered a magnitude of seven on the Richter scale, severely impacting the island. The disaster resulted in the loss of over 200,000 lives and affected more than two million people. However, the extent of the tragedy was not solely due to the natural phenomenon itself but rather to underlying economic, social, and urban vulnerabilities, the fragility of the state, and centuries of harmful international policies against Haiti, beginning with the imposition of a punishing foreign debt by the French after Haiti's revolution and abolition of slavery in 1804.

media event for many months to come. TV and radio news pundits began to describe the humanitarian effort in Haiti as a "third U.S. military front"—the first two being Afghanistan and Iraq, of course. Previously uninterested art critics were now eager to engage with contemporary Haitian art. The very artists who had given birth to the Ghetto Biennale in 2009, mostly to be ignored at the time, were celebrated in 2011 with the creation of a Haitian Pavilion at none other than La Biennale di Venezia. A particular conversation from 2009 pre-earthquake Haiti resonated in my mind in this new context. A man asked, "Do you know what our politicians are hoping for?" I shook my head, not knowing the answer. "Another disaster," he replied.

The *Art Biennials and Other Global Disasters* series takes its point of departure from this personal experience, which is obviously not exclusive to Haiti. Over the last few decades art biennials seem to have grown at the same rate as global disasters—a parallel that may instantly recall Naomi Klein's book *The Shock Doctrine: The Rise of Disaster Capitalism*, in which the author exposes the relation between predatory capitalism and global catastrophes.[2] Starting in 2010, my first artworks in the series were a set of research diagrams where I presented this partly absurd analogy between mega exhibitions and disasters in rationalist terms, as well as a set of monumental banners, where I provocatively paired well-known art events with global political, economic, or ecological disasters. Elaborated through a process of drawing, painting, and digital designs, each banner offers a different challenge to viewers and participants, by the sheer specificity of its double naming. The banner "Venice / Chernobyl" triggers very different associations and significations from "Sharjah / Kanungu" or "Kassel / Banqiao." Additional layers of meaning appear through the physical and cultural context in which these seemingly celebratory banners are placed, whether in an art gallery in Beirut (2013), at the Bienal de La Habana (2015), or in an art exhibition at a train station in Montevideo (2015).

Within the framework of these intentional provocations, I developed other works over the years to collectively reflect upon questions such as these: What analogies between today's preeminent global art events and international relief efforts might be relevant, beyond

—

2   Naomi Klein, *The Shock Doctrine: The Rise of Disaster Capitalism* (New York: Picador, 2007).

the expensive logistical operations that involve the temporary incursion of hundreds or thousands of people to both biennials and disaster zones? What constitutes a memorable event today, one that involves art but also goes far beyond it? What categories do we use to reconstitute the geographic links between cities in rapidly changing structures of culture, trade, and finance? What are the ways in which art has been used at a massive scale to legitimize oppressive regimes and economic systems? Can sites of disaster or armed conflict also be economic and cultural hubs, or are these two terms mutually exclusive? This book brings together, for the first time, an archive compiled from this multiyear artistic investigation, each chapter addressing specific contexts where new works were staged and produced. Included in the book and addressing some of these questions are also two essays by curators Octavian Esanu and Dannys Montes de Oca, both of whom brought the series to highly meaningful contexts in its early phase—Lebanon and Cuba, respectively.

The period from 2020 to 2022, however, gives this book its title and also marks the series' most intensive and final phase. Ghetto Biennale's 2022 presentation at St. Kunigundis Church in Kassel for documenta fifteen provided a meaningful cultural context to close the project, to come full circle, so to speak, and bring it back to its origins in Haiti, especially as reality had now connected the grassroots Haitian counter-biennial with one of the world's most highly attended, critically respected, and well-funded mega exhibitions. Global events provided the rest: Unprecedented environmental disaster, a global pandemic unlike anything we had experienced since the emergence of HIV/AIDS, and the powerful rise of new forms of right-wing nationalism. All three have posed key challenges to the historical claims and operational mechanisms of international art biennials and neoliberalism overall, and are therefore a central part of the most recent works in this book.

The artworks presented at documenta with Ghetto Biennale and Atis Rezistans appear under the name of *20 22: The Common Wind*, in reference to the year, as well as the brilliant writings by the late historian Julius S. Scott.[3] The same numbers 20 and 22, with a space in between, appear obsessively in every painting of

—

3   Julius S. Scott, *The Common Wind: Afro-American Currents in the Age of the Haitian Revolution* (London: Verso, 2018).

a cycle with that name, all painted over three years and sketched out during the worst lockdown period of the COVID-19 pandemic. These works are a desperate attempt to bring color to the gray monotony of a period marked by so much death and mourning, but they also aim to remember events and figures in a time when our individual and collective survival became the universal foreground that threatened to erase all else. In this publication, the paintings accompany quoted statements and ideas from fourteen prominent curators, who participated in a globally accessible online series I also produced during the Spring 2021 lockdown. Staged as a free, weekly conversation series, attended by over 3,000 viewers over fourteen consecutive weeks, *20 22 The Ongoing Biennial* addressed many of the topics mentioned above, also creating a permanent archive of this exceptional time.

It would be a mistake not to address the current documenta in relation to the topic of disasters. Personally, I think ruangrupa's documenta fifteen will be seen, in time, as one of boldest and most interesting experiments in cultural production of its kind, still too radical to be embraced by critics, curators, and collectors, many of whom were alienated from the outset by the collective's deliberate lack of reliance on the influence and resources of the professional art class, bypassing traditional mechanisms of validation and sup-port. The institution itself, however, seems to have been unprepared to deal with the intensity of the debates surrounding Palestine and anti-Semitism as these took over so much of the conversation for months before the show opened and up until its current final weeks. Global anti-Semitism, Nazi history, and the Holocaust have all been part of the series presented in this book since the introduction of the Degenerate Art exhibition [*Entartete Kunst*] into research diagrams (2010) and the figure of Goebbels into *Islands of Tragedy and Fantasy* at the Bienal de La Habana (2015). The history of white supremacy also appears prominently on the banner placed on the tower of St. Kunigundis Church when documenta fifteen first opened. Israel's illegal and violent occupation of Palestinian lands has likewise been addressed in the *20 22 Painting Cycle* through a painting referencing Gaza. Amid weekly threats of censorship, the avoidable removal of artworks, and a growing tendency of institutions and artists alike to posture rather than negotiate, it is with great sadness and concern for the future of art exhibitions that I close this piece. It seems to have taken a collective from Indonesia and an unprecedented number of racialized artists coming to documenta for Germans to accept that this international event is also first and foremost a German exhibition. For the sake of the future of this show and the other important exhibitions this book is devoted to, I hope these are but the painful signs of a new and better beginning.

Pedro Lasch, September 19, 2022, Kassel, Germany

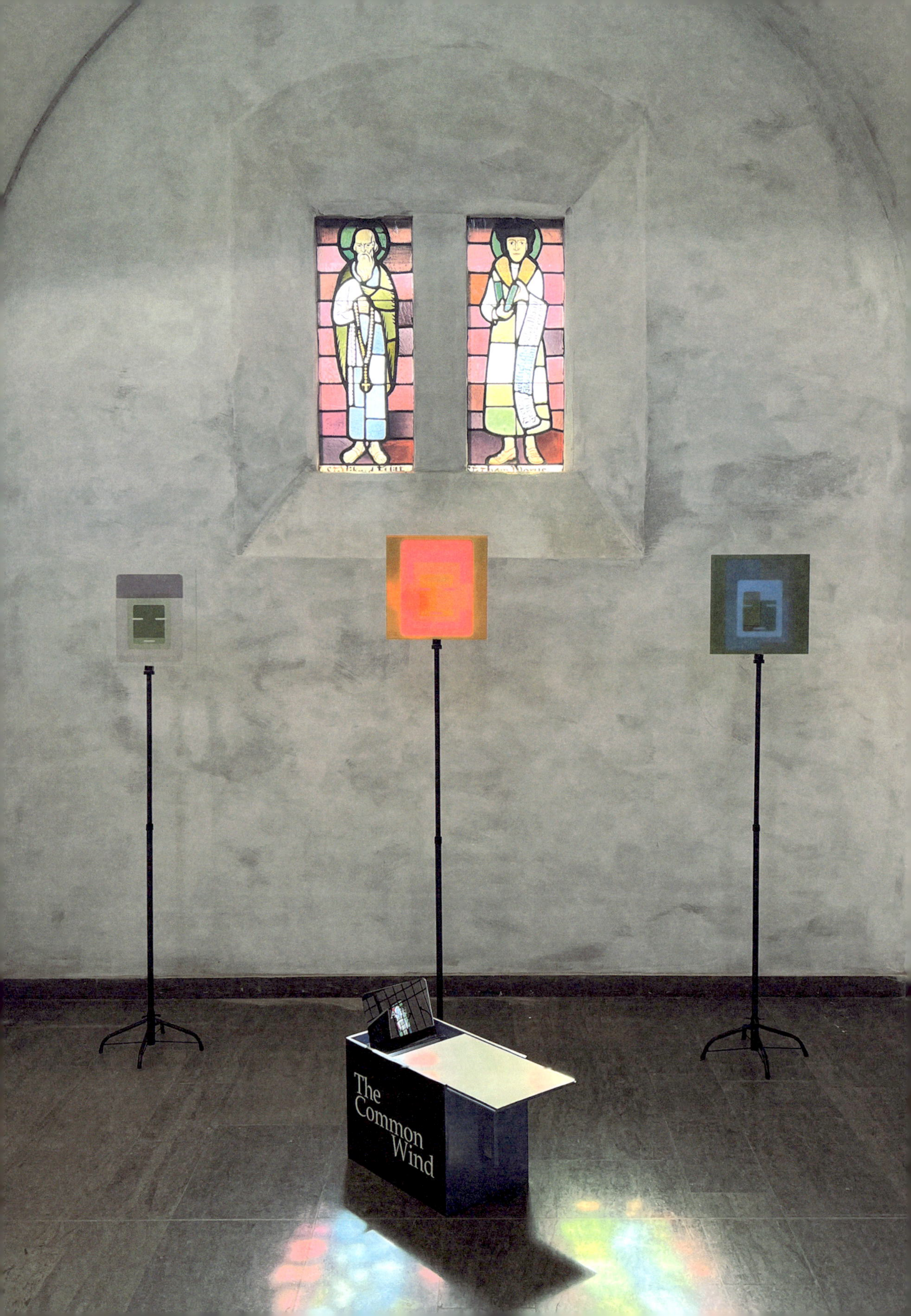
The
Common
Wind

The Common Wind: From the Ghetto Biennale to documenta fifteen

This chapter presents the arc that connects the works made in 2009 for the first edition of the Ghetto Biennale in Haiti with those produced for the collective during its 2022 participation at documenta fifteen. The following pages include texts and images for all works included in both exhibitions. The projects produced in Haiti in 2009 were a collaboration with Miguel Rojas-Sotelo titled *Bicentenario y Narcochingadazo* [Bicentennial and Narcochingadazo], and a series of *Naturalizations* mirror mask workshops created in collaboration with Esther Gabara. Both included the participation of Atis Rezistans members, as did the works presented at documenta fifteen. While it was the experience of the tragic 2010 earthquake in Haiti and its international response that triggered the beginning of the *Art Biennials and Other Global Disasters* series, it is important to stress that the works for Atis Rezistans at documenta are not rooted in disaster but very much the opposite. Framed as an homage to the writings of late historian Julius S. Scott in *The Common Wind*, these interventions echo his book's dedication to the informal communication methods and transnational social networks used by both Haitians and non-Haitians to amplify the message and impact of the Haitian Revolution. They are a joyful dialogue with several generations of Haitian artists in this shared path from Port-au-Prince to Kassel, a path filled with the richness of a long and inspiring political history.

Color Mask Prototypes No. 1–5, 2010
Naturalizations series, 2002–ongoing
Installation (12 × 12 × 0.25 in prototype, stands varying between
range of human heights)
Painted and laser-engraved acrylic sheets displayed on metal stands

Echoing the stained glass windows of St. Kunigundis in Kassel,
these experimental prototypes bring color to the otherwise transparent and reflective mirror mask series the artist has used in many
settings around the world, including the first edition of the Ghetto
Biennale in Haiti in 2009. The prototypes are unique, but all of
them change dramatically with the light's and the viewer's position
toward them, becoming abstract faces in dialogue with the audience
and the sculptures from Grand Rue.

TOP: *Color Mask Prototypes 1–5, 2010.* Trial installation. documenta fifteen, St. Kunigundis Church, Kassel, 2022

BOTTOM: *Color Mask Prototype 4, 2010.* Trial installation. documenta fifteen, St. Kunigundis Church, Kassel, 2022. Works on wall: Edouard Duval-Carrié, *Toussaint Louverture and Dutty Boukman, 2021*

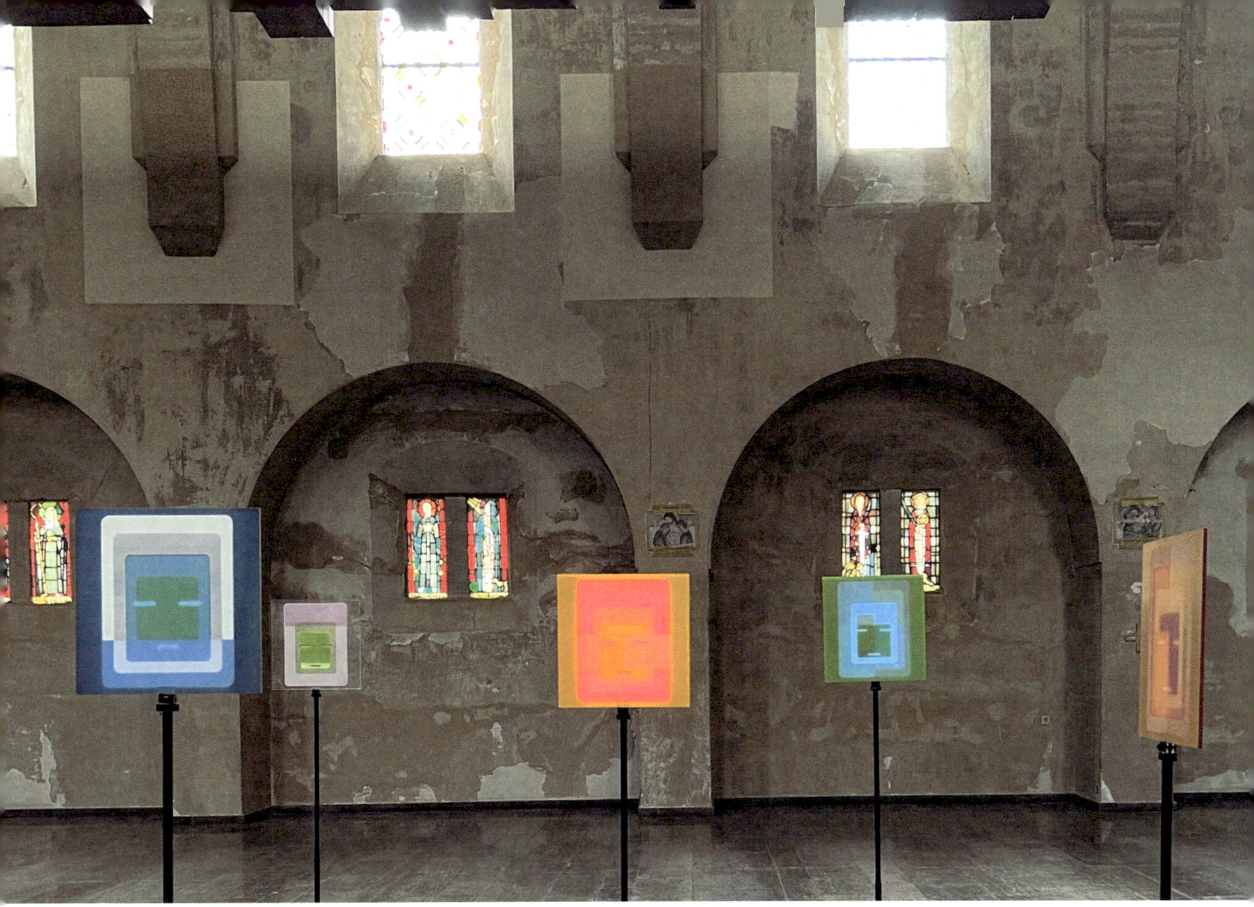

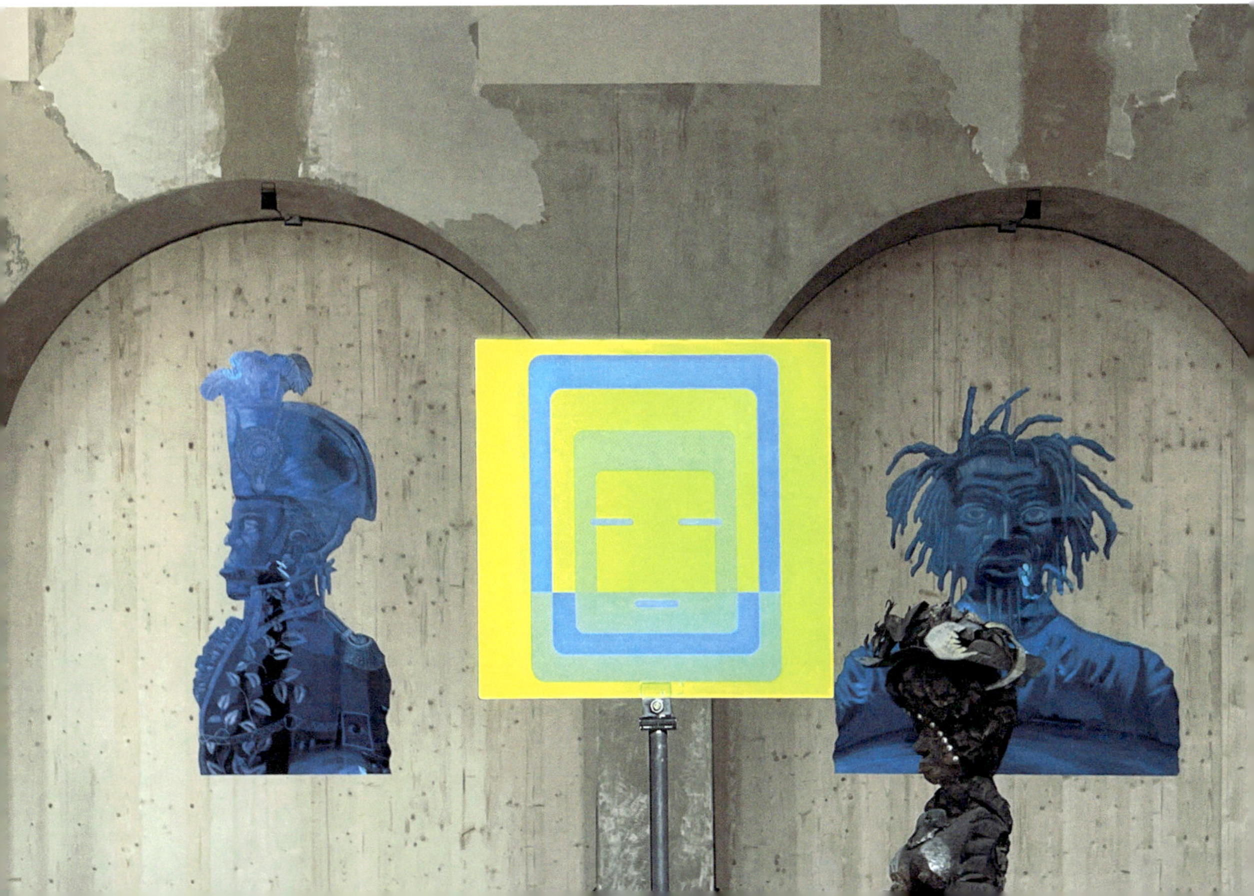

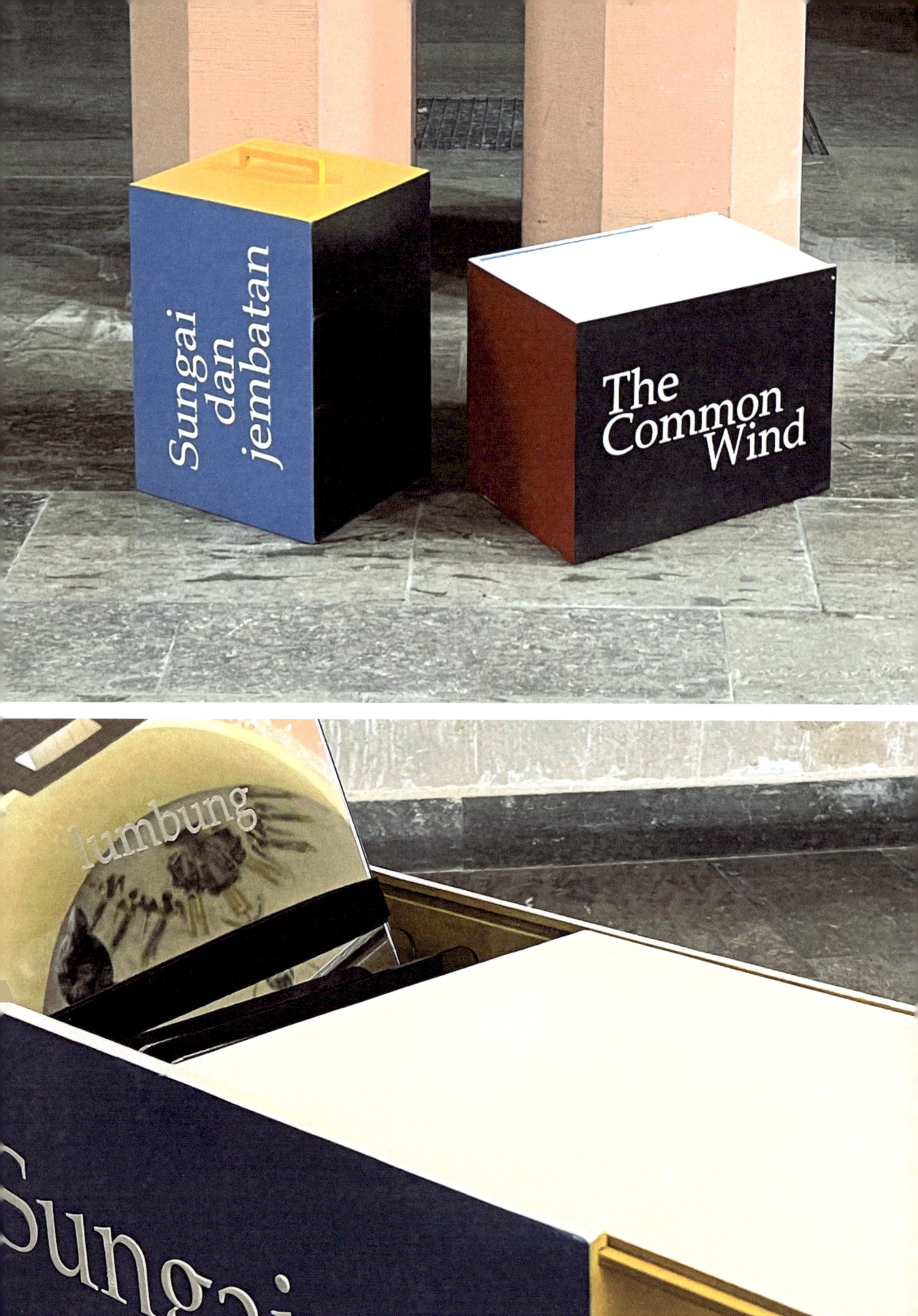

Sungai dan jembatan
The
Common
Wind
lumbung
Sungai

***The Common Wind and River and Bridge Mirror
Mask Box Sets,* Kassel, 2022**
***Naturalizations* series, 2002–ongoing**
Interactive sculpture, 12.5 × 16 × 10.5 in boxes,
each with twenty 8.5 × 11 in engraved mirror masks

At documenta fifteen, these masks were activated by revisiting the
way they had been used during the first Ghetto Biennale in Port-
au-Prince in 2009, as a kind of ambassadors of Atis Rezistans and
Ghetto Biennale, moving from the exhibition space into other areas
of the documenta. The first box focuses on the global impact of the
Haitian Revolution and the work of late historian Julius S. Scott. It
features the title *The Common Wind* in English on one side and its
Haitian Creole translation, *Van Momen An*, on the other. The second
box focuses on ruangrupa's metaphor of an exhibition like documenta or the Ghetto Biennale being a bridge that spans temporarily
over a much more complex continuous past, present, and future of
collective being, presenting the phrase *The River and the Bridge*
in Indonesian as *Sungai dan jembatan* and German as *Die Brücke
und der Fluss*. Participants of the workshops used these masks
to reflect the Atis Rezistans art on their own faces, taking with
them photographs that fused their body with the works, as well as
words engraved on the mirror that were chosen for their relation
to racial emancipation and collective organization. Facilitated by
Lasch and a team of art mediators (called *sobat-sobat* by ruangrupa) these workshops happened on a weekly basis throughout
the hundred days of documenta at St. Kunigundis Church, at the
Fridericianum with RURUKIDS, and throughout Kassel and its
many exhibition venues.

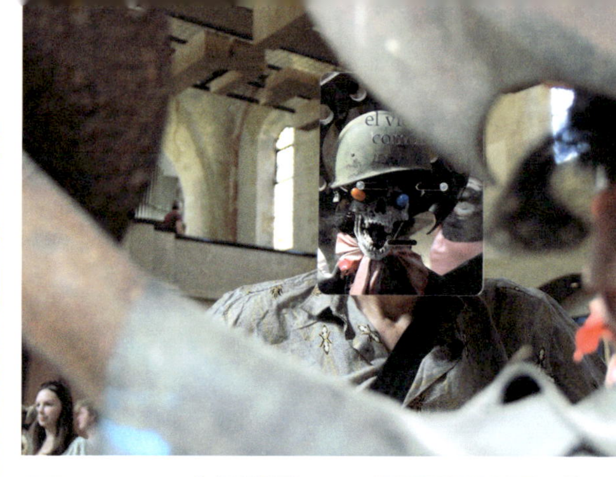
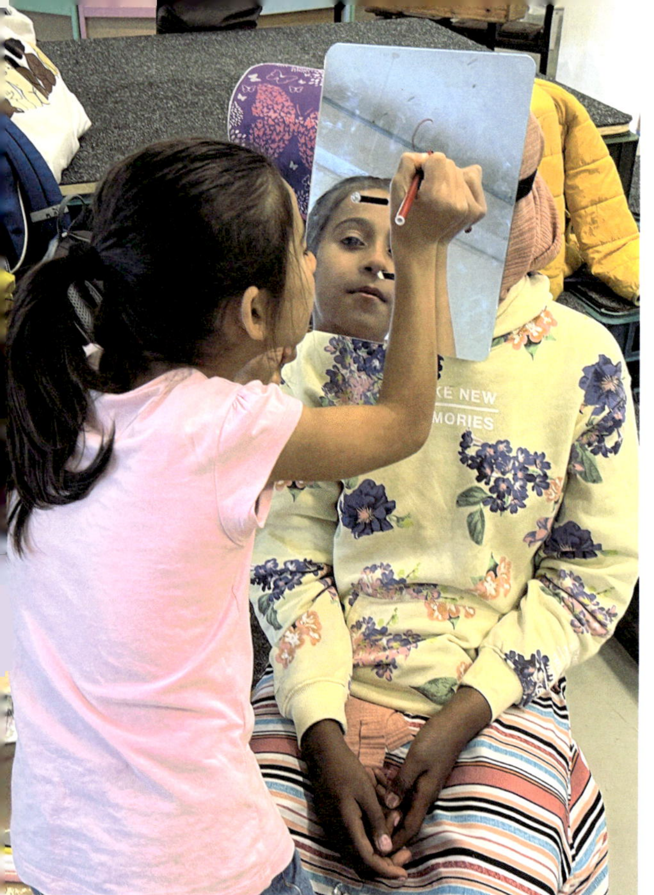
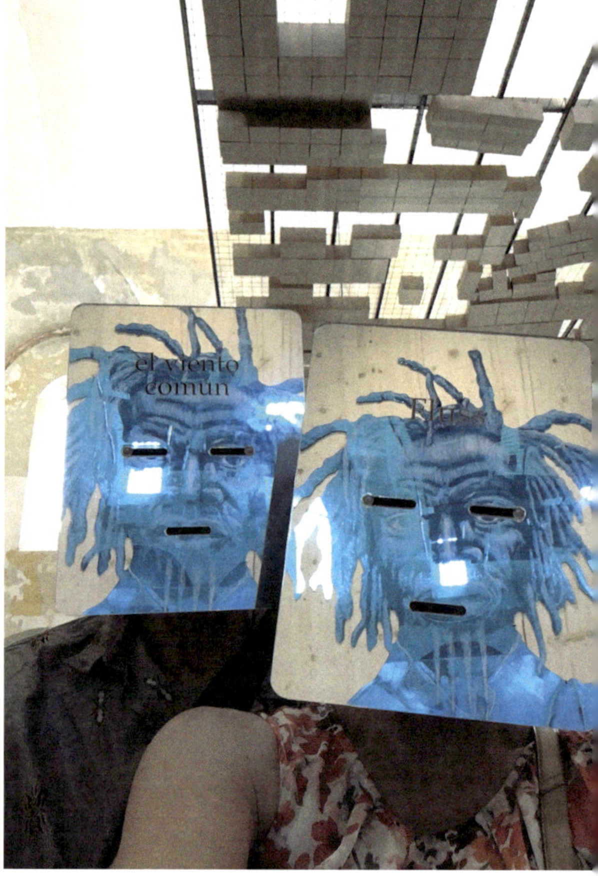
el viento
común
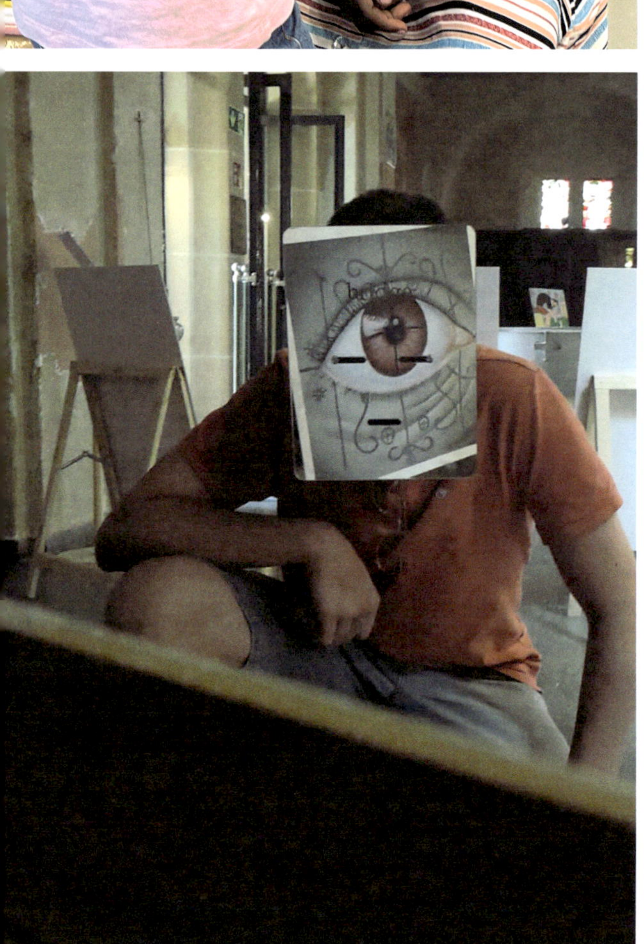
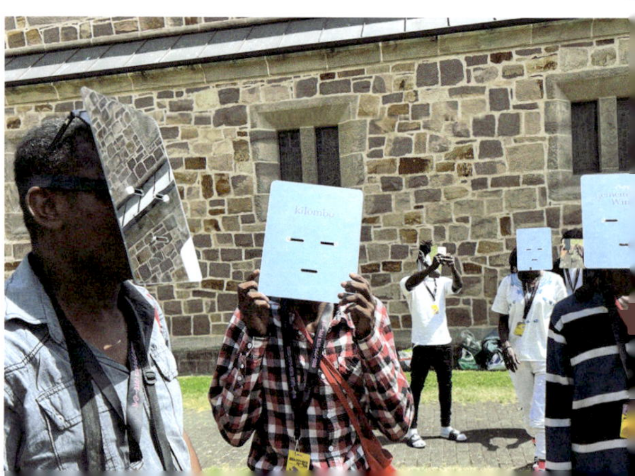

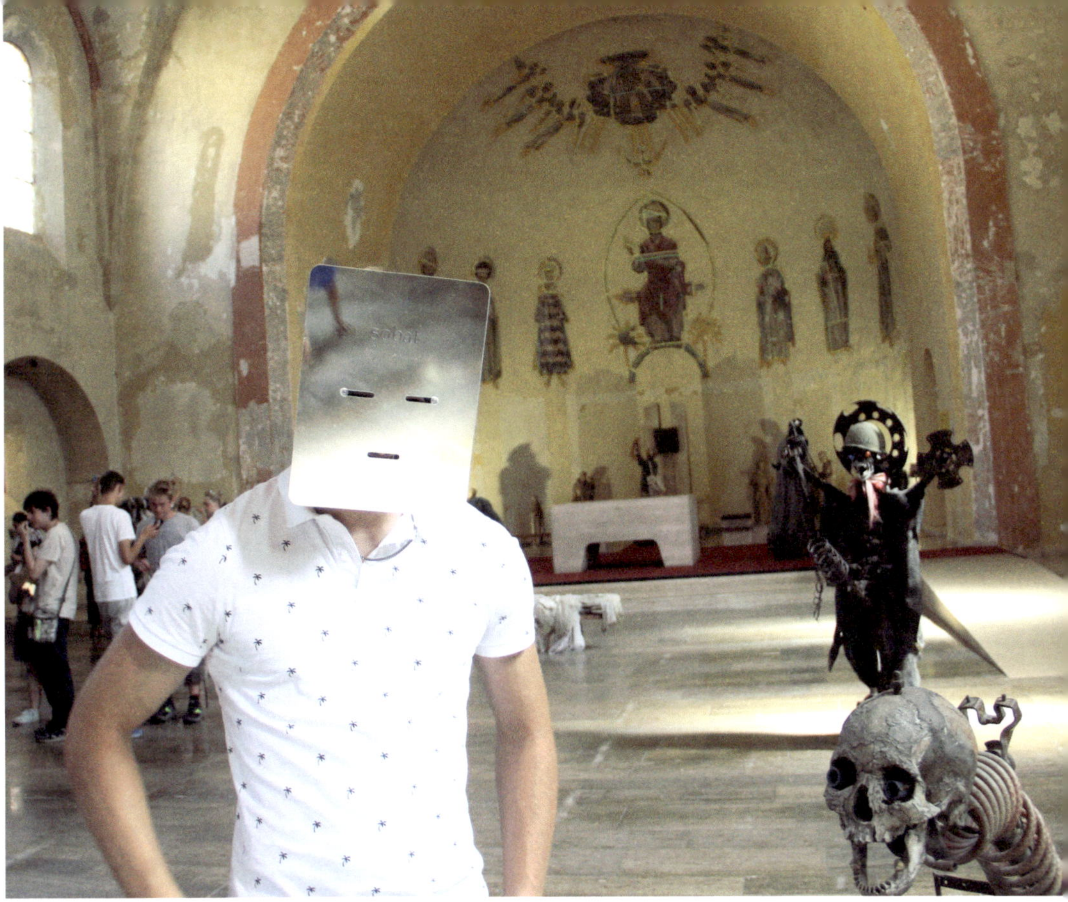

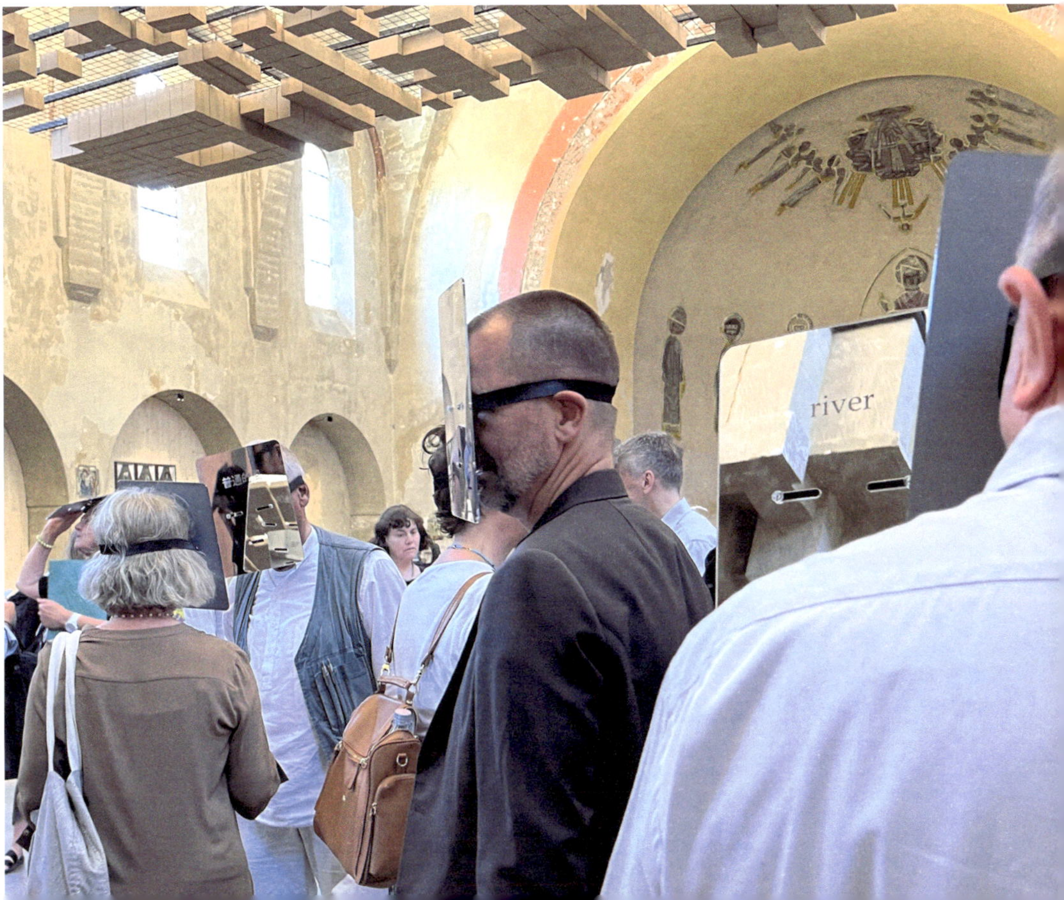

Mirror Mask Workshops. documenta fifteen, St. Kunigundis Church and Fridericianum, Kassel, 2022. Photography: Pedro Lasch, sobat sobat, Atis Rezistans, Robert Hötzel, students from Thomas–Morus–Gymnasium Daun

Grand Rue and Frantz Fanon Workshops, Port-au-Prince, 2009
Naturalizations series, 2002-ongoing
Community workshops in the Grand Rue
neighborhood and local high schools

These mirror mask workshops[1] were intentionally designed for two
very different contexts. The first happened during the beautifully
chaotic opening of the Ghetto Biennale in Grand Rue, with hundreds of people coming in and out, using the masks with very little
verbal interaction and in very unpredictable ways. The second set
consisted of highly focused activities with local high school students
where we took our time experimenting with the masks after exploring Frantz Fanon's *Black Skin, White Masks* and other writings,
the 1805 Haitian constitution's statement of "All distinctions of
color must cease… Haitians will henceforth be known only by the
generic appellation of blacks,"[2] as well as ideas and experiences
that participants brought to the work. All 2009 images shown here
belong to these workshops and were taken by Esther Gabara. A
visual essay entitled *Silent Absence,*[3] not reproduced here, was created by Gabara and Lasch from these images in 2010 to address the
mourning and devastation of that year's unprecedented earthquake.

—

1   For a full bibliography of past uses and methods from the *Naturaliza-
tions* series see: Pedro Lasch, *What Are We Before We Are Naturalized?*
(Washington: Provisions Library, 2015) and *Pedro Lasch: Entre líneas
/ Between the Lines* (exh. cat.), curated by Lucía Sanromán Aranda
(Mexico City: Temblores Publicaciones-INBAL, 2024).

2   *1805 Constitution of Haiti.* Retrieved April 4, 2025, from: https://
wp.stu.ca/worldhistory/wp-content/uploads/sites/4/2015/07/Constitu-
tion-of-Haiti-1805.pdf.

3   *Silent Absence* is an unpublished series of photos and wall texts that
Pedro Lasch was invited to create in 2009.

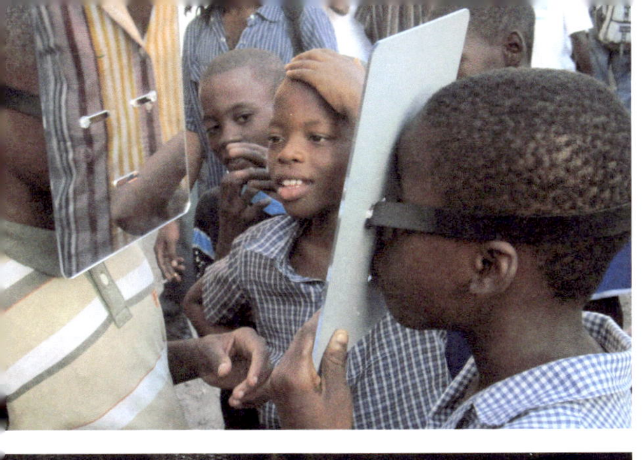
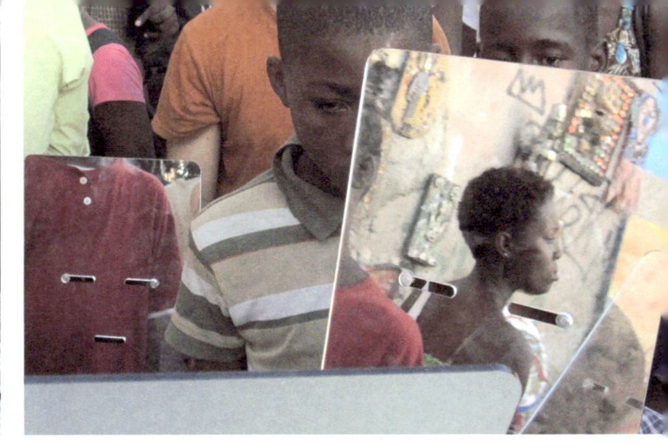
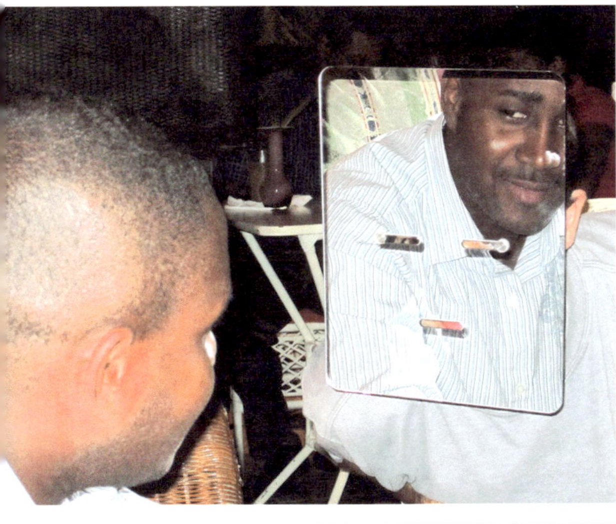
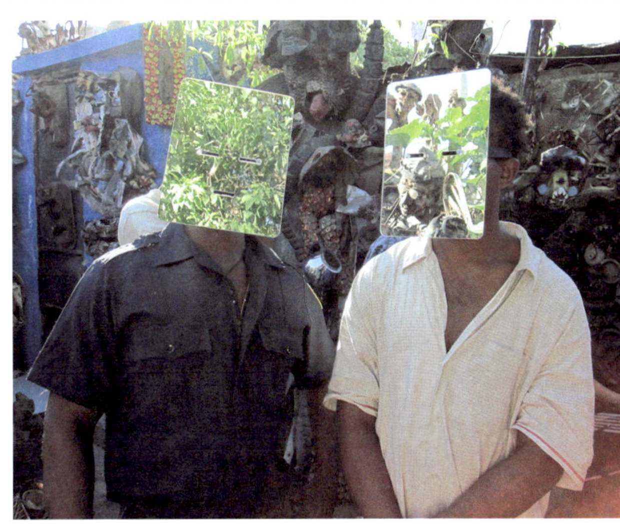
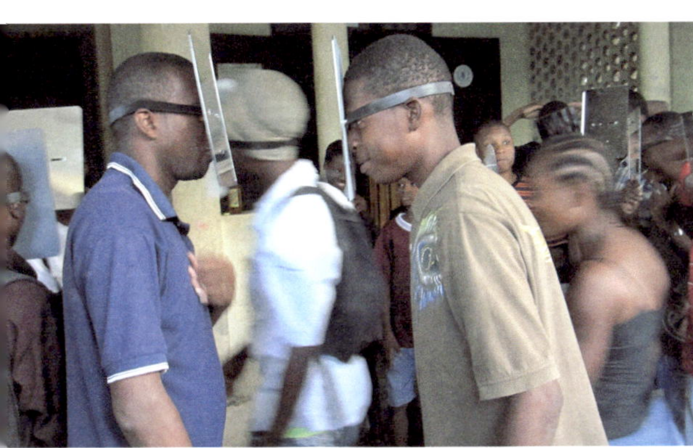
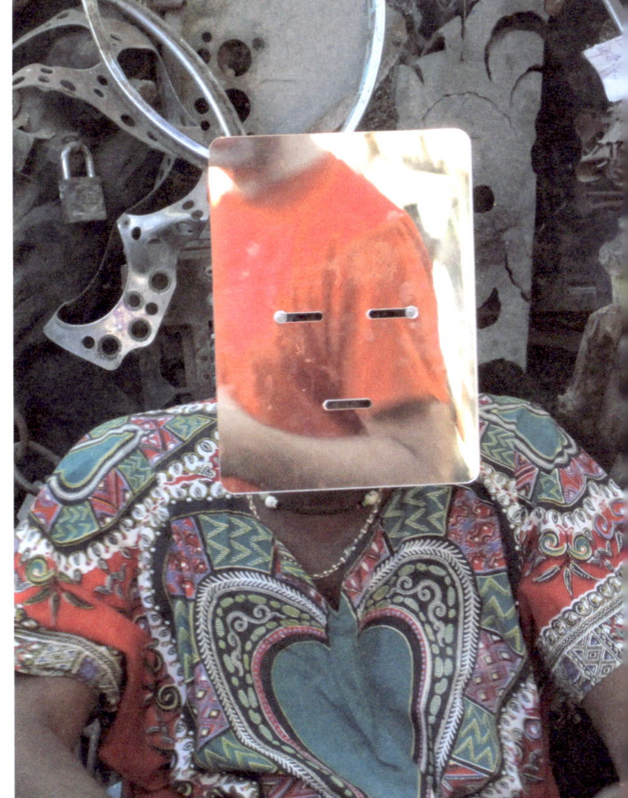
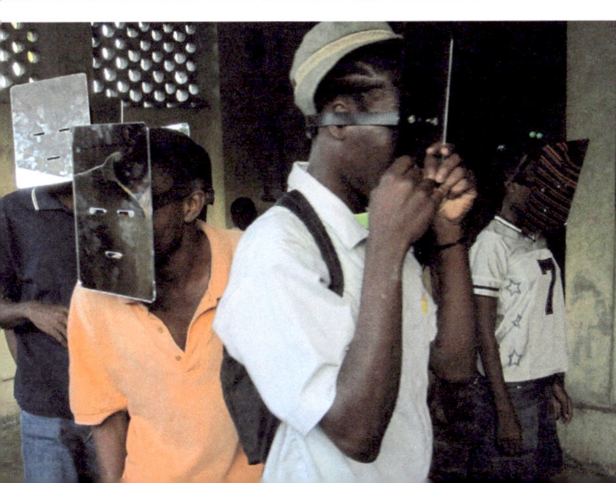

Atis Rezistans / Ghetto Biennale
Pedro Lasch

Museum Etikett No. 57, 2011 aus der *Labels Series*, 2001–2022

Dieses Werk spricht von der Bedeutung des Jahres 2009.

Atis Rezistans / Ghetto Biennale
Pedro Lasch

Label No.57, 2011 from *Labels Series*, 2001–2022

This work speaks of the significance of 2009.

Atis Rezistans / Ghetto Biennale
Pedro Lasch

Label No.61, 2022 from *Labels Series*, 2001–2022

"Poverty is the greatest form of censorship."

André Eugene

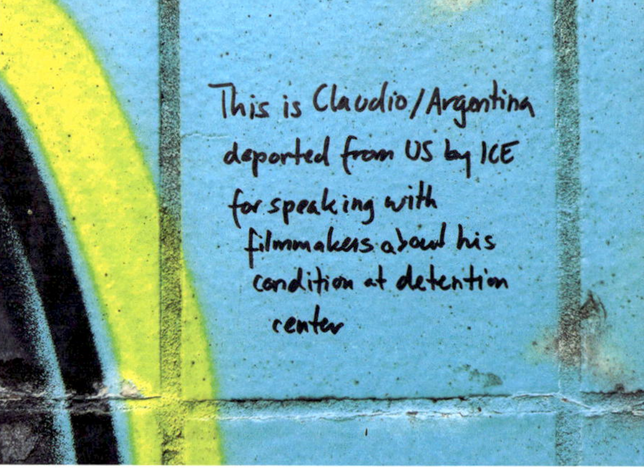

This is Claudio/Argentina
deported from US by ICE
for speaking with
filmmakers about his
condition at detention
center

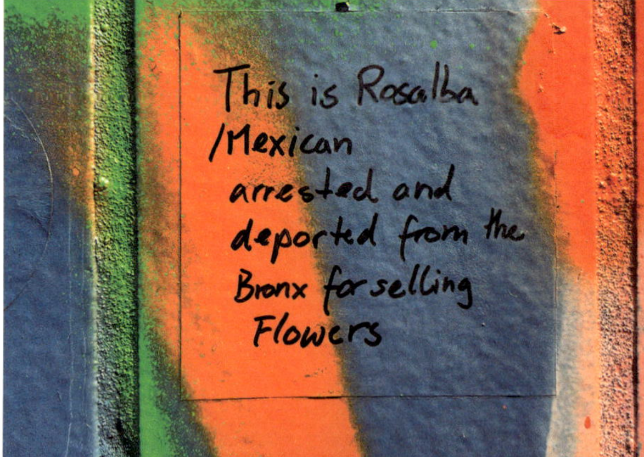

This is Rosalba
/Mexican
arrested and
deported from the
Bronx for selling
Flowers

***documenta Wall Labels*, Kassel, 2022**
***Labels* series, 2001–ongoing**
Standard wall labels with text (variable dimensions)
Print on paper, adapted to the venue in style and form

Starting with five labels at the St. Kunigundis venue, this new
installment of the artist's *Labels* series was applied in Kassel in the
form of succinctly placed museum labels, dispersed as poetic text,
speaking to the surrounding art and environment but written in
ways that escape their original context. Throughout the hundred
days of documenta fifteen, other labels appeared across venues
and collaborative platforms, functioning as ambassadors to Atis
Rezistans and the Ghetto Biennale.

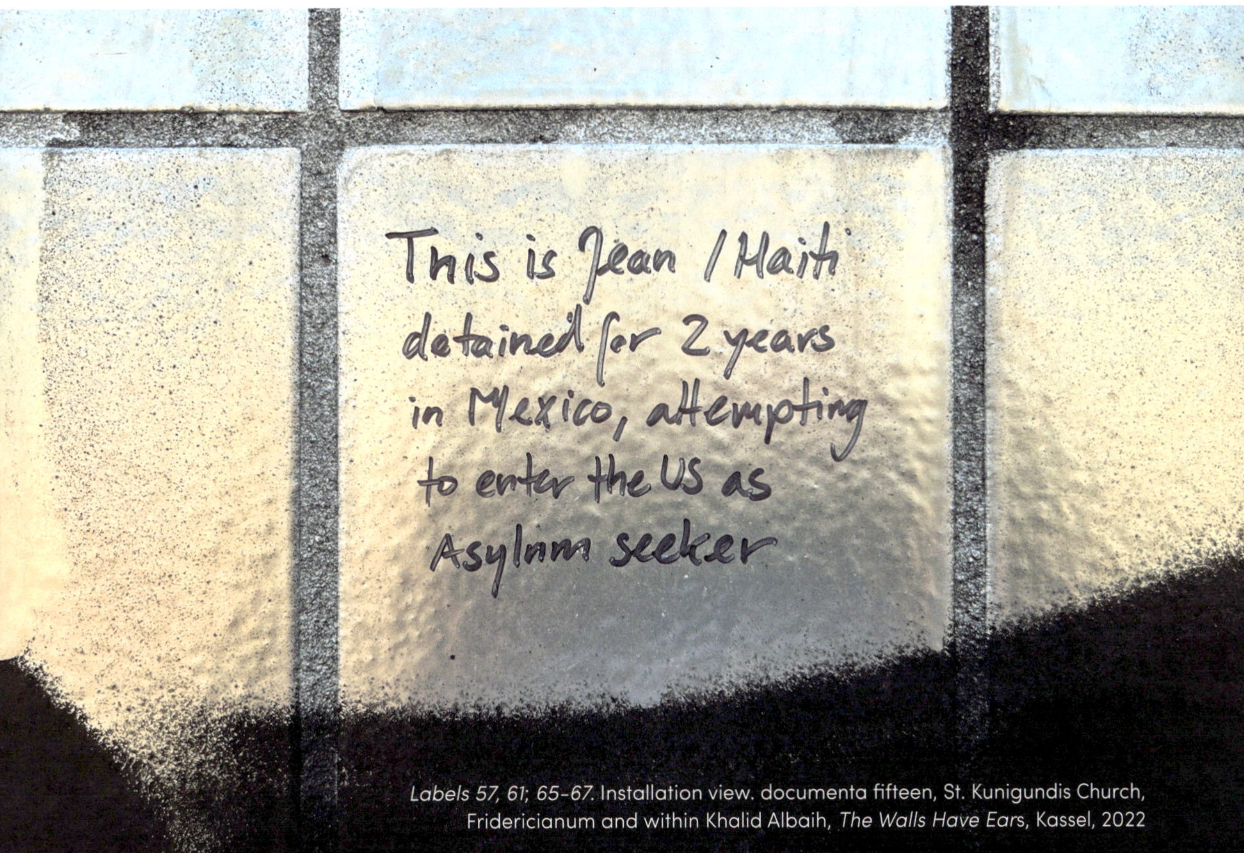

Labels 57, 61; 65–67. Installation view. documenta fifteen, St. Kunigundis Church,
Fridericianum and within Khalid Albaih, *The Walls Have Ears*, Kassel, 2022

Bicentennial & Narcochingadazo, Port-au-Prince, 2009-2010
Community workshops and mural painting in public sites

Developed with Miguel Rojas-Sotelo, as well as local individuals
and organizations at each site it appeared in, the *Narcochingadazo*
project was created under the heading of: *"contra las oligarquías
y sus celebraciones oficiales"* [against oligarchies and their official
celebrations]. The first stage of the project was launched in May
of 2009 on the internet and in a series of performances and social
actions in Spanish and Yucatec Maya in the city of Mérida, Yucatán,
during Arte Nuevo InteractivA IV. Mostly dedicated to establishing
connections with individuals and social groups who wanted to produce counternarratives to the innumerable official Latin American
bicentennial celebrations, this stage concluded with our contributions to the first Ghetto Biennale in Port-au-Prince in December of
2009. The goal was to place Haiti and the Caribbean at the forefront
of the debate and artistic creations around the 2010 bicentennials,
especially as the Haitian Revolution is continuously excluded from
official hemispheric and world narratives. Reproduced here are
images of the mural that Lasch and Atis Rezistans collaborators
painted during a community workshop on a prominent wall of their
Grand Rue neighborhood. To open the workshop, Lasch painted
the numbers 1810, 1910, and 2010 on the wall with a simple, blocky
font, in reference to Colombian artist Antonio Caro's *Proyecto 500*
and the various bicentennials being prepared in the Americas at
the time. After community activities and discussions addressing
important events that keep being erased from local and collective
memory, Atis Rezistans collective members proceeded to paint over
the year 1810, replacing it with the year 1804, associated with the
Haitian Revolution. The new number stayed up for the duration of
the international gathering, visibly integrated with other Ghetto
Biennale activities happening next to the wall.

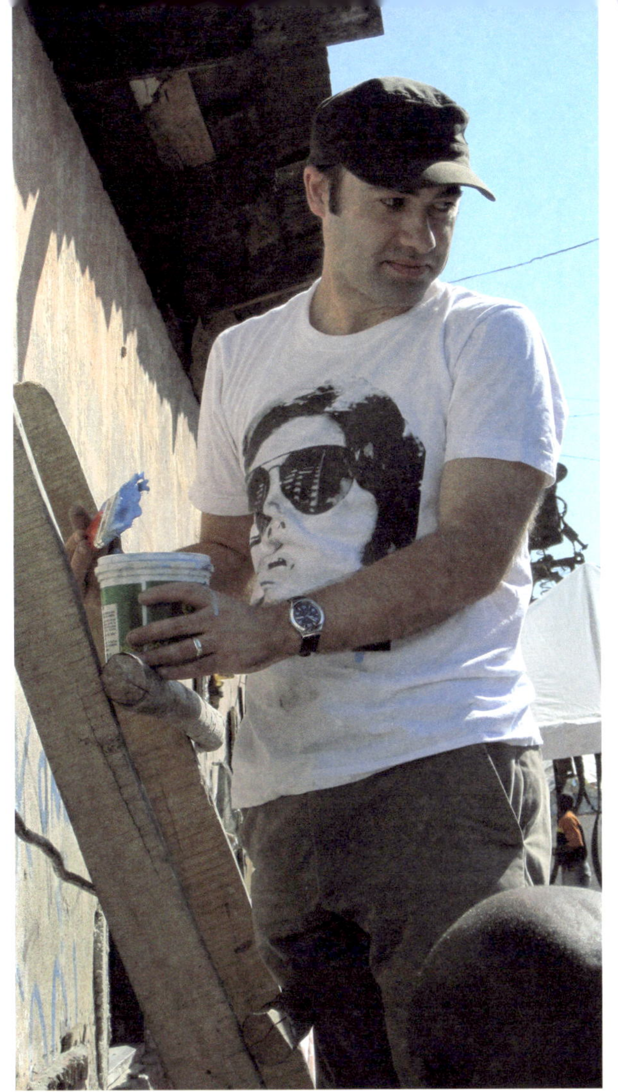
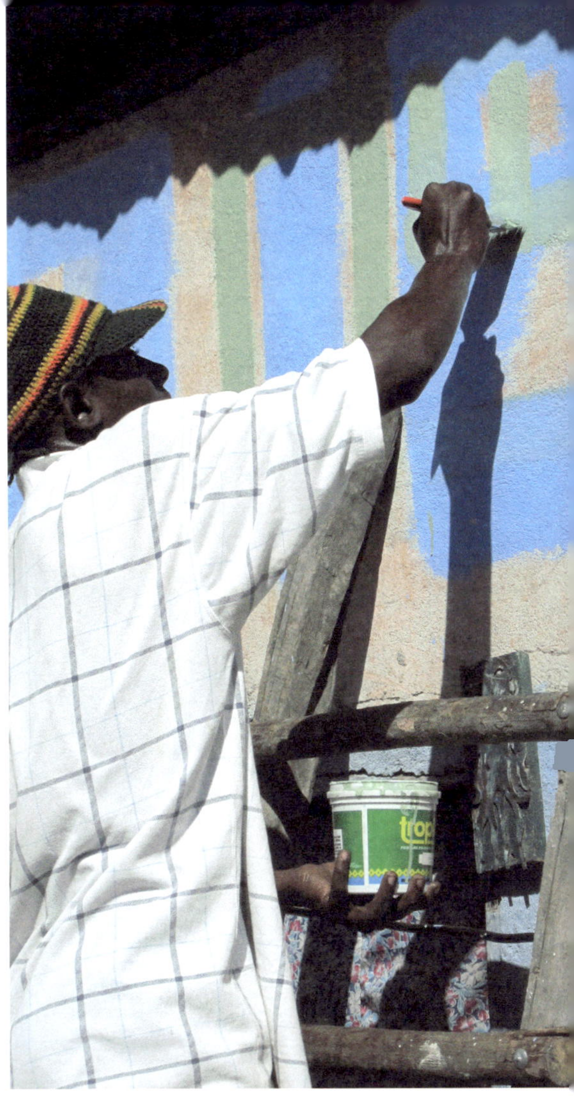

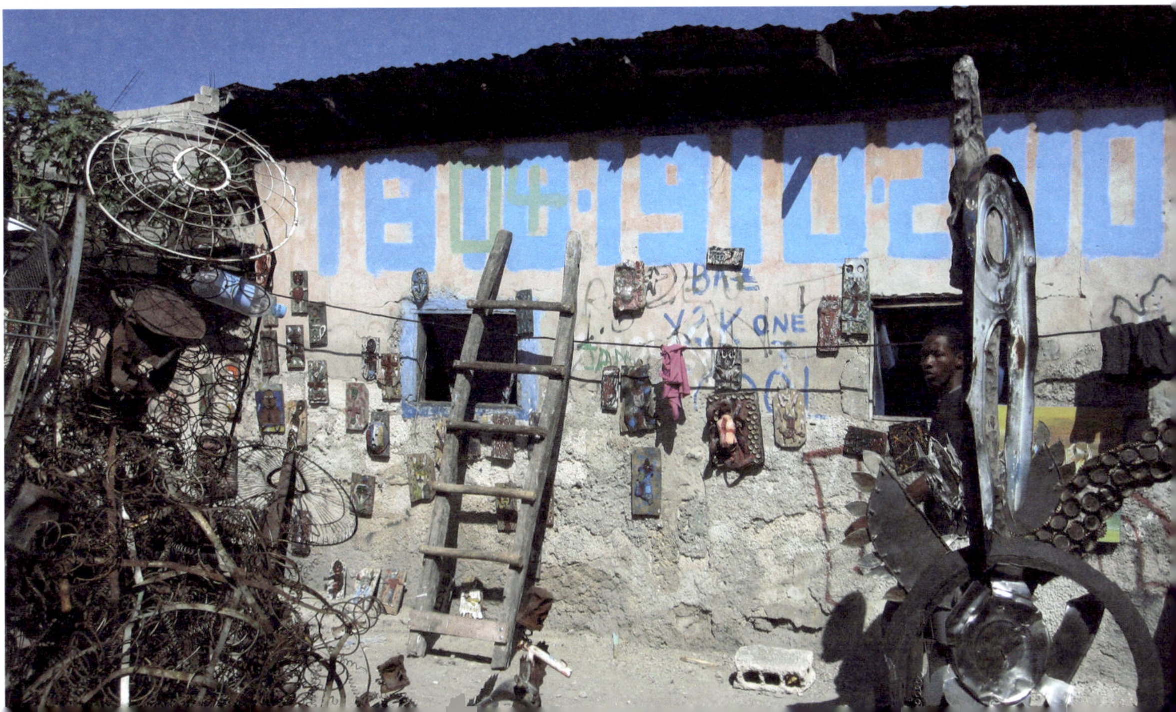

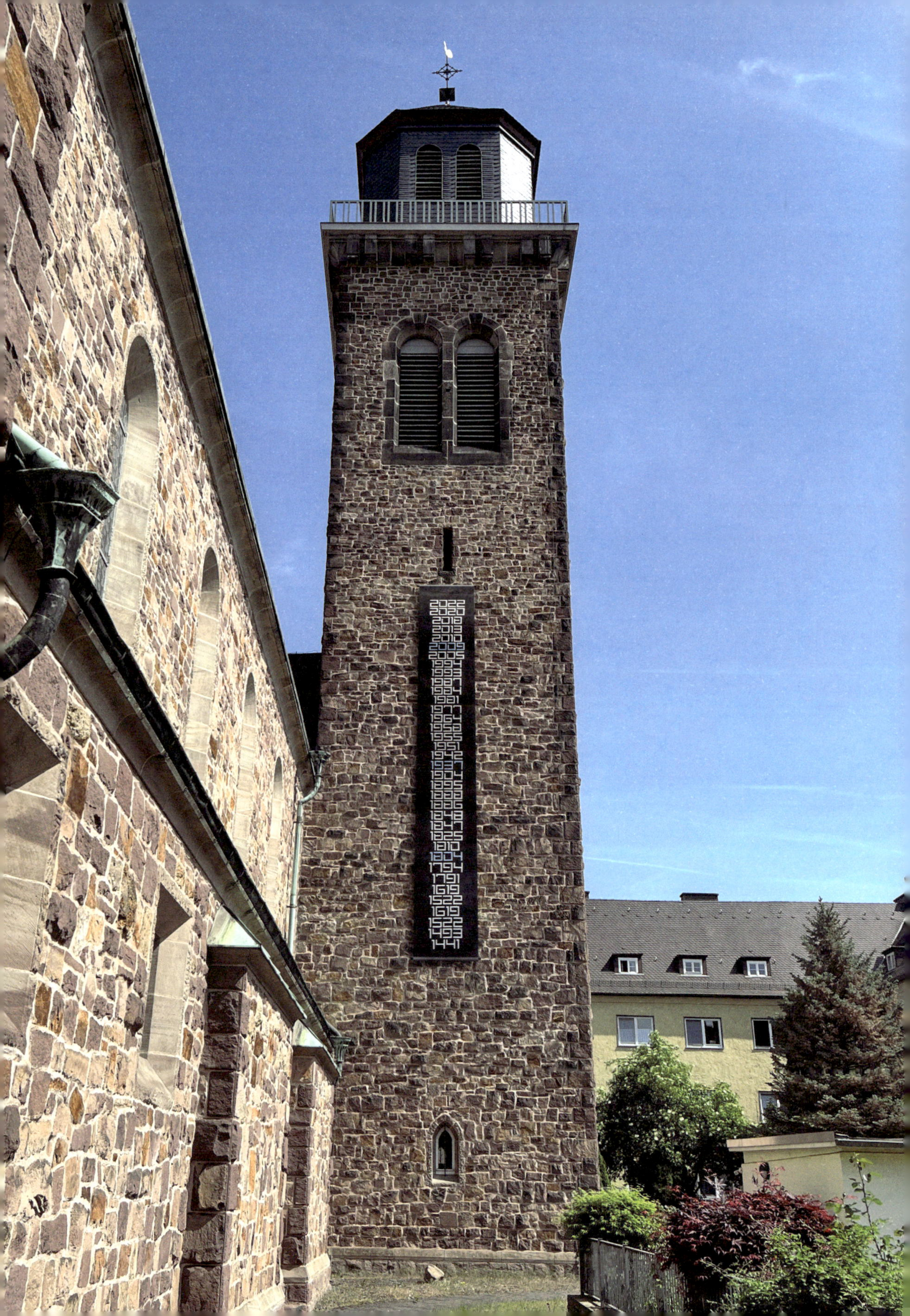
2022
2020
2018
2013
2010
2009
2005
1994
1993
1987
1984
1981
1977
1964
1958
1955
1951
1942
1937
1904
1895
1888
1886
1848
1847
1825
1810
1804
1794
1791
1619
1522
1619
1522
1493
1441

***St. Kunigundis Common Wind Tower Painting*, Kassel, 2022**
***Art Biennials and Other Global Disasters* series, 2010-2022**
Monumental banner hung from church tower
Hand-painted gesso and acrylic on color fabric, 34.12 × 3.94 ft

Hand-painted for the tower of St. Kunigundis Church in Kassel, this monumental banner bears only numbers. The years listed allude to the histories so many of us have been taught; the thirty-six dates appearing on it function like an abstract set of visual questions. A printed artist statement and list of events was circulated among participants as a starting point for workshops held throughout the hundred days of documenta. Revisiting the international relevance of the Haitian Revolution in the context of documenta, the dates on it refer to key events in the global struggle for emancipation. A contrasting set of numbers describes the global expansion of white supremacy and the history of the Euro-American slave trade, which should be part of our collective memory. Perhaps least expected, but also crucial to the project, are the dates that tell the story of global exhibitions, be they world fairs, human zoos, international biennials, or ideological displays like the Degenerate Art exhibition [*Entartete Kunst*] staged by the Nazis in 1937. The act of painting dates on a public site refers to one of Lasch's works for the first Ghetto Biennale in 2009.

List of events associated with dates appearing on the painting:

2022: Atis Rezistans and Ghetto Biennale at documenta fifteen in Kassel
2020: COVID-19 global pandemic
2018: Publication of *The Common Wind* by Julius S. Scott
2013: Biennale Park on Saadiyat Island set in the United Arab Emirates
      (UAE) on the largest human-made island
2010: Earthquake in Haiti/independence bicentennials celebrated
      across the Americas
2009: First Ghetto Biennale, initial mural honoring the Haitian Revolution
2005: Augsburg Zoo puts *Afrika-Dorf* [African Village] on display
1994: End of apartheid in South Africa
1993: First Sharjah Biennial
1987: First İstanbul Bienali
1984: First Bienal de La Habana
1981: Mauritania becomes the last country in the world to abolish slavery

1977: Djibouti becomes the last African country to
        gain independence from European colonizers
1964: United States Civil Rights Act
1958: Brussels World Fair includes the "last"
        human zoo, a "Congolese village"
1955: First documenta in Kassel
1951: First Bienal de São Paulo
1942: Wannsee Conference, Nazis develop the "Final Solution,"
        a plan of racialized murder, sustained also by the forced
        labor of Jews and many other persecuted communities
1937: Degenerate Art exhibition in Munich,
        millions see the touring Nazi exhibition
1904: The St. Louis World's Fair stages largest human
        zoo in history, with thousands on display
1895: First La Biennale di Venezia
1888: Brazil becomes the last nation in the Americas to abolish slavery
1886: Cuba becomes the last Spanish territory to abolish slavery
1865: United States Congress abolishes slavery with the
        13th Amendment/The Ku Klux Klan is formed
1848: Second French Abolition Act
1847: Liberia becomes the first African country to gain
        independence from European colonizers
1825: Haiti's exorbitant foreign debt is imposed by France
        and Europe as compensation to former slaveholders
1810: American countries gain independence from
        Spain/Mexico abolishes slavery
1807: British Parliament votes to abolish the slave trade
1804: Haitian Independence is declared, the country becomes
        the first in world to permanently ban slavery
1794: First French Abolition Act, invalidated by Napoleon soon after
1791: First World's Fair held in Prague/Vodou ceremony at Bois Caïman
        sparks the Saint-Domingue enslaved uprisings
1619: First sale of slaves in English colonies at Point Comfort, Virginia
1522: First major uprising of enslaved Africans in the Americas on the
        island of Hispaniola
1493: Columbus transports enslaved Native people, free Blacks
        arrive in Americas/expulsion of Jews and Moors from Spain
1441: In the early Renaissance, Portugal begins the
        European slave trade out of Africa

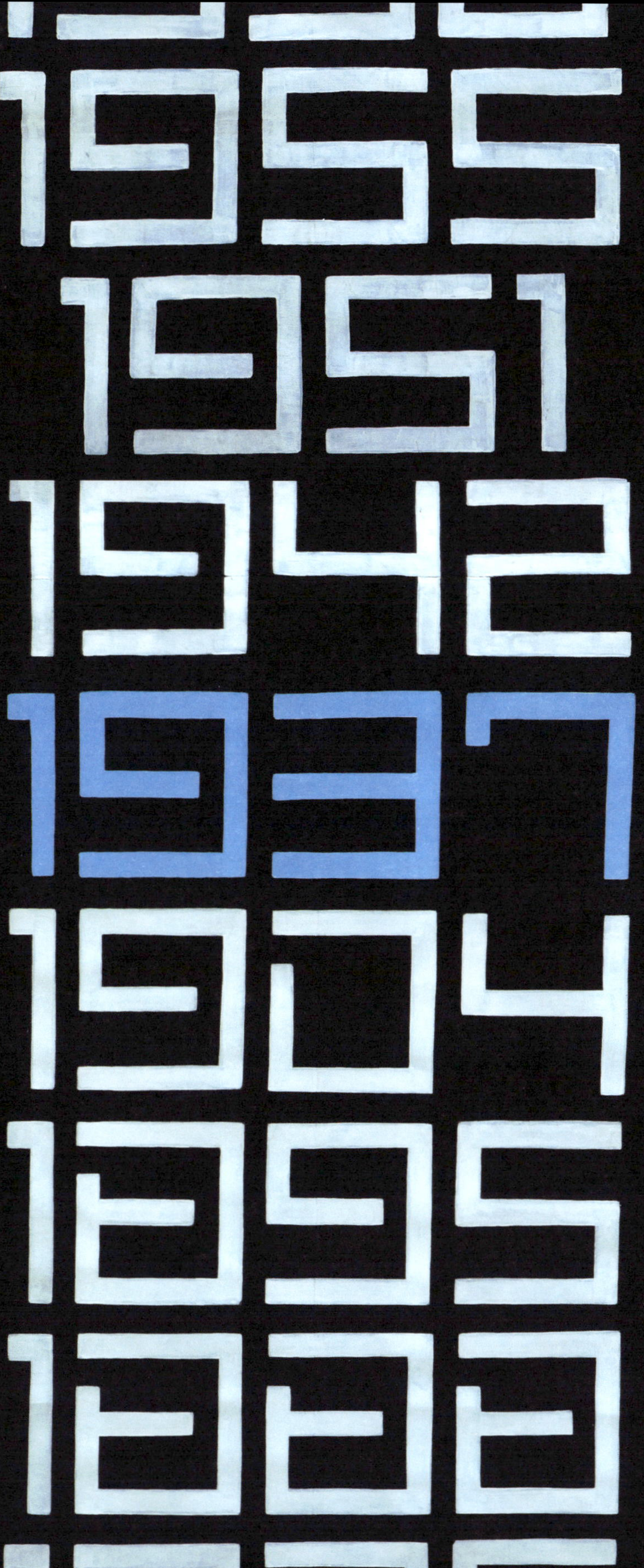

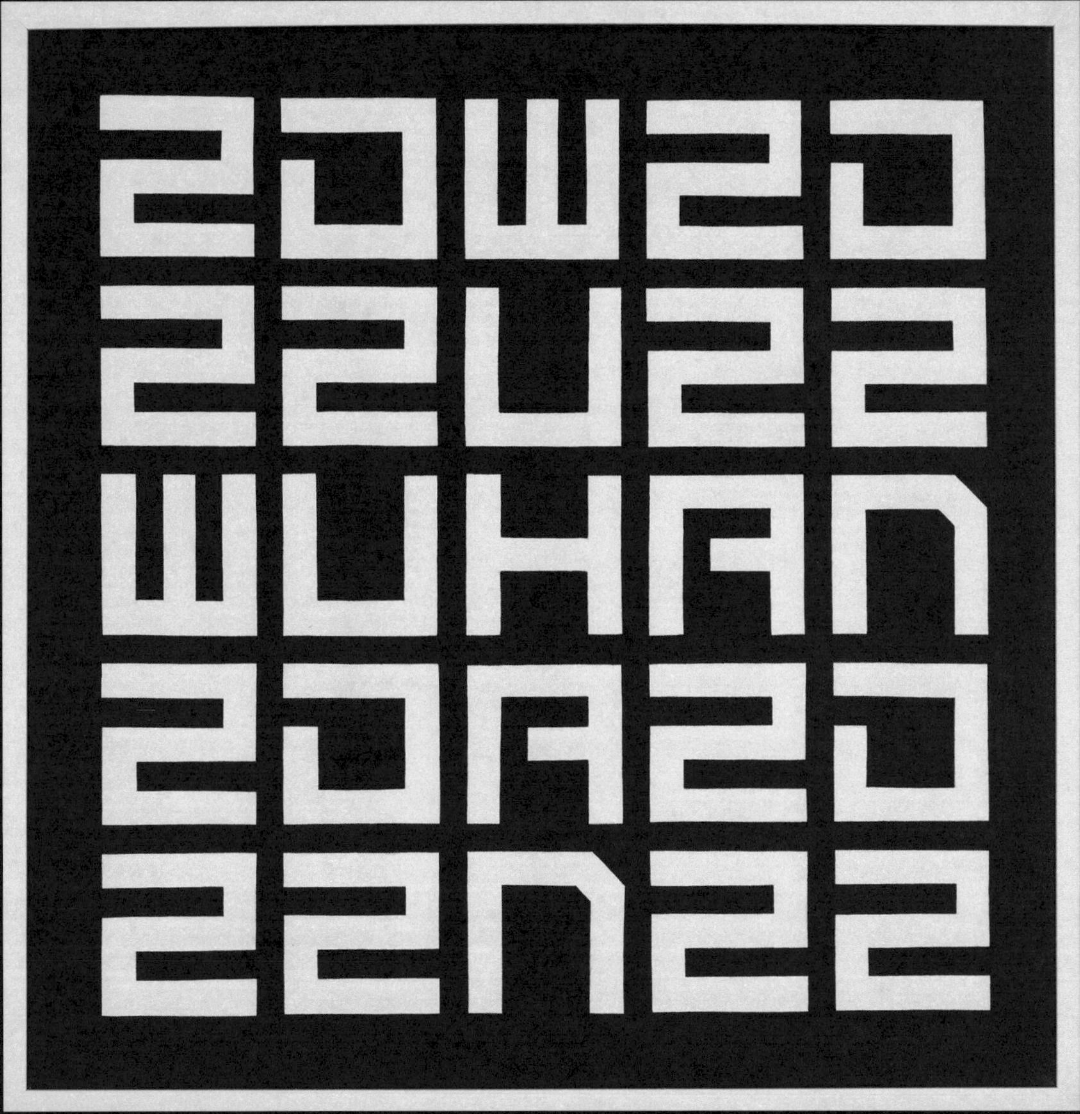

Wuhan, 2020. Oil on canvas, 30 × 30 in

20 22 The Ongoing Biennial Conversation and Painting Cycle, 2020 – 2022

Hoor Al-Qasimi, Carolyn Christov-Bakargiev, Andrea Giunta, Yuko Hasegawa, Rujeko Hockley, Candice Hopkins, Miguel A. López, Cuauhtémoc Medina, Gabi Ngcobo, Lucia Pietroiusti, farid rakun (ruangrupa), José Roca, Ralph Rugoff, Trevor Schoonmaker

Set in the context of an unprecedented pandemic, global shutdowns, and the rethinking of every aspect of art and exhibition-making, the works presented in this section developed as two parallel, yet related, series: a public, weekly online conversation cycle with international curators and a set of over thirty abstract word paintings addressing events from this time.

Organized by Pedro Lasch and the Franklin Humanities Institute Social Practice Lab (SPL) with support from the FHI World Arts Initiative at Duke University, *The Ongoing Biennial* conversation cycle included fourteen prominent curators and international art professionals. This event was attended live by over 3,000 remote viewers from dozens of countries between January and May of 2021. A permanent archive of the full conversations has been preserved at the FHI SPL site, where it can still be accessed by its growing public. For this publication, we have selected quotes from each guest in relation to biennials, global exhibition-making, and the challenges of this specific historical period.

The selections appear alphabetically, listing each curator's name and accompanied by paintings that Lasch developed in the same period. These were produced with a range of contemporary and traditional oil techniques on canvas, using a specially designed font that enhances the tension between visual play and legibility. The numbers 20 and 22 appear obsessively in every painting, in varying levels of abstraction. Bringing color to a time of gray monotony and mourning, the works spell names and events from a time when our individual and collective survival became the universal foreground that threatened to erase all other forms of collective memory.

Hoor Al-Qasimi

"For the first Lahore Biennale, the focus was very much on South
Asian artists. So when they invited me to the second edition, they
wanted to look outside of South Asia but also include artists from
the region. It was tricky because I really wanted to invite artists from
the so-called Global South, to spark a conversation about postcolo-
nialism and the shared histories that many of these countries were
facing. It was an opportunity to open up conversations between
many countries and continents."

"Growing up as an artist, I often thought about what I wanted from
a biennial. I grew up with the Sharjah Biennial, which started when
I was 13. Then in 2002, I took over because I was trying to control
everything, and they said, 'Do it yourself!' So it became my job. But
at the heart, I was just a young artist who wanted things to happen
in Sharjah. I didn't want to keep running off to Berlin, New York, or
London. It became a kind of responsibility to create and inspire the
next generations. Now, I've been doing this for nearly twenty years,
and there's been such a big difference in terms of the art scene, not
just in Sharjah but the whole region: the Gulf, the UAE—everything
is connected."

"In 2002, when I got involved with the Sharjah Biennial, I was just
asking a lot of questions, because I wasn't comfortable with the idea
of country representations. Many people are from more than one

country; there are diasporas, people from mixed heritages, and so on. There were so many issues around nationality and identity that I found the idea of representing a 'country' to be problematic, so that was one of the first things I changed."

"The UAE pavilion in Venice was really a museum show. I remember a fellow curator saying to me, 'You need to do something very quick for Venice, something that people come to experience and leave, like an experience or a gimmick.' I said, 'Well, if they don't have the time, they don't have to see the show.' That was important for me: this idea that a biennial is a spectacle with people just rushing around; that's not a reason to show something or not show something. And because this was really talking about the UAE, I wanted to do a historic museum show—which was not easy considering the space and conditions."

"Our online March Meeting forum was very well received. We had over 7,000 registrations, 4,000 attendees, and the average atten- dance for most panels was about 200 to 300, which you wouldn't get in our physical spaces. But we did miss getting together after the talks. For the next one, we're trying to see how we can combine the two formats, because it's great being able to have people from different parts of the world watching and being part of the Q&As and everything, so we are trying to see if we can manage to do both. "

"I struggled with virtual reality options because I refuse to have our exhibitions online. People get busy and lazy, and they say they've seen an exhibition because they saw it online. We need an audience. We need people to come to the museum. It's not the same experi- ence. I was thinking about Lahore as I was doing the presentation. You can't recreate an exhibition online. It's just not possible."

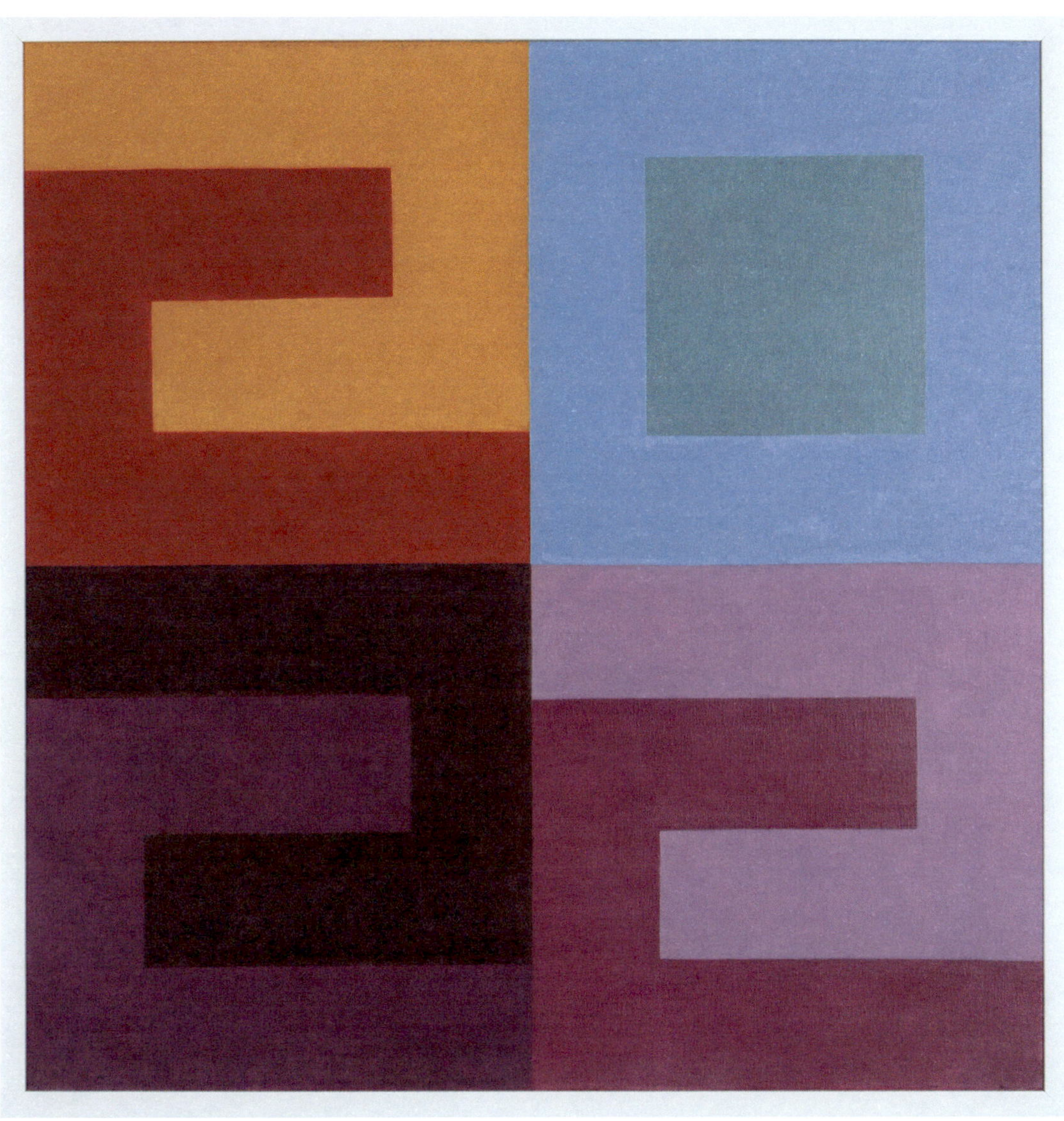

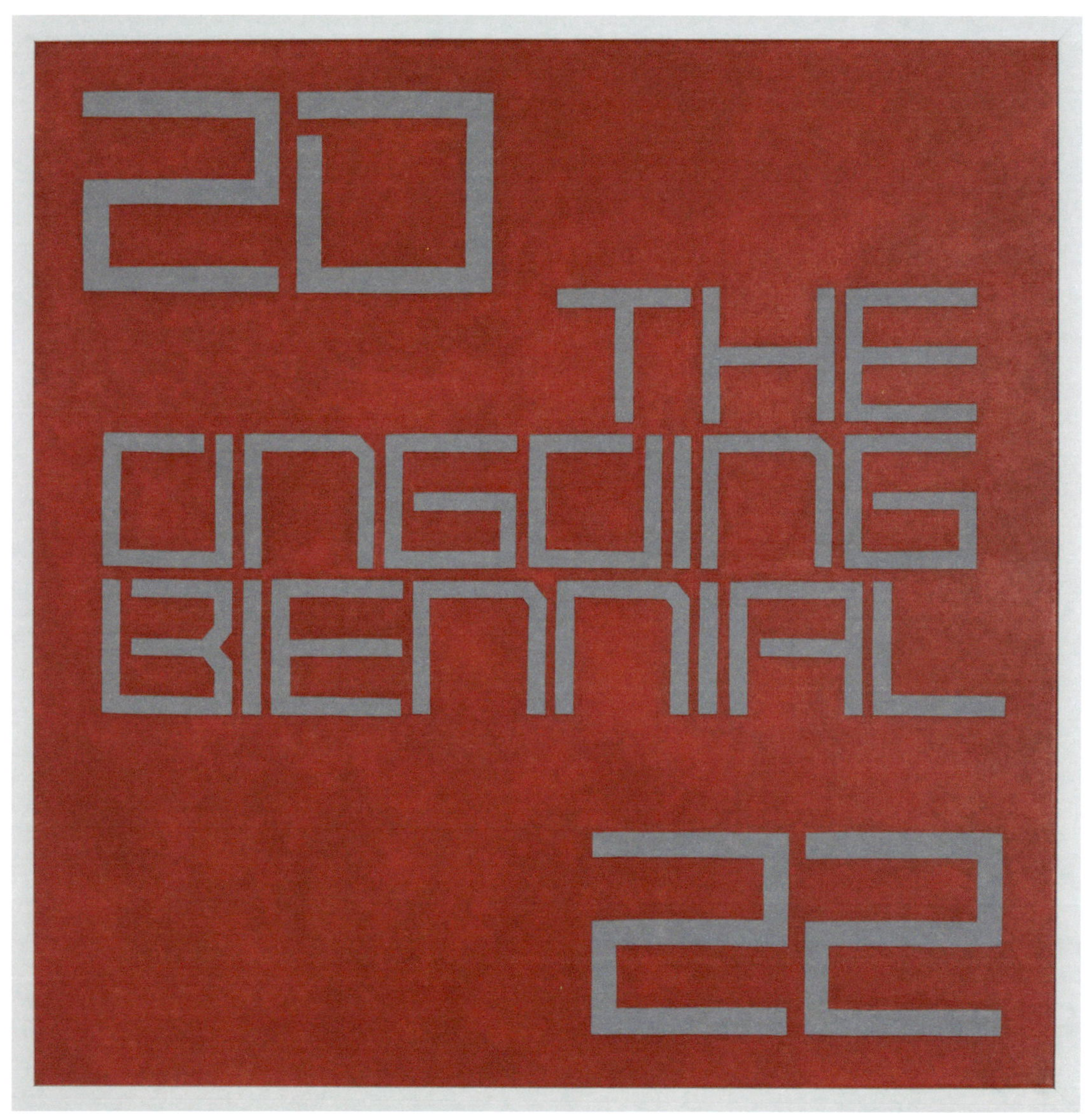

    The Ongoing Biennial, 2021. Oil on canvas, 30 × 30 in

Carolyn Christov-Bakargiev

"I was nominated to curate the 16th Sydney Biennale in 2008.
I decided it would revolve around the concept of *upside down*, in
a way—of going backwards, moving in a loop, reversing, spinning,
turning. It was basically an investigation into one question: Why is it
that artists who have been revolutionary in their artistic practice—in
terms of materials, form, structure, and technique—and who have
investigated forms related to reversal, inversion, repetition, and so
on, have usually been revolutionary in their politics?"

"There were great precedents to my 2012 dOCUMENTA(13) in terms
of invited artists. Personally, I am a bit boring, in the sense that I often
invite the same artists to different exhibitions over time—because we
share a life together. It's really about life, it's not about the exhibition.
It's about how you can traverse thirty, forty, fifty, sixty years, having
conversations and understanding the world as it changes with the
same people, yet at the same time, being very open to meeting new
artists. Every exhibition I've made has involved artists who have been
with me before and some new ones."

"You know, the reason I did that edition of documenta the way I did
was to stop something that was becoming a general opinion I did
not share. Biennials were being criticized as tourist traps—ways for
cities to legitimize themselves through tourism—and the art system
was moving toward auction houses and art fairs. It was the rise of

Art Basel, and the decline of the biennale system. The reason is that
the art fair, structurally, is more like the internet. The internet, in its
networked website structure, is closer to the art fair model than to
the biennale. So, at the time I needed to prove that the international
periodic exhibition still mattered—and I think I did!"

"I think the main danger right now is over-digitalization. You can
see it in where wealth concentrates. It's always about following
the money, and right now, it's all in digital. Digitalization certainly
helped during the pandemic—not just for buying things but also
exploring all events and online activities. Thanks to the internet,
certain marginalized groups have been able to move more in the
forefront. I'm certainly not against the thinking of someone like
Legacy Russell or of young people who see this as an emancipatory
opportunity. However, I do think there is a risk: in the future, ecological movements and hyper-digitalization will form an alliance to
save the planet—by making people stay at home and be online all
the time. A kind of a matrix risk."

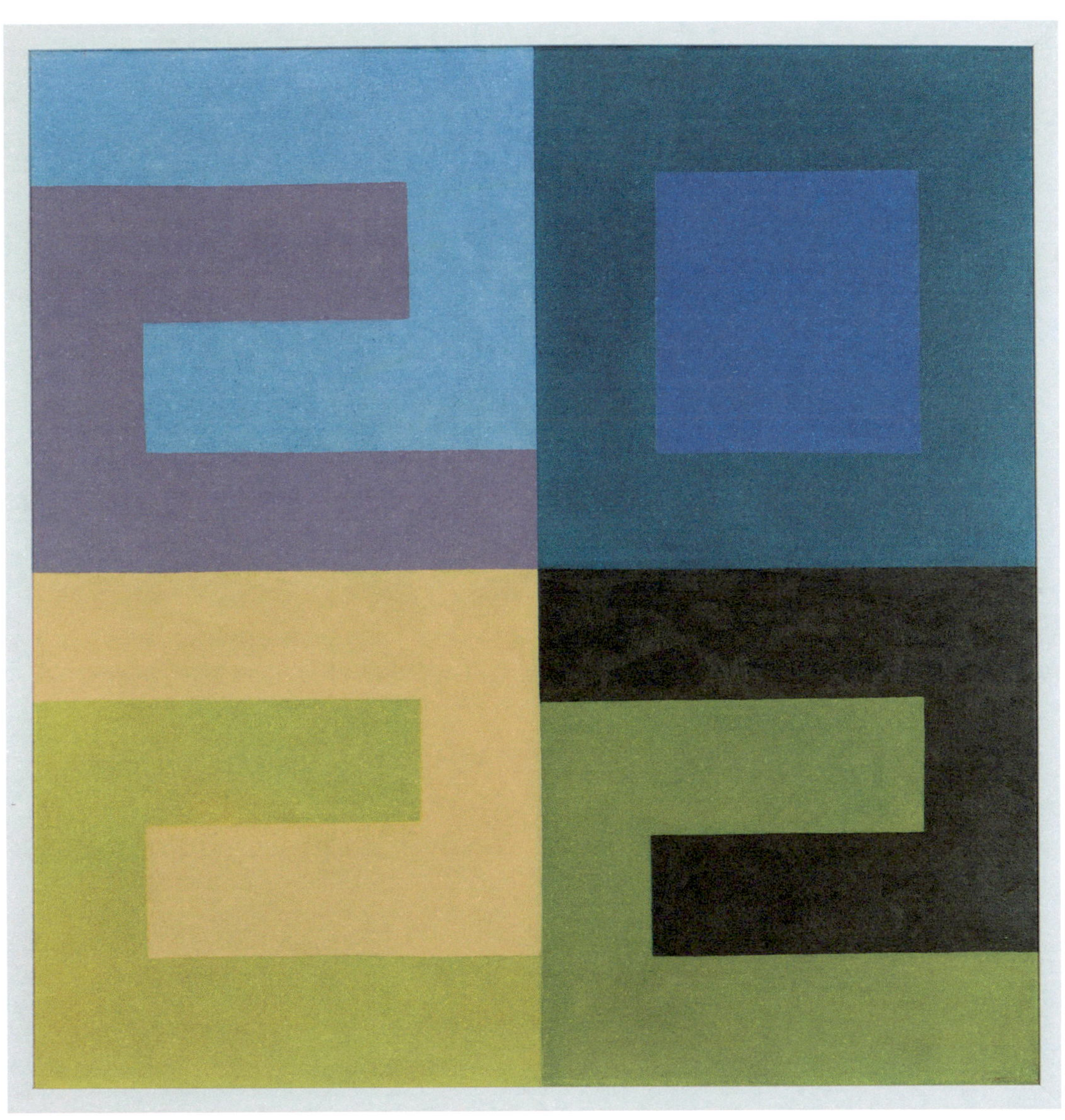

Abstraction No. 2, 2020. Oil on canvas, 30 × 30 in   37

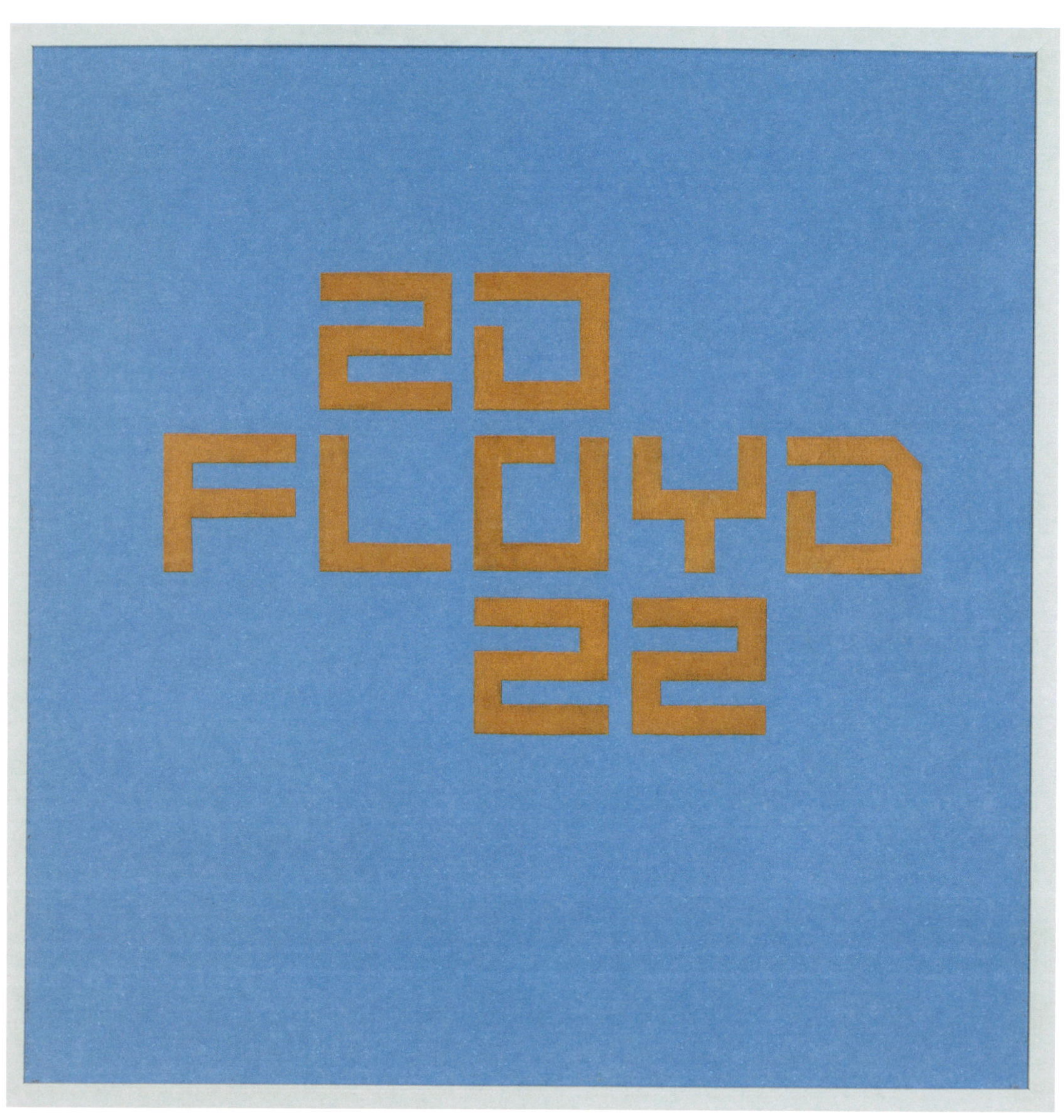

38   *Floyd*, 2020. Oil on canvas, 30 × 30 in

Andrea Giunta

"I think that every time art has the possibility to occupy a space, it should. And for me, the challenging thing is not to criticize the biennial but to see what the biennial allows me to criticize—or to change something that has to do with the world. I would never use the biennial forum to make an empty criticism of the system. I want a celebration of art that has a significant opportunity to make a powerful intervention."

"When I arrived in São Paulo at the end of the *Radical Women* exhibition, Bolsonaro came into power. The same thing happened in the United States, because when the exhibition opened at the Hammer Museum, Trump went into power. So, an exhibition that was conceived in a particular context became very radical in this new one. This is really important, because you might have an idea of the intentions, but it's the context that makes it spark."

"It is the responsibility of the historical exhibition to have a concept, to understand the framework, and to work with responsibility in researching that period. In a way, a historical exhibition is a kind of corset—it's more structured. I think the biennial gives you more freedom. But the responsibility you carry toward history in a historical exhibition makes you rethink contemporaneity. And if you want to reactivate works from the past in the present... then you don't make a historical exhibition just to box the past in."

"Many colleagues decided that, at a time when museums were closed, we shouldn't do anything—because art should be essential, and the experience of being directly in-touch with a work of art cannot be replaced by any other experience. But at the same time, I think we had an enormous responsibility because the first thing we saw when the pandemic occurred and everything shut down was that many museums decided to fire an important part of their staff, particularly educational staff. Departments were dismantled, and many central institutions made those decisions. I think we need to be more committed to education because around the world schools are closed. So what's going to happen with education?"

"Regarding the Bienal do Mercosul, which took place right at the start of the pandemic, the online biennial was not able to offer the best solutions, as we were in between two spaces: the physical and the digital. And we did the best we could having to make this move in less than a month. The curatorial team was in crisis because we had different positions. Some of them didn't want to do anything. I agreed because, of course, in such an extreme situation, everybody had to feel and do in whatever ways they could. Then, I wrote a letter to all the artists, just asking how they were. After ten days of not knowing what to do, the responses started coming in and were so emotional. They needed to be in touch, so I proposed that they send a short film, made with a cell phone. That became our first activity."

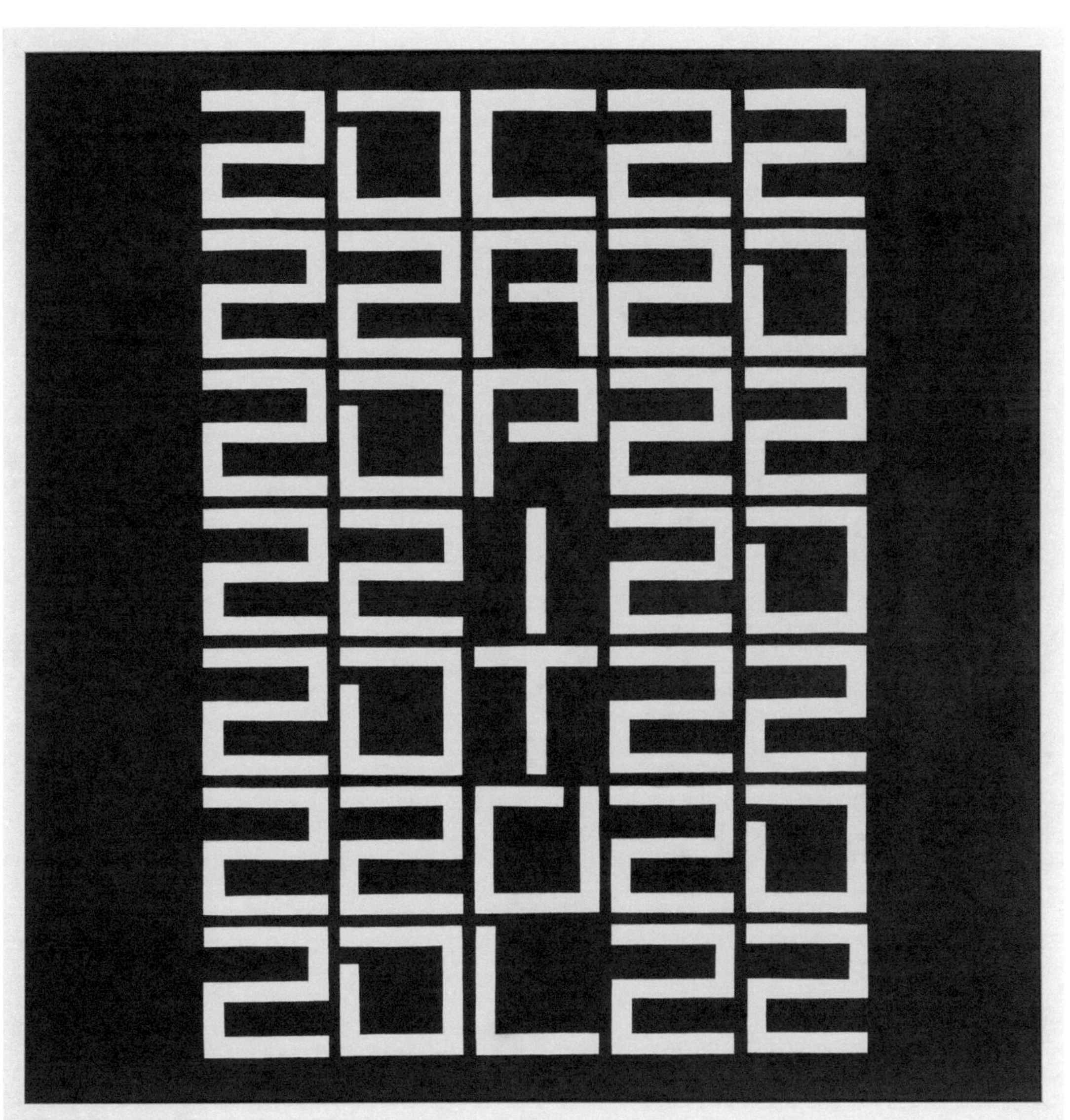

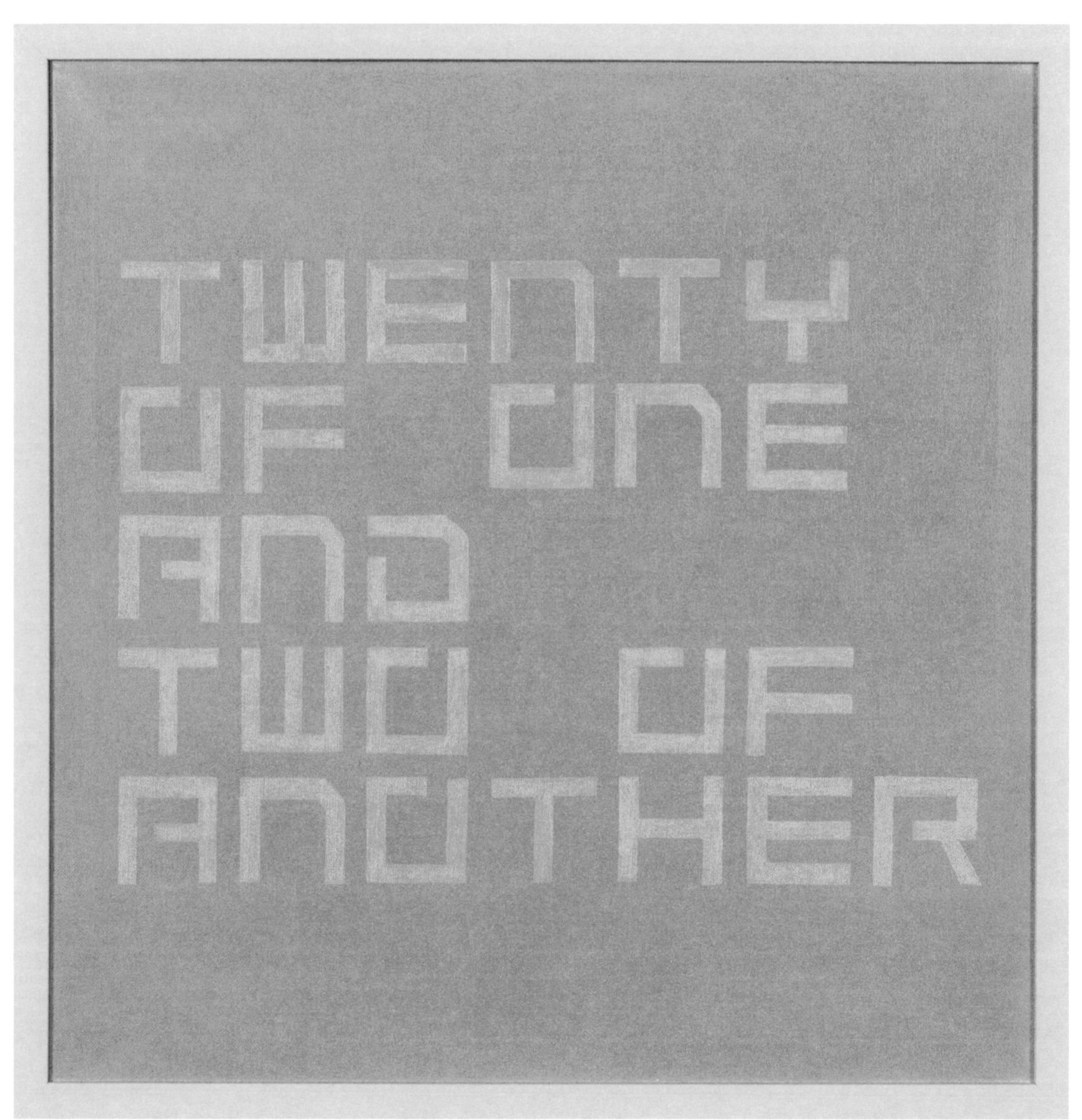

   Twenty of One and Two of Another, 2020. Oil on canvas, 20 × 20 in

Yuko Hasegawa

"The curator's role is increasingly vital because people crave narratives. A narrative provides a kind of familiarity—especially in relation to particular sensory experiences. This makes it substantial; when confronted solely with big data, one often cannot truly engage with it. Yet some artists possess the ability to craft compelling visualizations that facilitate such engagement."

"Some curators approach biennials without anchoring them to a strong conceptual framework, simply selecting artists and presenting their work. For me, however, the theme/concept functions as a crucial tool. It allows me to construct a trajectory, to establish a certain coherence. My first biennial, in Istanbul in 2001, coincided with the start of the twenty-first century—a period marked by global instability and uncertainty. At that time, I articulated a curatorial framework based on what I called the three m's and three c's. The three m's represented dominant twentieth-century forces: men, symbolizing individualism and egoistic attitudes; money, representing wealth and capitalism; and materialism. These forces drove immense development yet left profound consequences. The three c's, conversely, served as a corrective mechanism oriented toward the twenty-first century: coexistence, collective intelligence, and consciousness."

"For the 7th International İstanbul Bienali, I organized the exhibition around the three m's to the three c's, integrating my research on sensory languages. I titled the edition *Egofugal*—a neologism not found in any dictionary. It signifies movement from the center to the periphery, a flight outward, reflecting a departure from one's own ego. This approach embodies the principle of caring for others as one cares for oneself, blending Western individualism with Eastern collectivism."

"I traveled to the Taklamakan Desert to investigate the boundary between East and West. It may have been a somewhat whimsical endeavor—I simply wanted to locate that border, literally where the 'West' ends and the "East" begins. Istanbul itself functions as a geopolitical border, and it became a compelling site to explore the notion of the egofugal within a hybrid space, a zone of intercultural communication between East and West."

"My mentor, Uzawa Hirofumi, a mathematical economist, emphasized the importance of social common capital. At a time when many were declaring the end of capitalism, he reminded me that capitalism never truly ceases; rather, we must rethink how capital can be generated in novel ways. According to Uzawa, social common capital provides members of society with essential services and institutional arrangements that sustain human and cultural life. It consists of three categories: natural capital, social infrastructure, and institutional capital. Natural capital includes the natural environment and resources, such as the Earth's atmosphere. Social infrastructure encompasses roads, bridges, public transportation systems, and utilities. Institutional capital comprises hospitals, educational institutions, judicial and police systems, public administration, financial and monetary institutions, and cultural capital. In this framework, curatorial practice can locally activate and regenerate these forms of social common capital, fostering programs and initiatives that build trust and participation within the community. This process forms the foundation of my curatorial approach."

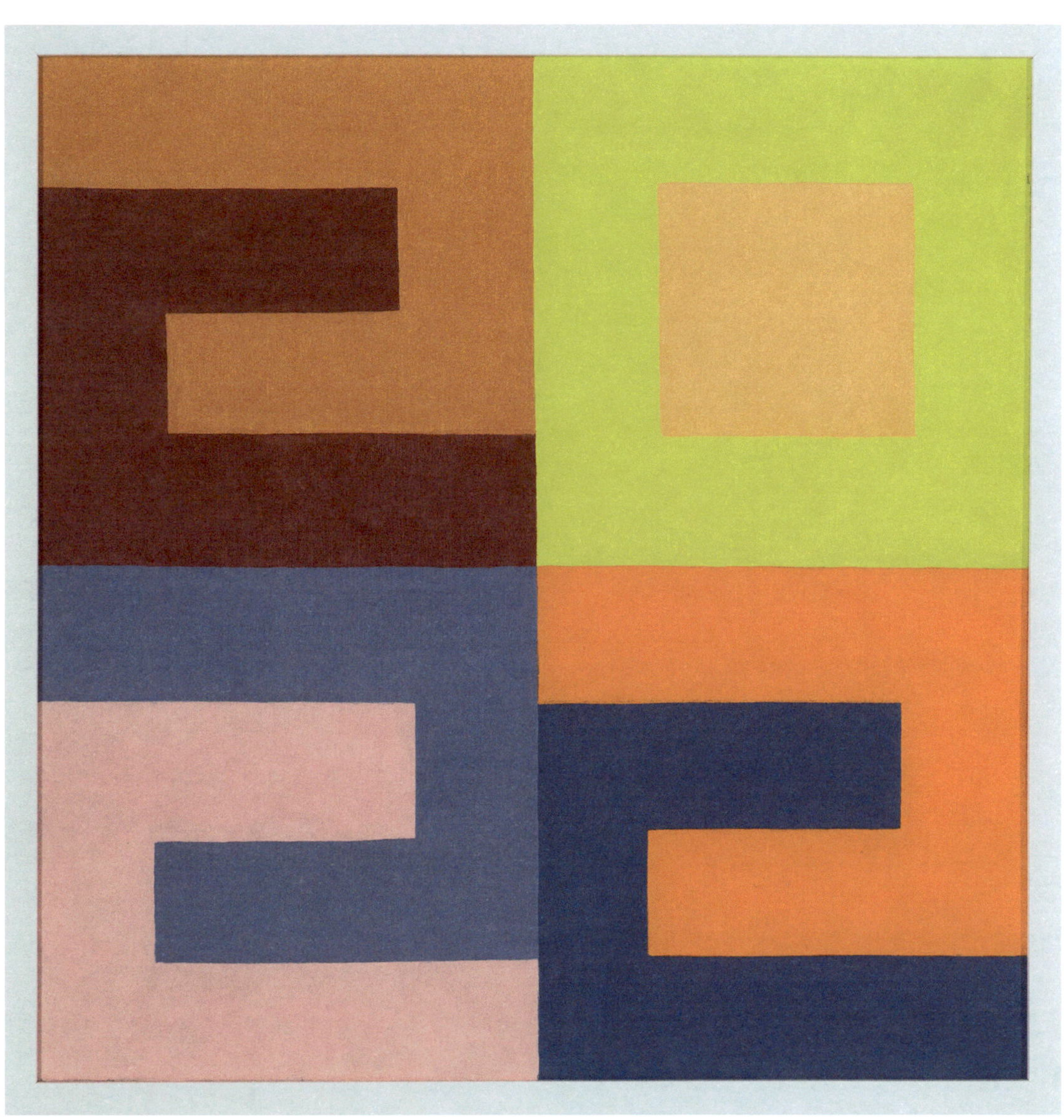

Abstraction No. 3, 2020. Oil on canvas, 20 × 20 in   45

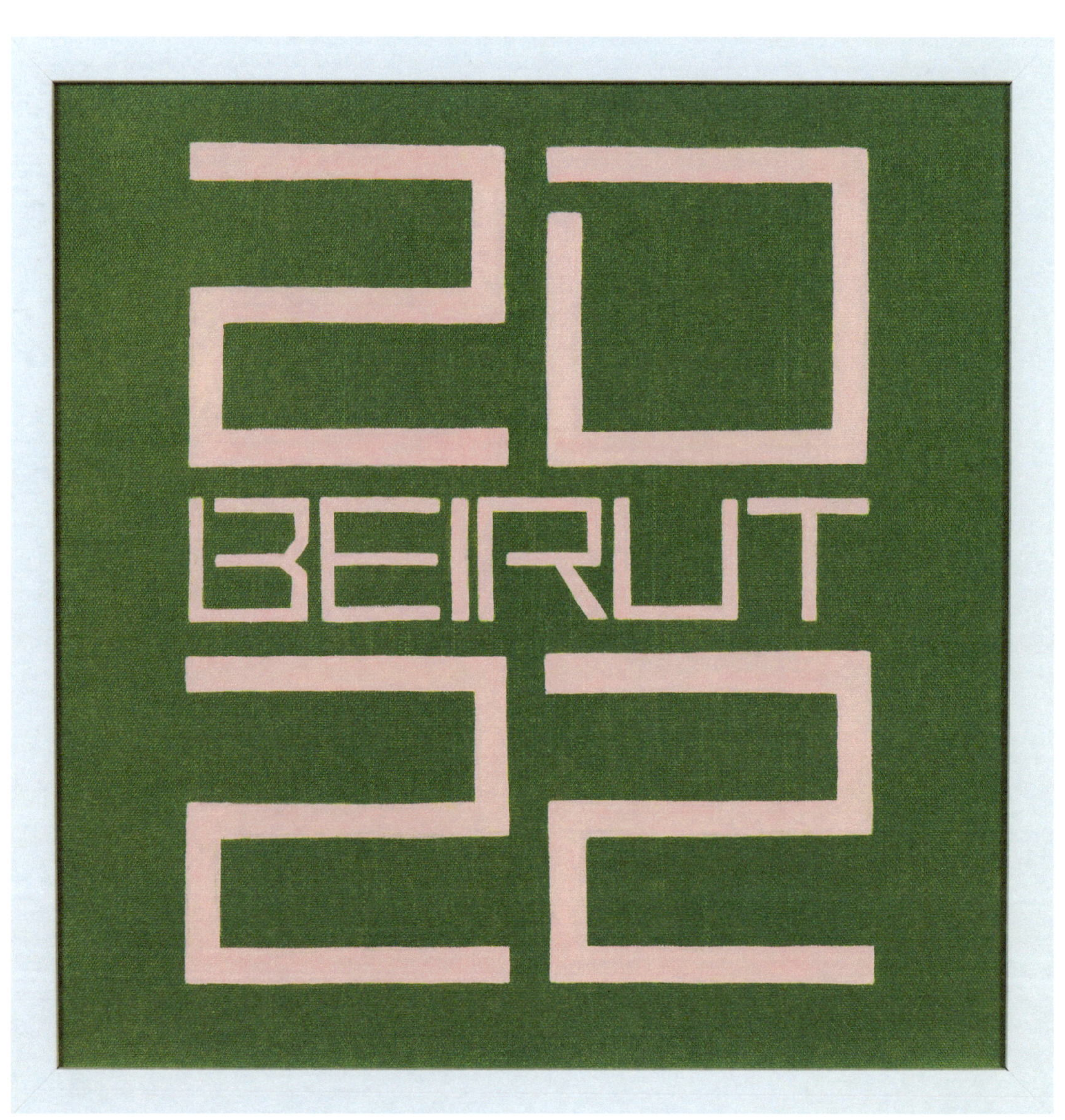

46   *Beirut*, 2020. Oil on canvas, 20 × 20 in

Rujeko Hockley

"As a curator, I like this idea of speaking directly from your own experience, from your own identity. It is not about one group, idea, artist, or approach being more valuable than another—it's that each person deserves their own perspective, through their own specific lens. So whatever work, artists, or ideas you choose to put forth as a curator into the world, your responsibility is to find that specificity, find that lens, to share it clearly with audiences, so that they—regardless of their own identity, interests, background, education, or knowledge—can access another person's subjectivity, and other groups' subjectivity."

"When I think about my job as a curator, I try to do exhibitions and work with artists that I believe are truly important and create conversations that bring them into a broader world through this platform. I'm the one who has to be compelling. I'm the one who has to believe in it. I need to walk into rooms where no one looks like me and where people might not think we share anything in common. But it's not about making myself palatable or legible, so that they feel like we have something in common. It's about being enthusiastic, heartfelt, and so serious about the thing that I'm talking about, that they feel this is also for them."

"Do we no longer have a public in the way that we had historically? In the future, will we continue to travel all over the world to see exhibitions and give talks? Or will we mostly do it like this—on Zoom? Many more people can attend this way. We should never give that up. Not because of the numbers, but because it means people from all over the world are able to participate and hear from these incredible thinkers and makers in a way that would otherwise never happen. There are also the questions of accessibility for people who are physically here but not able to attend, or who, for whatever reason, cannot come to a museum. Some of these things disability rights activists have been asking are suddenly possible. That, to me, is one major improvement."

"In terms of movements for social justice, I think that side of it, sadly, is not unprecedented. We have generations of police brutality all over the world, not just in the United States. We have generations of activism, agitation, co-optation, and squashing by the state. This is a cycle we see repeated again and again all over the world. What's been interesting is to see the broader art world come to some of the same interests I grew up with, to develop some of the same kind of consciousness. I'm thinking of institutions—I've only been an institutional curator, so I cannot speak for independent curating, but I do think institutions are going to look very different. Some institutions will not survive because of the pandemic, just because of the financial pressures. But also because what the public is demanding of us has changed. And they have every right—so if we can't get with it, that's on us."

"We've been stuck in the binary for many generations, especially in the context of Black art history, Black cultural production, and visual culture. It's either positive imagery to uplift, or it's deep trauma, the worst thing—because all that ever happens to us are bad things and trauma, right? I think that binary is completely unproductive and unhelpful. Not just because it's not accurate, like most binaries, but because it doesn't leave any space for nuance or specificity, for the fact that there can be joy even in difficult circumstances, or that trauma can exist in things that are supposed to be positive. Life is more complex."

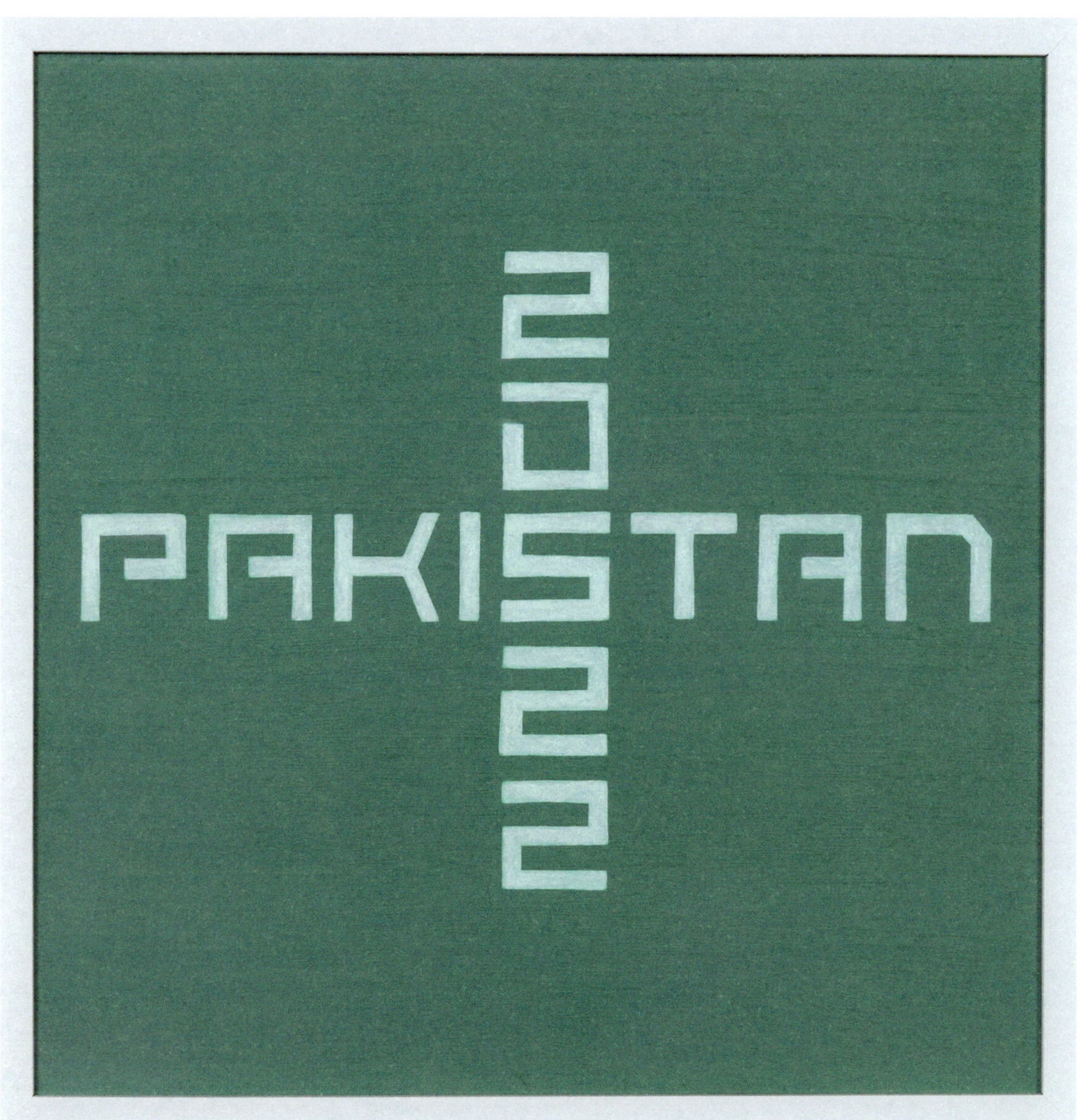

Pakistan, 2022. Oil on canvas, 20 × 20 in   49

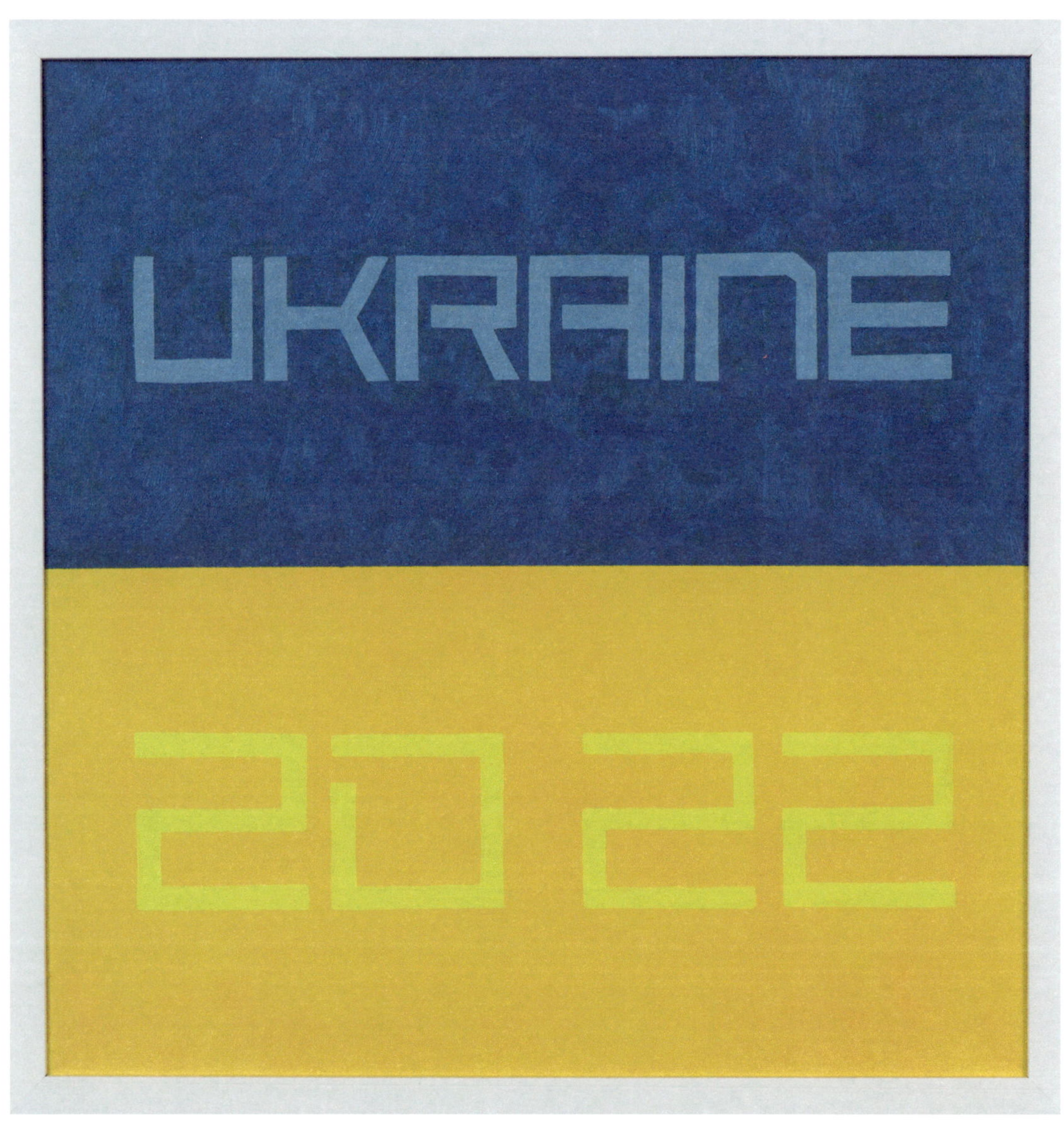

 Ukraine, 2021. Oil on canvas, 20 × 20 in

Candice Hopkins

"I think for a while there was a trend with biennials to either completely dismantle the exhibition that came before or do something entirely different. So it seemed like, especially in the 90s, biennials were mostly vehicles for forgetting—while also generating new ideas. For the SITE SANTA FE, we were instead thinking about how these recurrent exhibitions can draw a thread through, and that informs the work that we did. I think people are now thinking more critically about the structure of biennials—what they offer, how they can be areas of deep scholarly research, not just spaces showing what's new, underrepresented, or unknown."

"For the exhibition *Sakahàn: International Indigenous Art*, I realized that there were a lot of networks—as seen in political movements for Indigenous peoples—that hadn't really been represented before in an exhibition. Oftentimes, earlier exhibitions of international Indigenous art were tethered to a single language group or a single kind of relationship to original colonizers. We decided that we wanted to focus on artists who had had a major impact in their communities, as well as those that were starting to do that within their practice."

"The wealth of Indigenous people really fueled the development of the Renaissance—and people forget this [literally through the extraction of gold from the Incan Empire and other Indigenous lands]. Other examples would be how the Surrealists were looking

at masks and other cultural belongings from Africa, but they were
also specifically looking at Northwest Coast art, as well as Inupiaq
masks. I thought this was a fascinating relationship because it showed
how important Indigenous art was to the development of European
modernism. I saw an opportunity to expose these connections. It
was more about creating these tethers, these relationships that
were floating beneath the surface of art history."

"As many people know, documenta 14 was criticized, particularly in
Athens, for being a form of neocolonialism. It's a charge that was
hard to hear, but it got me thinking about many things—not only
the rights of people, but also about the rights to land and whether
people want these large exhibitions to descend on them. We were
thinking a lot about the potential of resonances—of whether it might
be possible to not only practice the form of deep listening but to listen
beyond. How do you listen beyond colonial resonances to something
else? That kind of grounding in sound and resonance and listening
changed the way that I worked on that exhibition and it changed the
way a lot of artists approached it as well. One of the things I think a
lot about is: How do we give agency to not just people in a place, but
the place itself?"

"Raven Chacon and I coauthored a score called *Dispatch* [written
in response to the water protectors at Standing Rock], which was
based on the analysis of who was there, what roles they were performing, and whether this might become a kind of framework for
other kinds of actions. It was a way to think about the role of art but
also the political role of sound—which is something that we've both
been thinking through a lot lately. One of the outcomes of that score
might be sonic fragments. One of the more insidious effects of white
supremacy is to divide us, right? And one of the ways that we can
work against that is by coming together. It is what I call *sounding the
margins*—bringing together people who might have been forcibly
dispossessed, even if we are never dispossessed in our ideas."

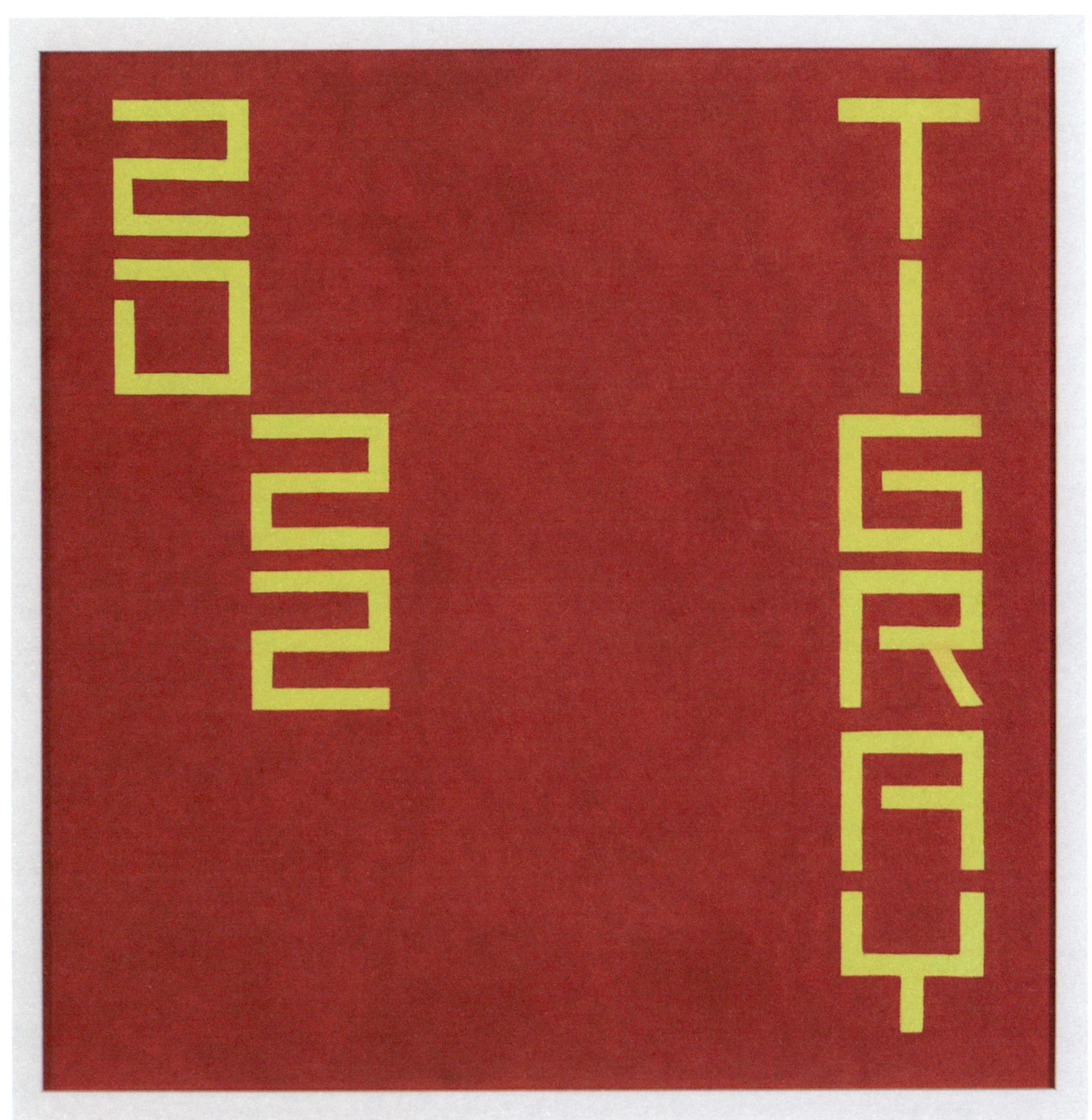

Tigray, 2021. Oil on canvas, 20 × 20 in   53

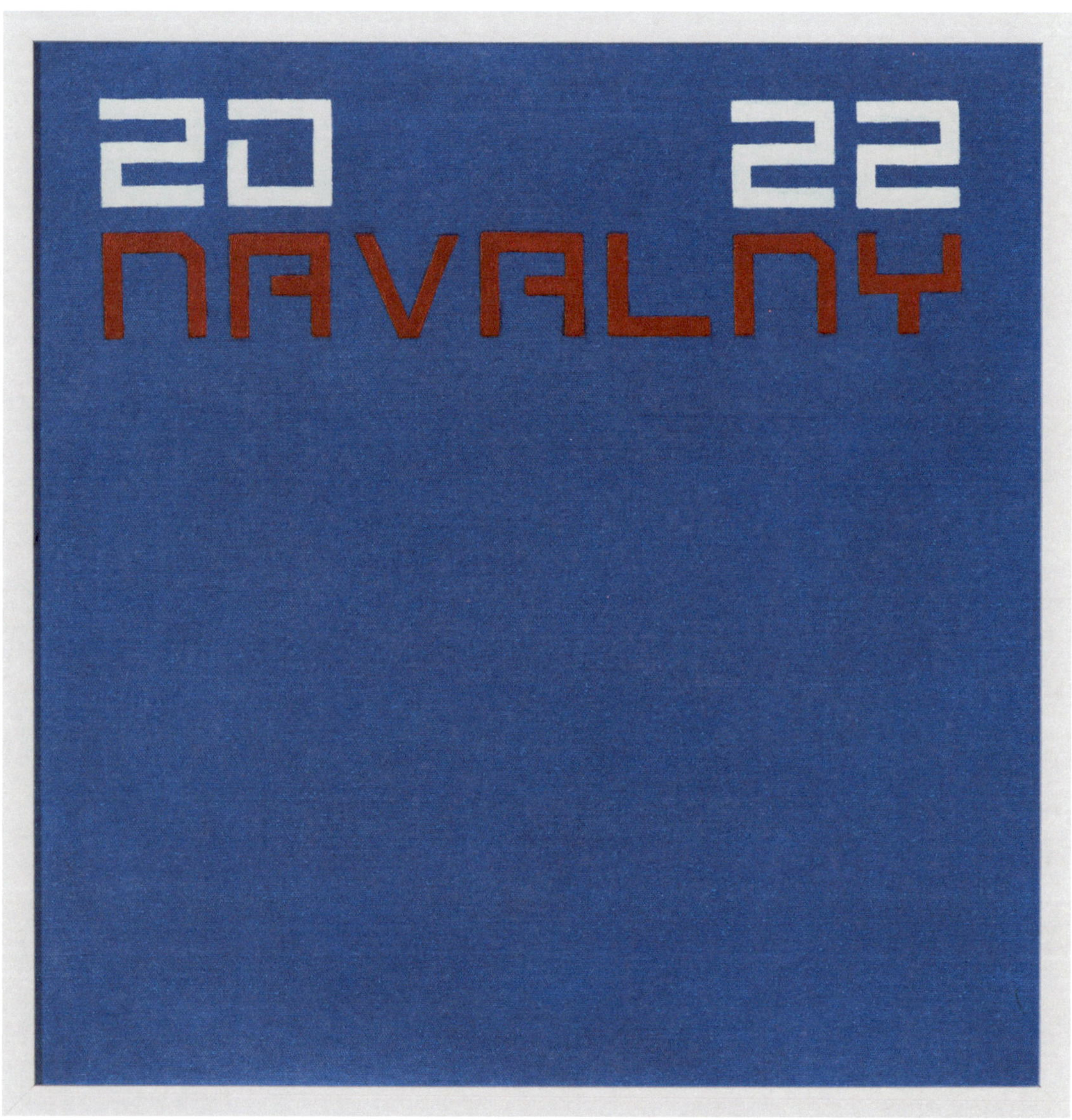

   Navalny, 2020. Oil on canvas, 20 × 20 in

Miguel A. López

"For the curatorial team of the 31st Bienal de São Paulo, it was important to propose a biennial addressing—or grounded in—conflict, understanding conflict not as a failure, but as a productive condition. Conflicts are integral components of a democratic project—precisely thinking about how tensions might be addressed or can be managed without turning into violence."

"Before the Biennial, I had already been working with the group Red Conceptualismos del Sur and later on a project titled *Perder la forma humana* [Losing the Human Form] (2013-2014), an exhibition that sought to bring together artists and collectives from the 1980s that had explored gender theatricality and *travestismo* (cross-dressing) in tension with dominant religious and political imaginaries. For São Paulo, I was interested in continuing that reflection by thinking about a constellation of specific figures—Ocaña from Catalonia, Nahúm B. Zenil from Mexico, Sergio Zevallos of Grupo Chaclacayo in Peru, and the Chilean duo Las Yeguas del Apocalipsis—who began working in the late 1970s and 1980s in response to crisis, violence, or armed conflict. In some cases, they witnessed political transitions from military dictatorships to democratic regimes, as was the case in Spain and Chile. Their practice critically channeled these contexts through *travestismo* as a form of political and aesthetic disruption, revealing how even within so-called democracies, nonnormative bodies continued to be targeted or rendered unintelligible. They were uncomfortable figures due to their deliberate marginality and aesthetics of excess, but also because of the alliances they forged with social movements and forms of grassroots activism. I was drawn to how each of these artists had proposed a different intervention within religious imaginaries—Zenil, for instance, imagining forms of reconciliation between homoerotic desire and spiritual devotion—and how their work was deeply intertwined with reflections on race and nationalism."

"In curating a section for the Bienal de São Paulo, I saw Giuseppe Campuzano's *Museo travesti del Perú* [Transvestite Museum of Peru] as offering a radically different framework for thinking about history, representation, and the museum itself. The work was an attempt to undo the expectations of scientific truth and total legibility that often defined Western museums. Instead, the project mobilized experimental strategies through narration, invoking concepts like therapeutics, duality, epic, *mestizaje*, and choreography to propose alternative modes of organizing history. The *Museo travesti* built a space that avoided falling into a traditional idea of community formation based on fixed identities, but rather operated through a promiscuous logic, taking the drag body as its *locus of enunciation*: a false body, a prosthetic body, whose nature is uncertainty, as Giuseppe liked to say. It opposed a logic of stable identity, favoring ambiguity and contradiction over coherence and embracing an unclassifiable body as the site from which all stories could be disorganized."

"The Bienal de São Paulo was controversial, among other things, for its bold and critical engagement with religion. In the days leading up to the opening, religious groups organized a series of protests targeting specific sections, notably *Deus é bicha* [God is Queer] (including Ocaña, Nahúm B. Zenil, Sergio Zevallos, and Las Yeguas del Apocalipsis) and the *Museo travesti*, along with three other projects, accusing the Biennial of promoting abortion, blasphemy, and sacrilege. These reactions, I believe, highlighted the biennial's desire to intervene in the public conversation and engage critically with ideas that shape social life. In this sense, I think the biennial was both timely and brave, addressing politically urgent issues in the midst of presidential elections. It also tragically prefigured the rise of far-right conservatism in Brazil."

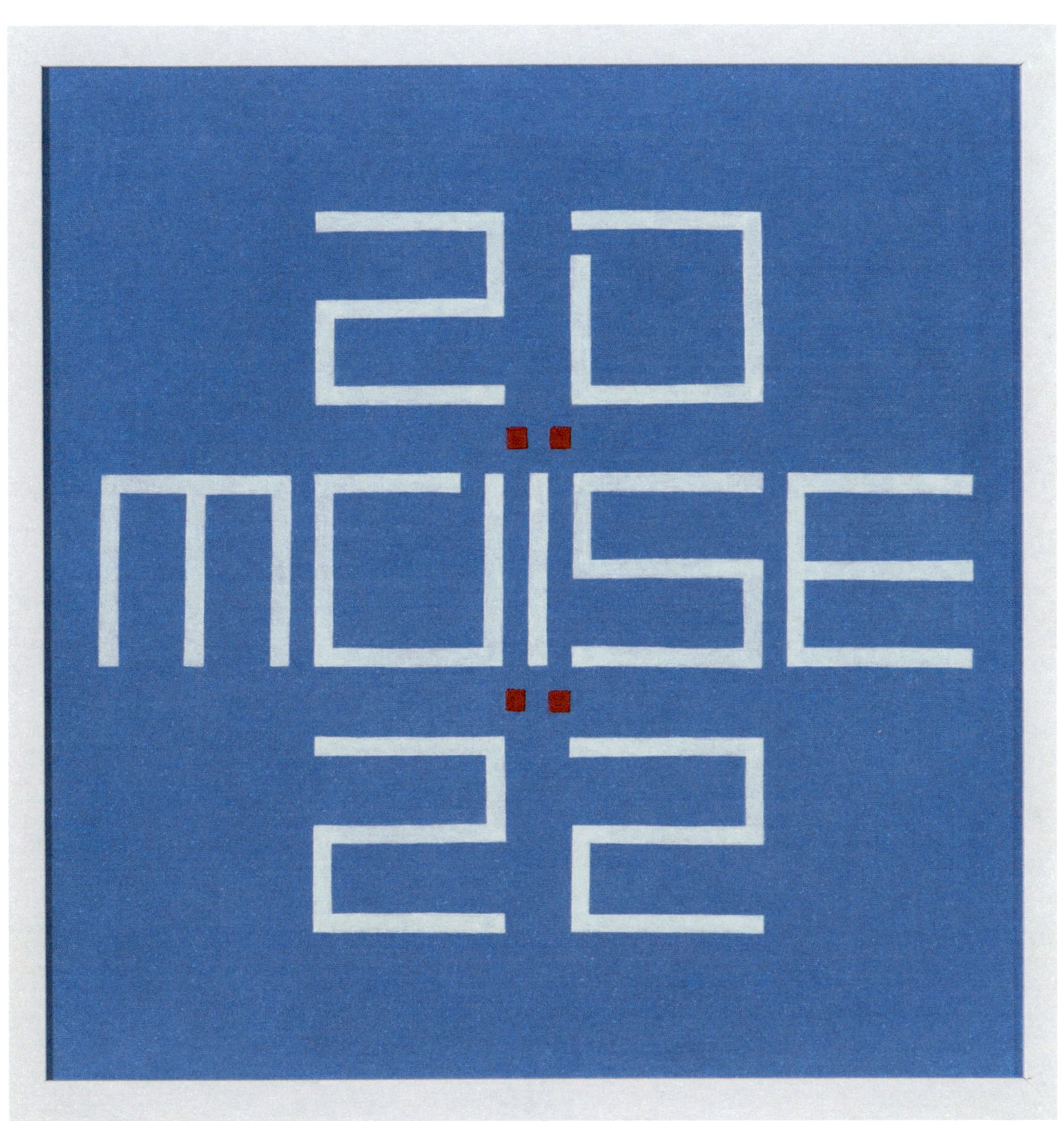

Moïse, 2021. Oil on canvas, 18 × 18 in   57

58   *Dobbs*, 2021. Oil on canvas, 16 × 16 in

Cuauhtémoc Medina

"One of the things I find most extravagant is the way many of my colleagues make presentations expressing discontent with the existence of biennials, and explaining all the reasons why they shouldn't be doing them. I'm convinced, committed, and totally sold on the importance of doing biennials. I believe that the energy I felt in producing them has to do with that commitment."

"Biennial art produces something very viable—a constant tension between autonomy and circumstance, specificity and individual practice. Somehow the polarities under which we work are produced by the biennial situation, in a similar way that art in the nineteenth and twentieth century was produced by the museum space."

"While preparing to curate the 12th Shanghai Biennale, I noticed this word invented by E. E. Cummings: *pro-regress*. I thought it was a very interesting idea because it summarized the present as a deep ambivalence and ambiguity of values and historical directions. So, I organized an exhibition that was trying to cover four areas of ambivalence: between war time and peace time; between our understanding of nature and culture; between the notion of freedom and control (like the inability to divide the liberal from the dictatorial side of our current structures of governments); and finally, between the notion of culture and art, which in my view suggests that we are always producing with a certain view of barbarism."

"This is related to a 'reputation-producing game' from one part of
the contemporary art system that relies on biennials and institutions.
A biennial that is not thought of in relation to advancing the reputa-
tion and the significance of artists is a poorly executed biennial."

"I was hoping to concentrate on one issue: the right to breathe.
What we are living through today is not just about the pandemic,
but also the political revolutions in the United States, in India, while
we are trying not to die of this disease. Our abilities have extended
through different means of technological communication, and we
are creating a different social system and a different mode of production through this crisis. The Black Lives Matter movement, the
George Floyd protests, and the question of breathing—how dying and
the impossibility of breathing has several connotations in terms of
health, ecology, and political equality—has become my obsession
over the past year."

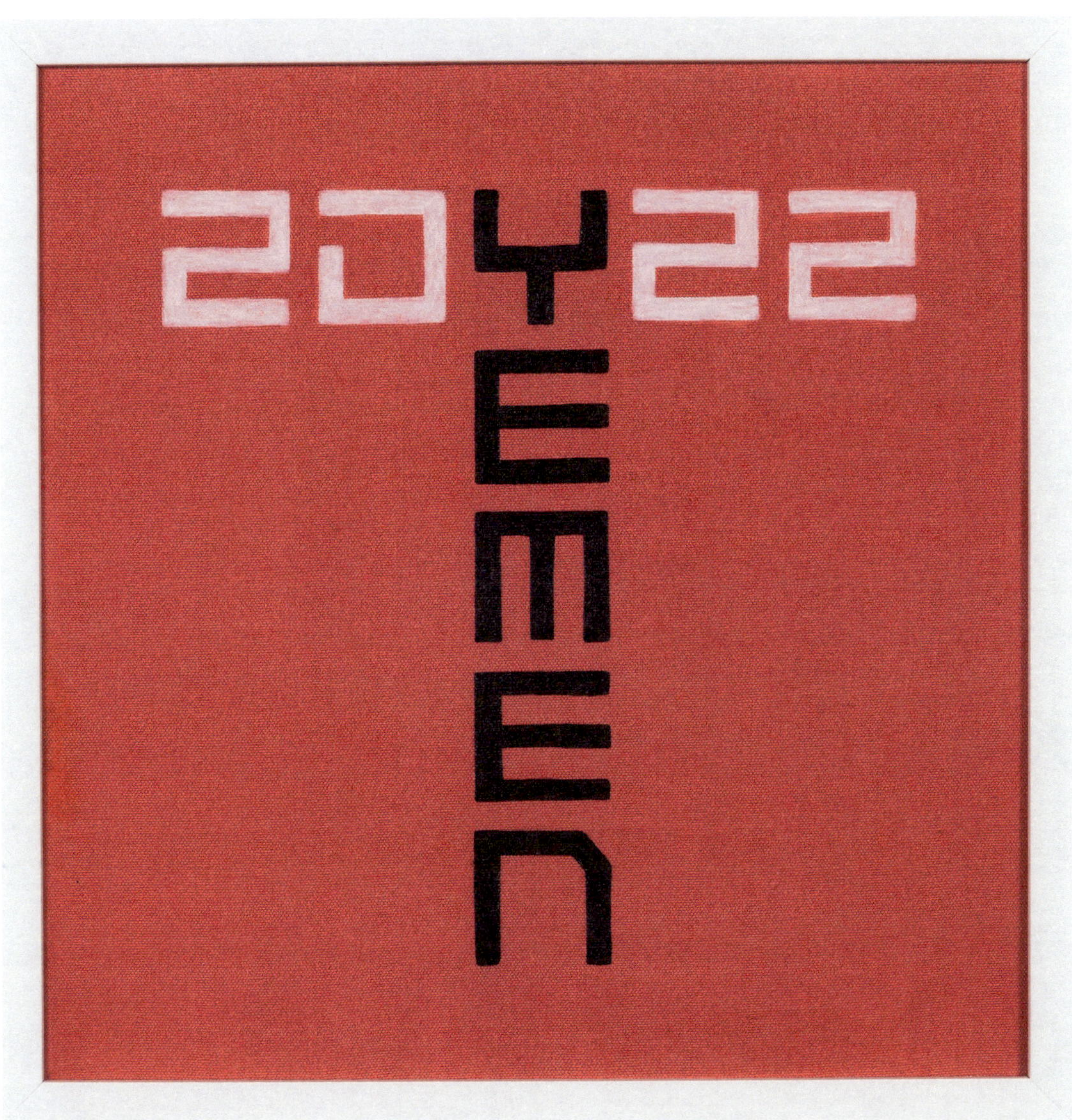

Yemen, 2021. Oil on canvas, 16 × 16 in   61

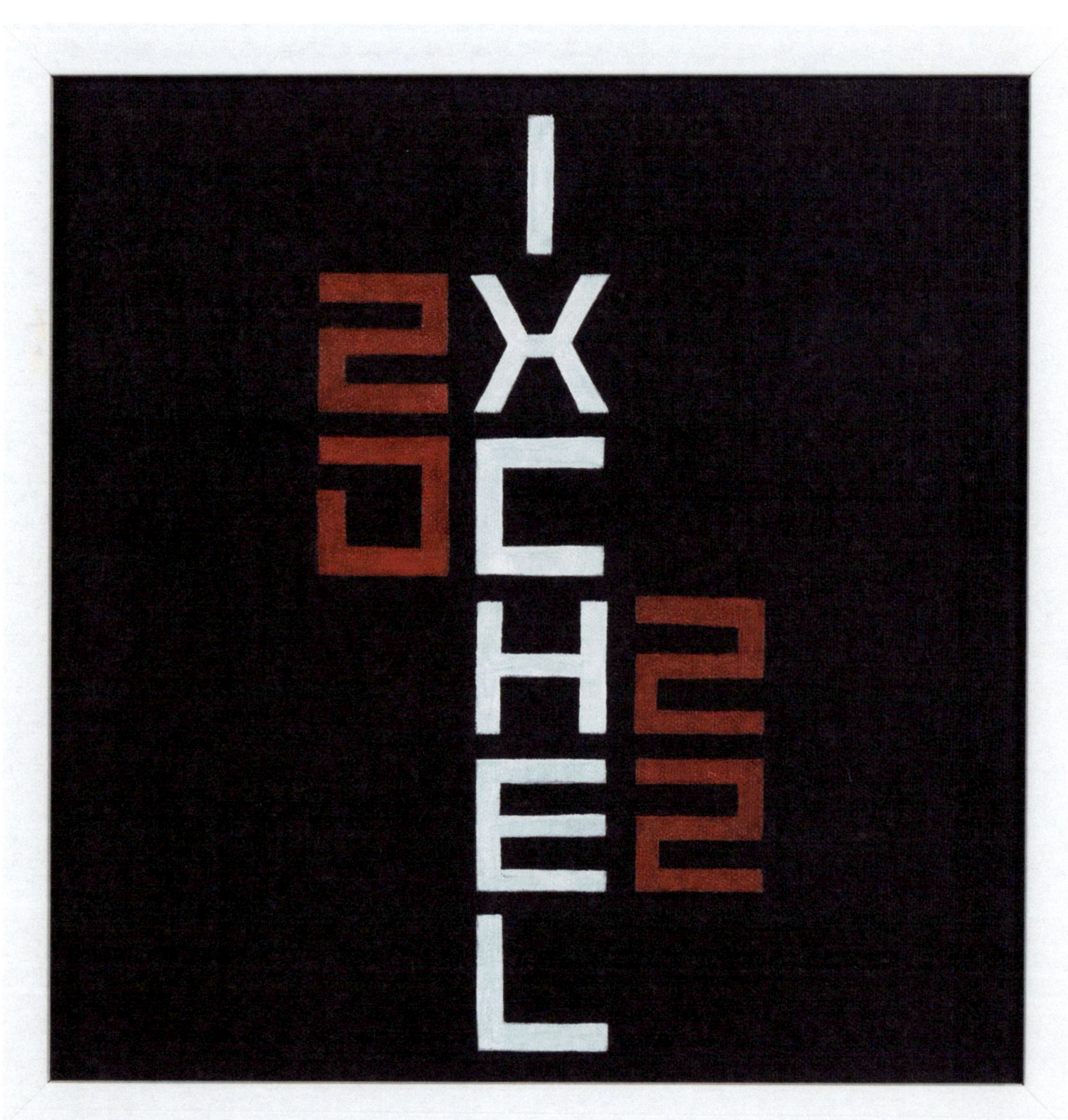

     Ixchel, 2021. Oil on canvas, 16 × 16 in

Gabi Ngcobo

"I think it's quite interesting that Cape Africa Platform (CAPE), also
happened twice, like the Johannesburg Biennale. In the context of
South Africa, things somehow don't last. You can do it twice, and
that's it. But they do shape something, expose something, and help
some artists figure out their grammars of being in the world, so they
will not be taken for granted, so to speak. Personally, this event really
shaped my thinking. I felt after CAPE 07 that I could do anything,
even if I didn't have anything—that what you need are ideas."

"Something that interests me is how things happened in the past, or
in history. If you bring them forward, they seem like they're talking
about the present. We're really thinking about the spiraling of history.
Sometimes it feels like you're just spinning in place, unable to break
free from a particular way of thinking—or from how others think
about you as a subject."

"I remember a public panel four months after being appointed as
curator of the Berlin Biennale, and the moderator just said, 'The
theme of your biennale is postcolonial, right?' Things like this—where
it is assumed how postcolonial looks to me but how it doesn't look to
you. So, it is important to distribute the responsibility in that we are
all postcolonial and need to take care of this mess, as it's not only the
work of certain people."

"I work chaotically. I don't sit around and make lists, which can be
frustrating. I work from my body, I work from memory. I have a way
of trusting myself, and my first rule is: I don't leave myself at home
when I go somewhere. I have to bring myself, and I have to look
at things from my perspective. And if I look at things from my perspective, then I want to see what kind of world one can create. I'm
inspired by the Combahee River Collective and especially the statement that when Black women are free, it means that everybody will
be free. I like thinking about how what I do as a Black woman would
reflect that kind of freedom for everyone to feel invited in a place
that they didn't feel invited before."

"Regarding critiques of the Berlin Biennale—not all, but those coming
from white men who did not find themselves addressed—we are so
used to that in our work. This whiteness and white supremacy, which
is quite tiring, pulls us back, wastes our time. It is like Toni Morrison
said: "The very serious function of racism is distraction. It keeps you
from doing your work." We wanted to really do things in a particular
way, without addressing whiteness—which is a broad thing because it
also exists within many of us. We are so used to looking at the world
in a particular way that, when it is not presented as we are used to,
a certain destabilization happens. And I was very much interested in
the destabilization of things as we have known them."

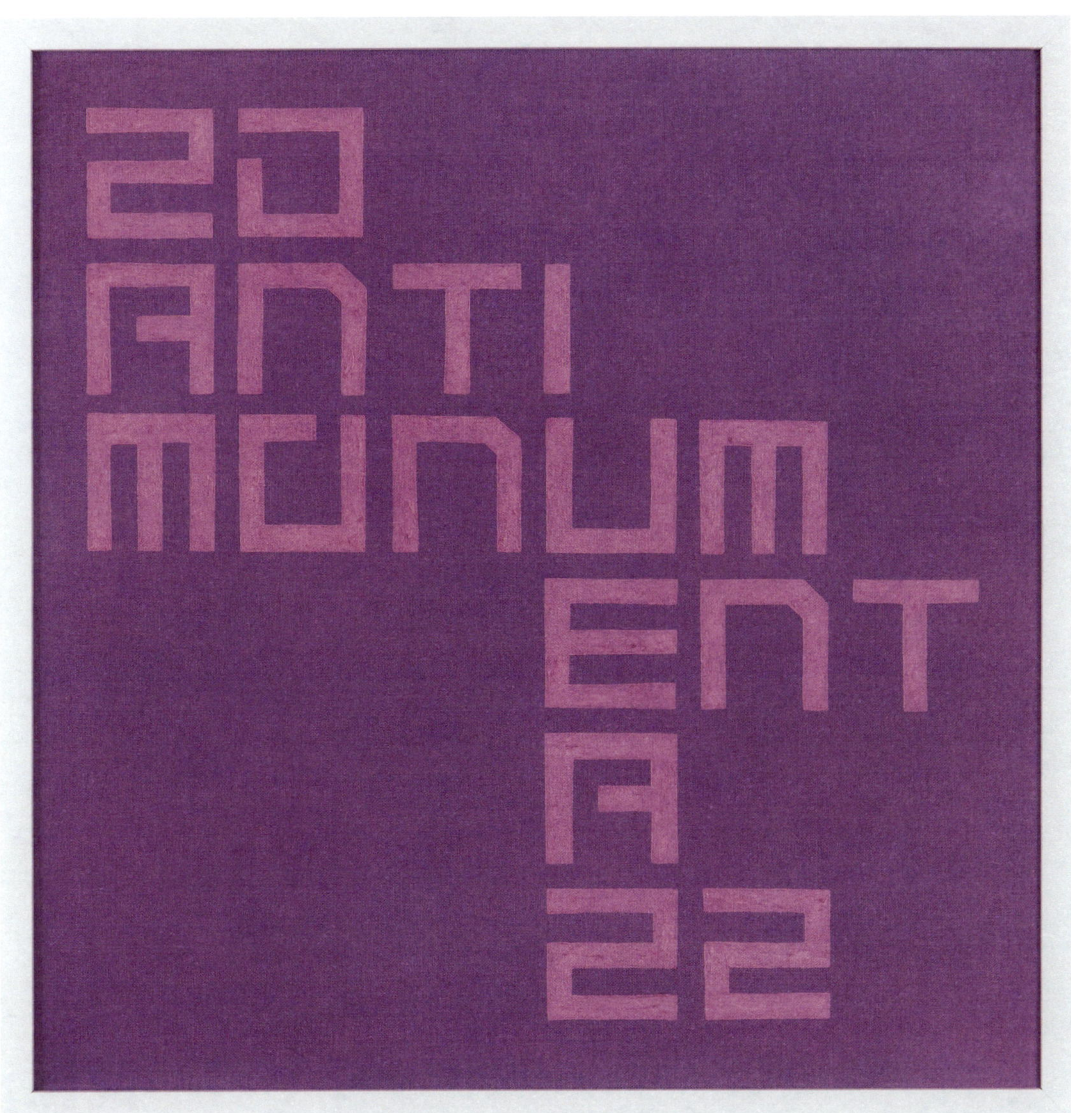

Antimonumenta, 2021. Oil on canvas, 24 × 24 in   65

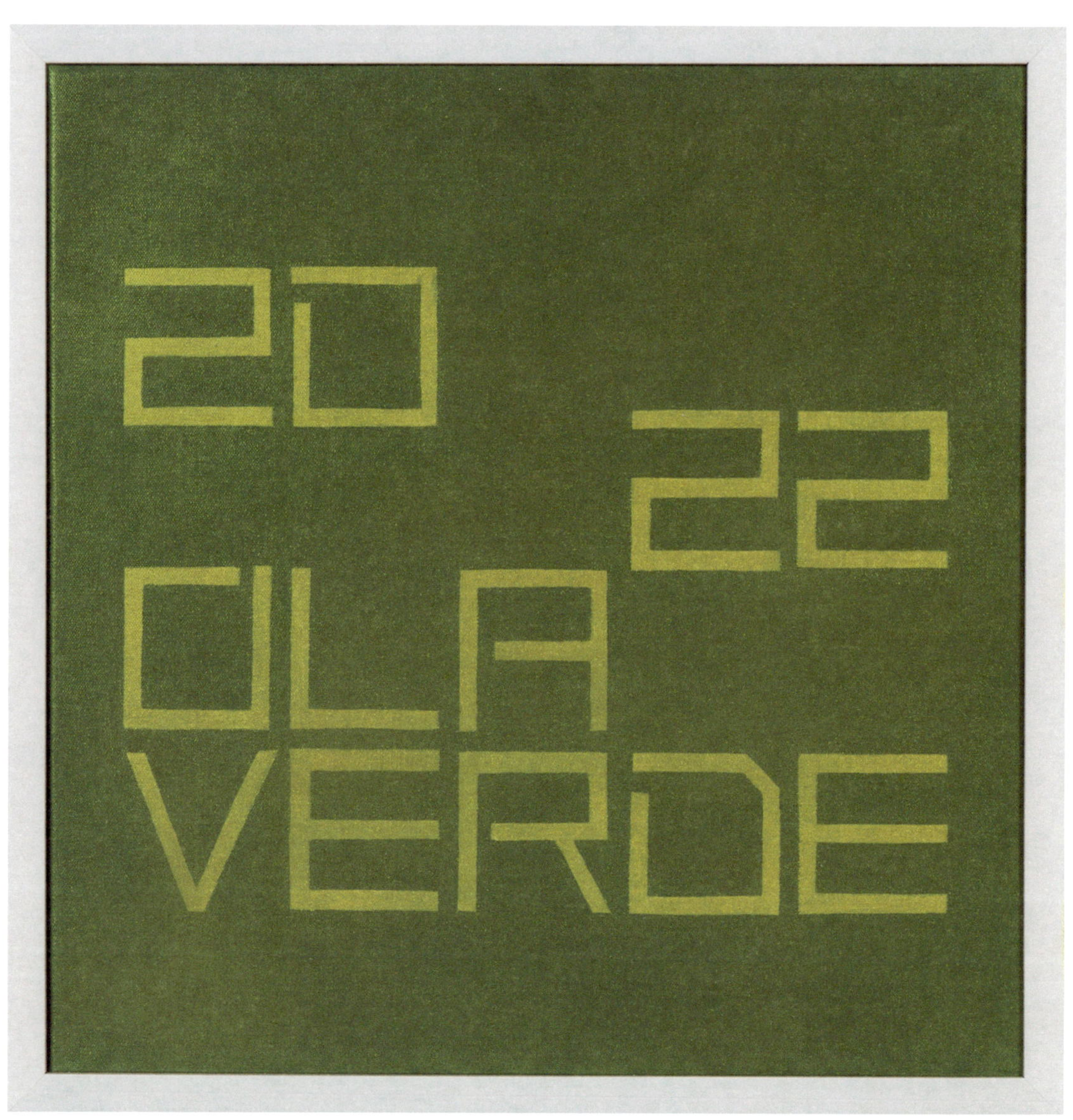

  Ola Verde, 2021. Oil on canvas, 20 × 20 in

Lucia Pietroiusti

"*General Ecology* emerged from spending a lot of time at the Serpentine Galleries before leaving for a year to have a baby and coming back, having learned all kinds of weird things about existence and how my own brain had changed. I have a background in gender studies. Before that, I was the curator of public programs at the Serpentine. So when I came back, I discovered this mysterious insight into what felt like interspecies communication by communicating with an infant, through the method of care, responsibility, and obligation, rather than language. That surfaced this entirely new notion that communication is not really about translation. So, I started to write a project for the Serpentine that would essentially necessitate a transformation of the role—to be obsessively, continuously, and forever dedicated to ecology."

"Every organization's mission statement has something about sustainability and resilience. But when you look deeper, you find that what they mean by sustainability and resilience, more often than not, has to do with the organization's *own* sustainability and the organization's *own* resilience. So, I was interested in whether you can bake that into the structure of an organization—and it's not done. It's like a work in progress. It's not just a mission of presenting art but also an extended, entangled kind of field of responsibility that has to do with planetary justice. I would say thrive-ability rather than sustainability."

"In the context of environmental justice and balance, can we think
of a different way to center the human—one shaped more like some
weird, radical anthropomorphism? And what I mean by that is: The
unequal distribution of the climate catastrophe is literally stacked
and built on top of the very same lines of colonial violence and
extraction—it maps onto them one-to-one. So, when we talk about
anthropocentricity, we're not actually referring to humans as a species but to a very specific kind of self-appointed group of humans,
with quite devastating consequences. Scientists say you shouldn't
anthropomorphize a tree. I find it much more stimulating to think:
What if saying a tree is capable of love, generosity, humor, or even
curating. Let's say art is not anthropomorphizing a tree, but that
being anthropocentric actually means assuming that love, generosity,
humor, and art in humans are emergences out of planetary versions
of those same things?"

"The ecological field and activism have traditionally had quite a lot of
blind spots, particularly around the notion of conservation because,
embedded or baked into the notion of conservation, is the fact of
some kind of 'untouched' land. But oftentimes, to call a piece of land
'untouched' promotes a political project of colonization—in order to
disavow the actual real existence and coexistence between peoples
and more-than-human species on those very lands. I'm also quite
conscious of the fact that, just like there is the extraction of rare earth
materials, there is a sudden emergence of Silicon Valley discourse
around Indigenous wisdom traditions. We need to be quite mindful of
not doing to ideas the same things that we are doing to mountains,
lands, and rivers. It would be untrue to speak about ecology without
speaking about racism, colonialism, extraction, Indigenous land,
restitution, and the like. It would be inaccurate."

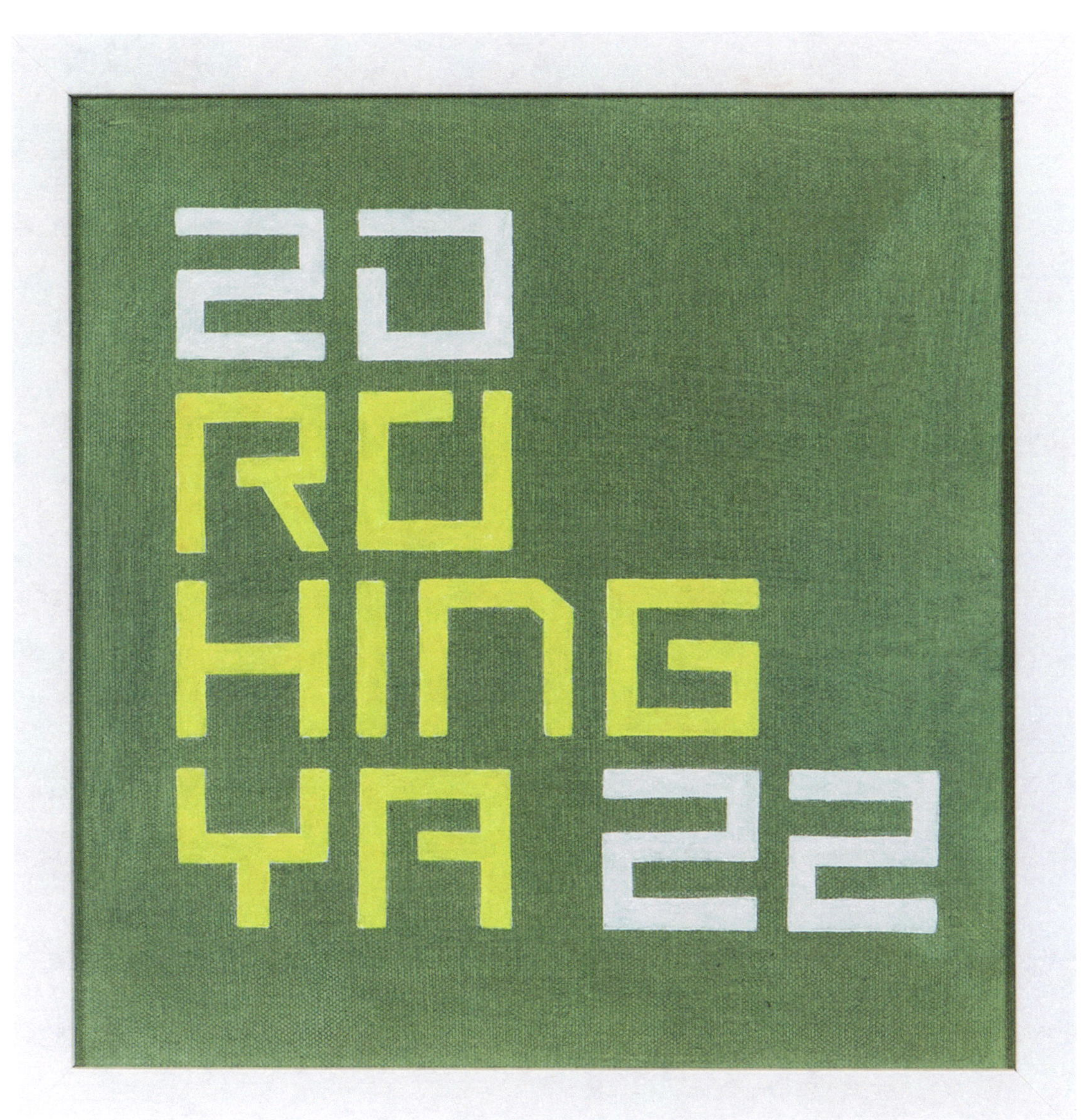

Rohingya, 2021. Oil on canvas, 12 × 12 in   69

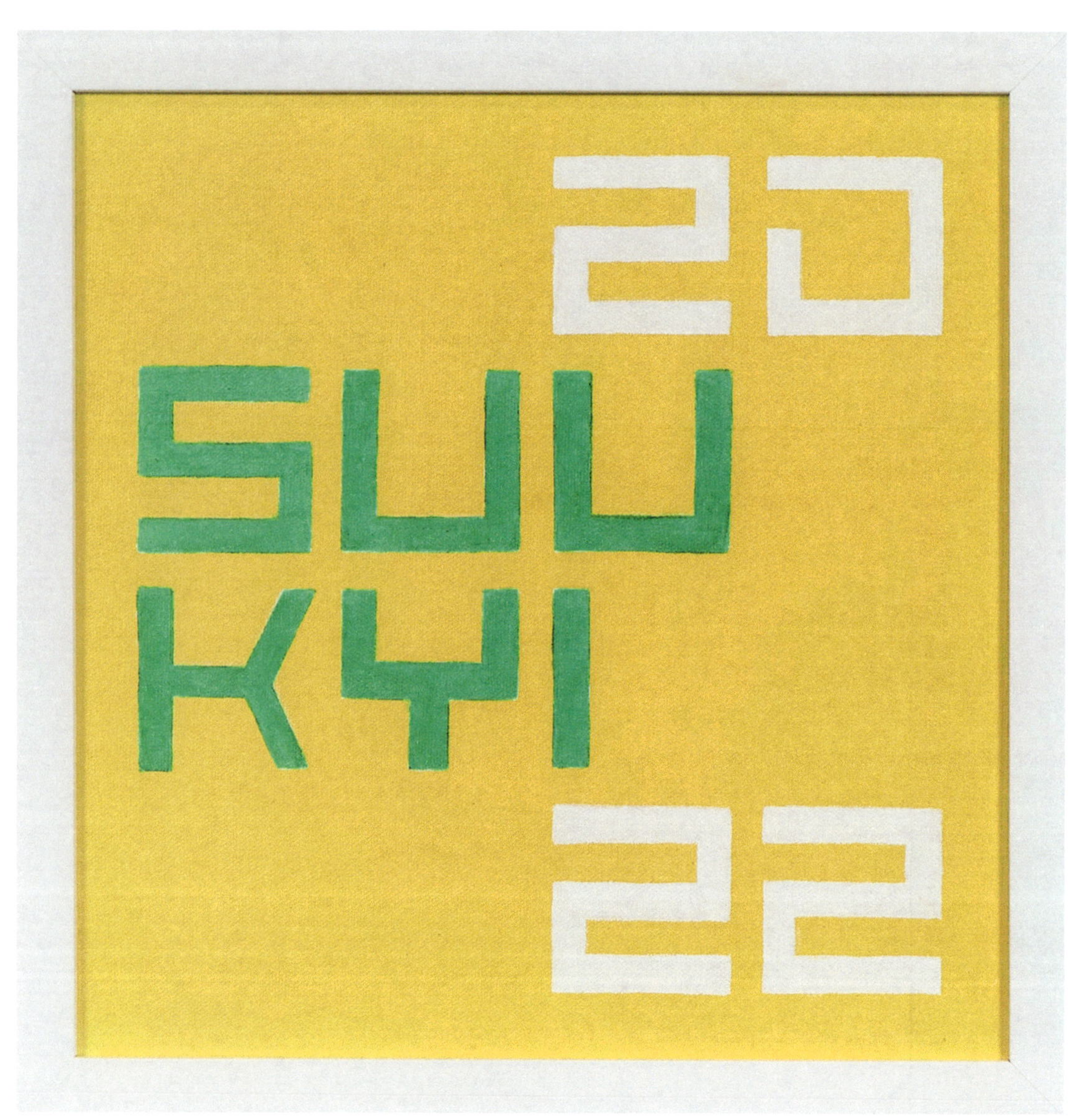

70   *Suu Kyi*, 2021. Oil on canvas, 12 × 12 in

farid rakun (ruangrupa)

"ruangrupa was formed in 2000 in Jakarta by six artists. I'm not one
of the founders; I met them around 2003, during my student days,
and worked with them sporadically until around 2010. Then I came
back and decided to stay in Jakarta, and ruangrupa was a big part of
that decision. Jakarta is one of the most expensive places in the country, and most of us couldn't afford a studio, so the street became
our canvas, let's say—our exhibition space."

"We were trying to engage with video art, although none of us were
experts, especially not in 2003. So we used the festival form as a way
to invite works or people that we deemed to be interesting to hear
from, or to learn from, and then to give away free artworks."

"Around 2007 came a proliferation of invitations from biennials, so
we built our artistic practice collectively through participation in
them. Working with locals became our modus operandi. For example,
at the Bienal de São Paulo, we invited local collectives to work with
us and to fill the space that was given to us in the pavilion. A lot of
the works were from *paulistas* themselves, as well as workshops held
by them. Many projects were initiated by them, but we worked with
them closely for a couple of months. That is why some argue that our
artistic practice holds similarities to curatorial practice as well."

"In 2015, ruangrupa was working with other collectives from Jakarta. It became a collective of collectives, and we came up with the term *lumbung* for our process, a vernacular word meaning 'rice barn.' It's just a shortcut for us to talk about what we were trying to do at that moment, this collective governance of things—let's say, how we work together. That's what we had been doing when documenta became interested in us."

"We are used to a type of approach which is parasitic. When invited by a large institution, the default approach or sensibility was to ask: 'What can we get from this institution?' But now, we're trying to do things differently. Instead of taking the back door and becoming a parasite, what if we take the front door? We need to become transparent. So, that's the thing that we are dealing with right now."

"Lumbung is a method, not a concept, not a theme. We're not trying to prove lumbung is something that we know well. And if others have other kinds of methods of collective governance, let's combine them. That's the main reason we're doing this. We also want to celebrate this agricultural term of 'harvest.' If this is a harvesting process, what we're doing—planting, sowing, taking care of, maintaining, harvesting, and then eating, of course—then, I think that's what we are. That's how we understand what we're doing right now. And also learning from others."

"The hyper-nationalism that is happening right now, which we realize can be a threat, has also proven to be a savior at times—let's say, for these local types of practices, ours included. Revisiting nationalism is one thing and collectivism is another. Those two things are a result of trying to do things differently, so it's interesting right now, at least for me, how actually the separation between right, left, and center in the political realm doesn't hold that strong anymore. Maybe we can come up with another type of approach, not seeing it as binary. We might also have another answer, but we don't want to repeat mistakes from the past, of course. So it is important to not fall into that."

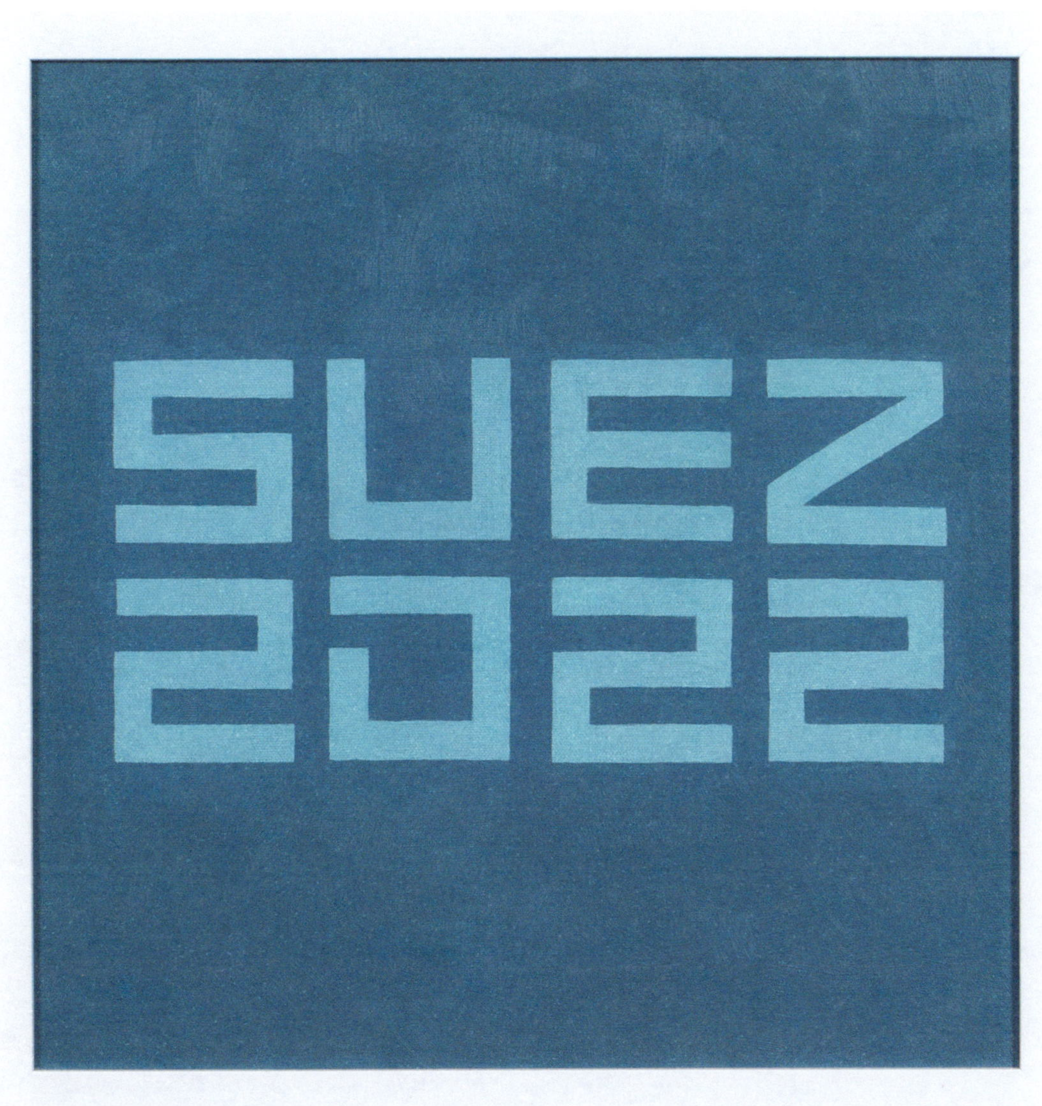

Suez, 2021. Oil on canvas, 12 × 12 in   73

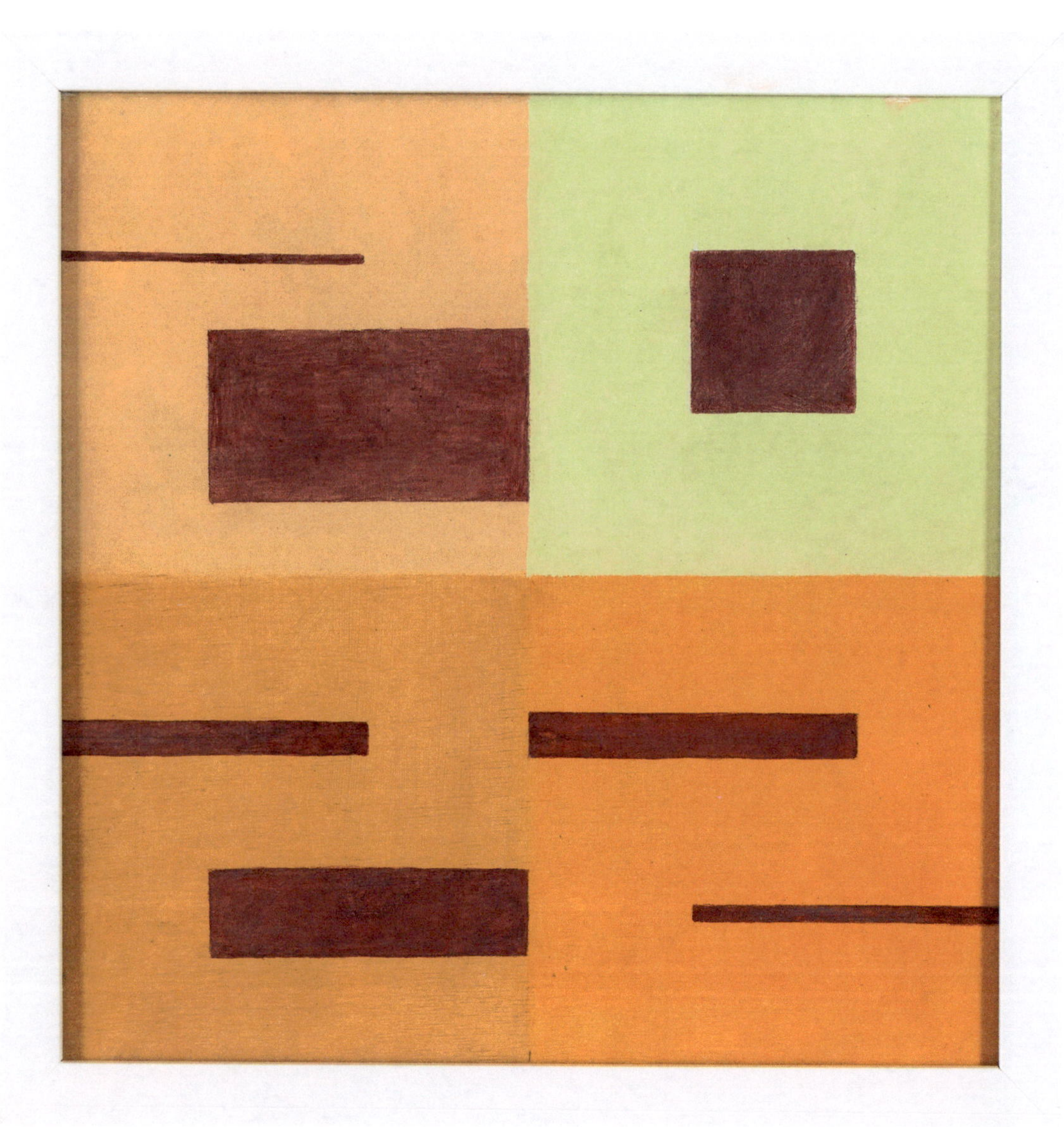

74   *Abstraction No. 4*, 2021. Oil on canvas, 12 × 12 in

José Roca

"I think the biennial model has a lot of possibilities and some problems. One of the problems is that, in some cases, cities that only have the biennial end up funneling all the resources into a single short-lived spectacular event, and then, there is no funding for the arts during the period outside of the biennial. Biennials are recurrent but also discontinuous. So, how do we connect what happens between one incarnation and the next so that the city doesn't suffer from the lack of programming between one incarnation of the biennale and the next? I think that's what I tried to do for the Bienal do Mercosul."

"Twenty-five years later, I was asked to bring back the Bienal de Arte de Medellín. In a way, I said, 'Well, it's probably not wise to do that. Let's think of another project, something that really addresses the needs of Medellín.' Medellín prides itself on being a very hospitable city. But in fact, if you had seen the program of the museums and institutions, they were primarily showing the same group of local artists. The canonical group of contemporary artists in Colombia had never been shown there, for example. I thought this notion of hospitality could be a good starting point. We decided not to call it a biennial, because the very concept can be problematic and we didn't want to tie it to a specific regularity. So, it was called the Encuentro de Medellín, and its first incarnation happened in 2007. We put in place several ideas there. One, that the theme would also be a strategy: What can hospitality and this tension between the host and the guest teach us about museum practice? The other thing was that this wasn't going to be a two- or three-month event; it was something that would be extended in time and space. It was scattered all over Medellín because we thought we didn't need a large activation; we needed something that would reweave together the loose threads of the artistic community that had been heavily hit by years of cartel power."

"In the 8th edition of Bienal do Mercosul, I tried to bring all I had learned from the previous experiences about geopolitics from the standpoint of art into this project. So, we developed what we called the 'activating strategies.' These were meant to activate a scene but not necessarily lead to an exhibition. Then, there were the exhibition strategies, which were the biennial proper, and the pedagogical project. One key component took place six months earlier, when nine artists traveled through the region, retracing the historical roots of colonial penetration in Rio Grande do Sul. It was very successful in activating the region before the biennial took place."

"In the 23rd Biennale of Sydney, rivers and other waterways feature prominently. But rivers are only the departure point. To continue the metaphor, they are the source that is then enriched by tributaries. Everything in the river's path makes it stronger and more diverse, and as it approaches the mouth, it branches out in a delta of other possibilities. So, this is the point of departure and what the biennial is about. In addition, we explore many other things, like the rights of nature, the voices of nature. If some rivers and other waterways have attained legal personhood and can be represented in court, can they have a voice in a biennial, for example? That is something we're asking ourselves. This biennial also articulates creation stories from different Indigenous groups, speculative science, collaboration between artists and scientists, and a slew of other themes."

"One thing that I've learned by doing these different biennials here and there is that there is no model that works for every place. Activating the local scene meant a lot in Medellín in 2007, for example, but maybe is not as necessary nowadays, since the Museo de Arte Moderno de Medellín has been revived and has an incredible program. So, every situation in time and space calls for a different sort of tailored model."

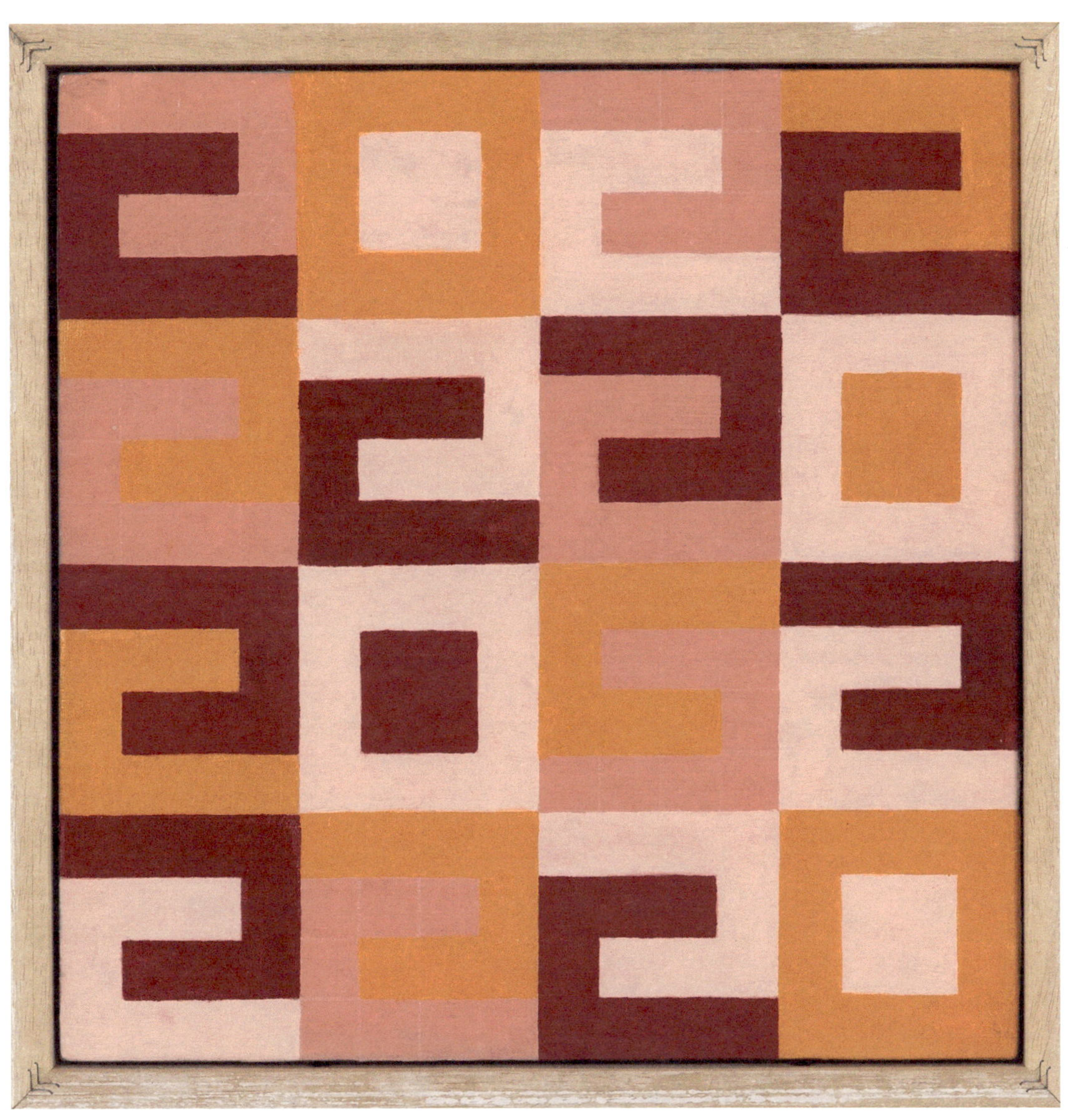

Abstraction No.5, 2021. Oil on canvas, 12 × 12 in

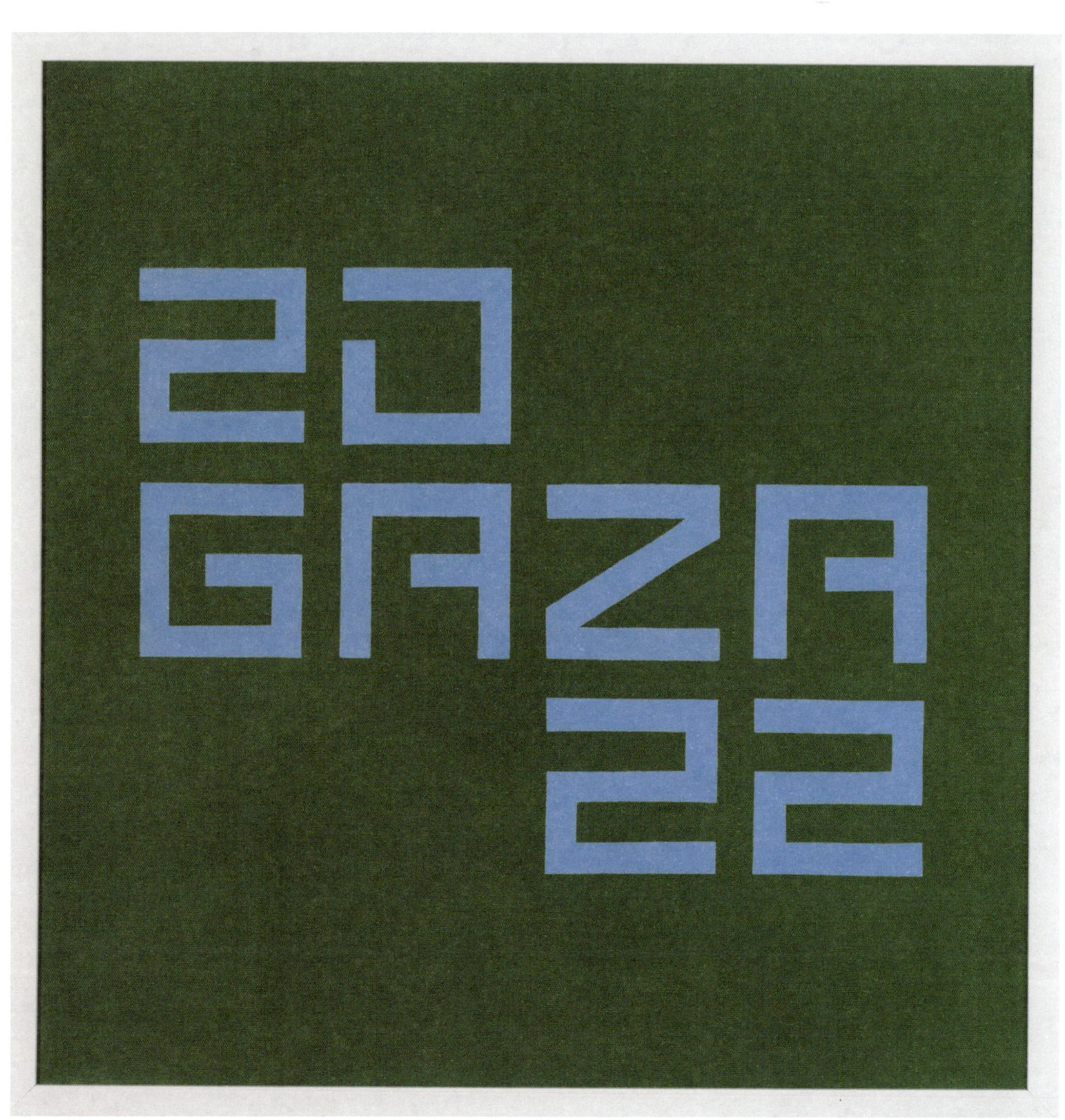

     Gaza, 2021. Oil on canvas, 24 × 24 in

"In organizing the 58th La Biennale di Venezia, I was thinking about this idea that a fact might not just be a relationship that exists in the world, but maybe there are alternative or parallel facts. In parallel with that is the idea that our political discourse is getting Twitter-ized; things are getting more and more simplified. It seems to me that art is one of the last places in our culture that allows for a kind of complex, multilayered discourse. That is, the opposite of simplifying things; it's actually connecting different possible path-ways of thought. For the Biennale, I wanted to show fewer artists and highlight the way those artists created complex, contradictory, ambiguous ways of making art—something generative rather than something that closes down meaning."

"I also feel that art takes a lot from its physical surroundings and how it is installed. I thought of this A and B format to suggest that you could make an infinite sequence of shows with the same artists. So, this A and B format in different buildings would emphasize that the same artists might do something completely different and that an artist's identity was not defined by a particular type of work. I hoped that people wouldn't realize, unless they were reading the labels, that these were the same artists in both venues. But once you do realize, then the challenge is to try to engage with the thinking underneath what superficially look like very different types of art."

"The overwhelming majority of biennials follow a very similar format, and the emphasis tends to be on a theme—and I'm slightly distrustful of curatorial themes. I have an uncomfortable relationship with those grandiose curatorial statements that the artworks are supposed to illustrate."

"I really think the curator's role is to be a bridge between the artist and the artwork and the audience. It is to find ways to make things as obvious, compelling, and inviting as possible to visitors. And if people can move through an exhibition in different ways, I think it also creates a sense of discovery and exploration. That is why I try to find ways to help the audience feel in the best spot, where they can really engage fully with artwork."

"One of the things that happens when you suddenly can't go to a gallery or museum is that you start to think about all the things you miss, and I think one of them is the public nature of that experience. It's not the same sitting in front of your computer. So, I started to pay attention to what was in the street. It became like a kind of gallery, and I really enjoyed that. I think that an important part of this lockdown moment was finding ways to keep an ongoing public conversation."

"Since the Hayward Gallery couldn't be open, we commissioned artists to make portraits of essential workers who had to work throughout the pandemic. I'd never tried to think of an outdoor exhibition, but we ended up with about sixteen large-scale visual artworks and poems from six poets, all responding to the pandemic. That began a new strain of work, doing things outside and working with a number of artists who are also artists from our neighborhood."

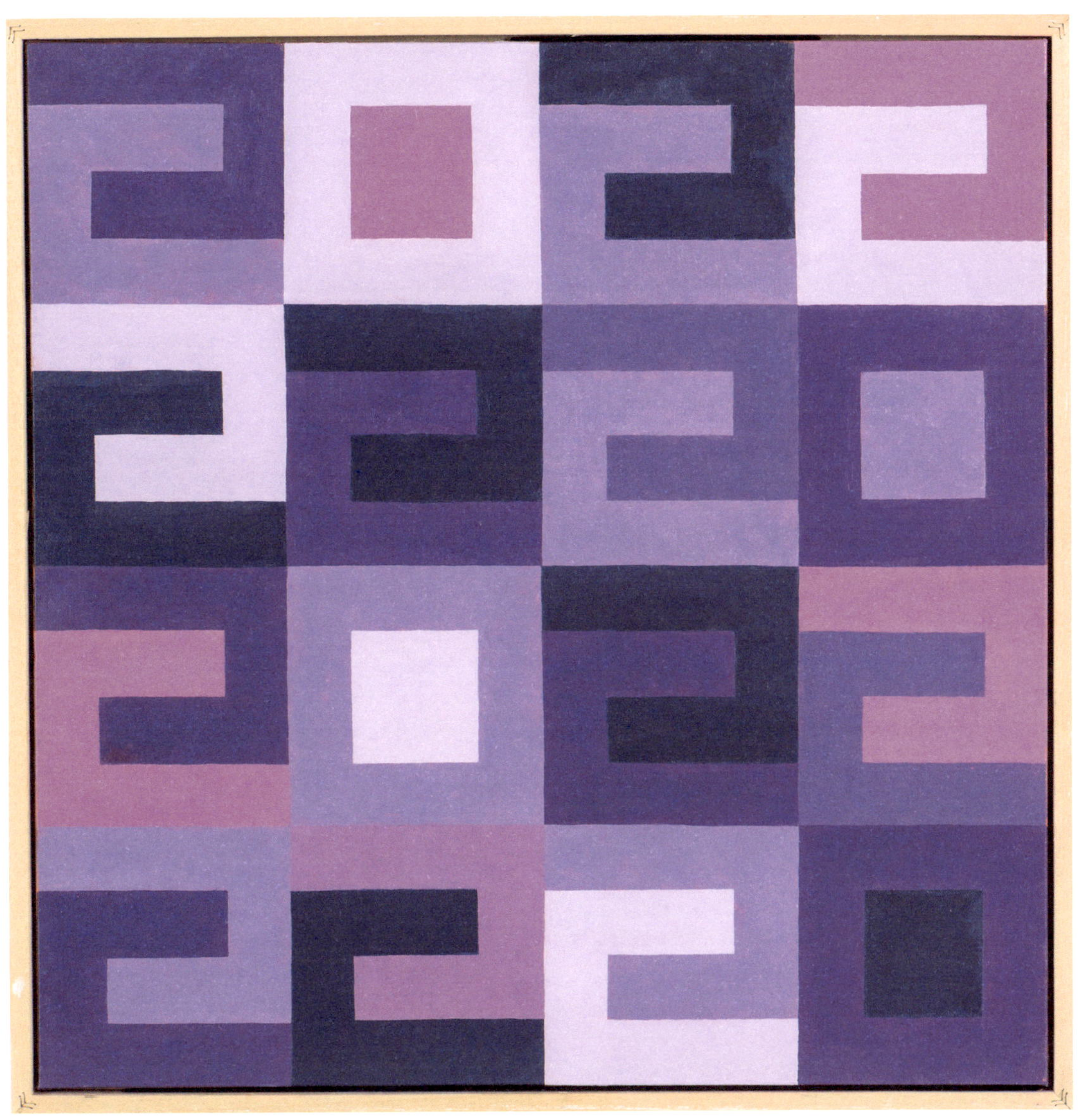

Abstraction No. 6, 2021. Oil on canvas, 24 × 24 in   81

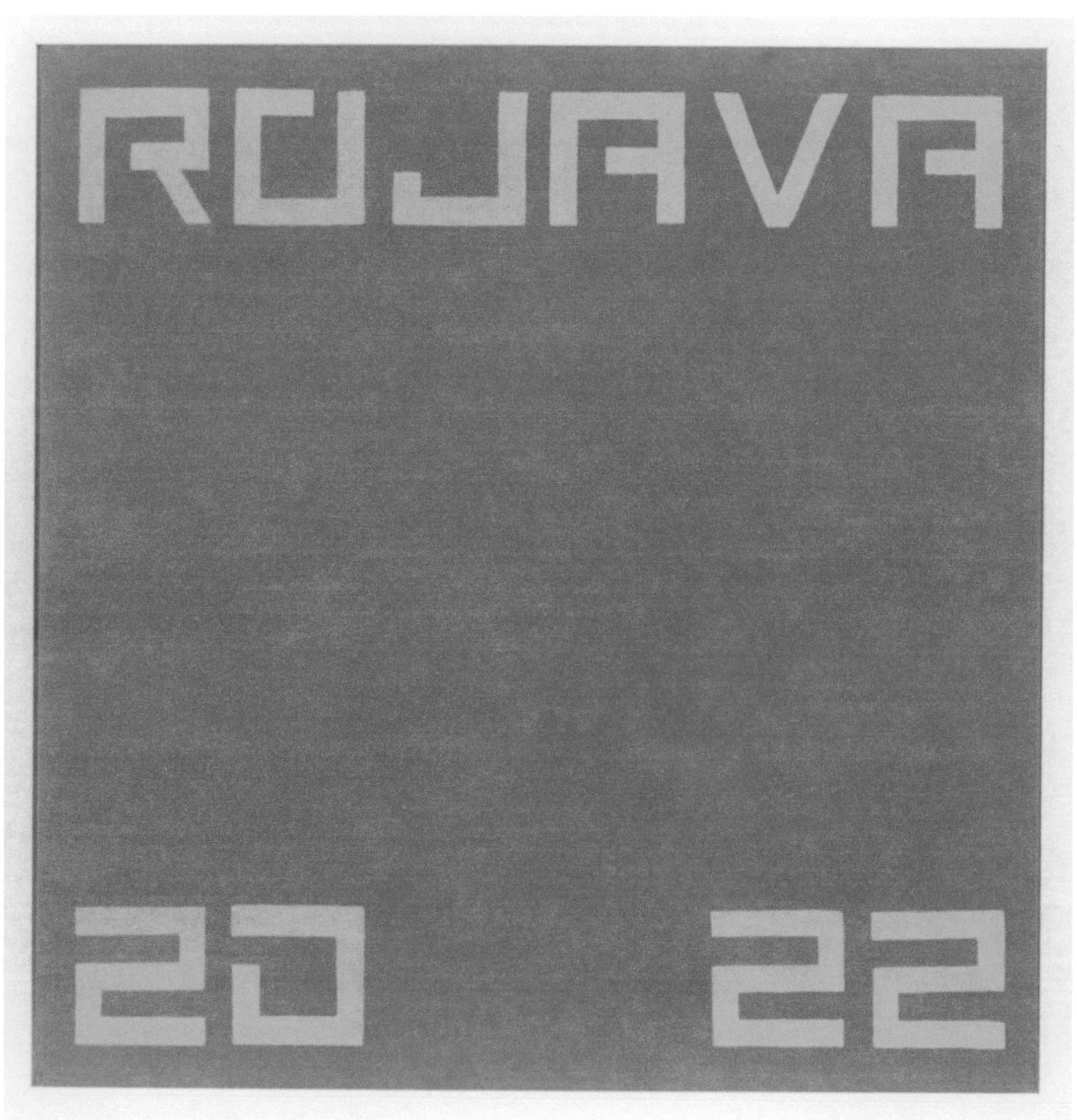

    Rojava, 2021. Oil on canvas, 24 × 24 in

Trevor Schoonmaker

"What I did in Prospect.4 was essentially pull together artists who hadn't had significant exposure. I tried to curate something that, frankly, I wanted to see myself. And working with artists repeatedly is part of that—it's something that is significant for me, because there's a relationship being built with the artists that I feel very strongly about. For me, curating is entirely subjective and incredibly personal. It's not a process where I'm a detached researcher. It's about projecting—not reflecting. I'm not just mirroring what's happening outside; I'm projecting what I want to say, from a place where I might feel more. It may show my personal interest, but it's also about finding a niche where there is an activist bent. I like to shine the spotlight on artists who have historically been overlooked and marginalized. But it's also reflective of my own experience. And that may sound odd when you look at me—as a straight white male—but my peers, my family, and my experience is perhaps not what you might anticipate."

"Curation is a creative process for me. It's not strictly an intellectual or research process. It's more like the idea of producing something— creativity as an embodiment of hope, in some way. You hope to make a difference. You hope to impact change. You hope to provoke dialogue. And if you have great ambitions, maybe you start to move the needle on the canon."

"Everyone was in crisis mode because of the pandemic and its health concerns—but also because of a racial reckoning. The pandemic really pulled off the veneer and exposed all the inequities in US society and around the world. Carrie Mae Weems's project makes it painfully clear that these two things are not two different crises. There are two sides of the same coin, and it beautifully—and at times painfully—illustrates that. The project illustrates how COVID-19 has disproportionately affected racialized communities and allowed us to pursue collaborations that we didn't even know were possible with local organizations and individuals."

"The pandemic crisis has revealed some things, like greater connectivity through forced virtual platforms like this one. Beyond our immediate environment, I feel more connected internationally and nationally—without having to get on a plane, burn fossil fuel, and spend money. So that's positive. I think museums had a hard time at first figuring out how to pivot, how to adjust, whereas performing arts, film, and time-based media already had the content. They couldn't just say: 'Look, here's this performance, here's this film, you can enjoy it.' I think that really pushing the technological side—the virtual component—can help augment what we do in person."

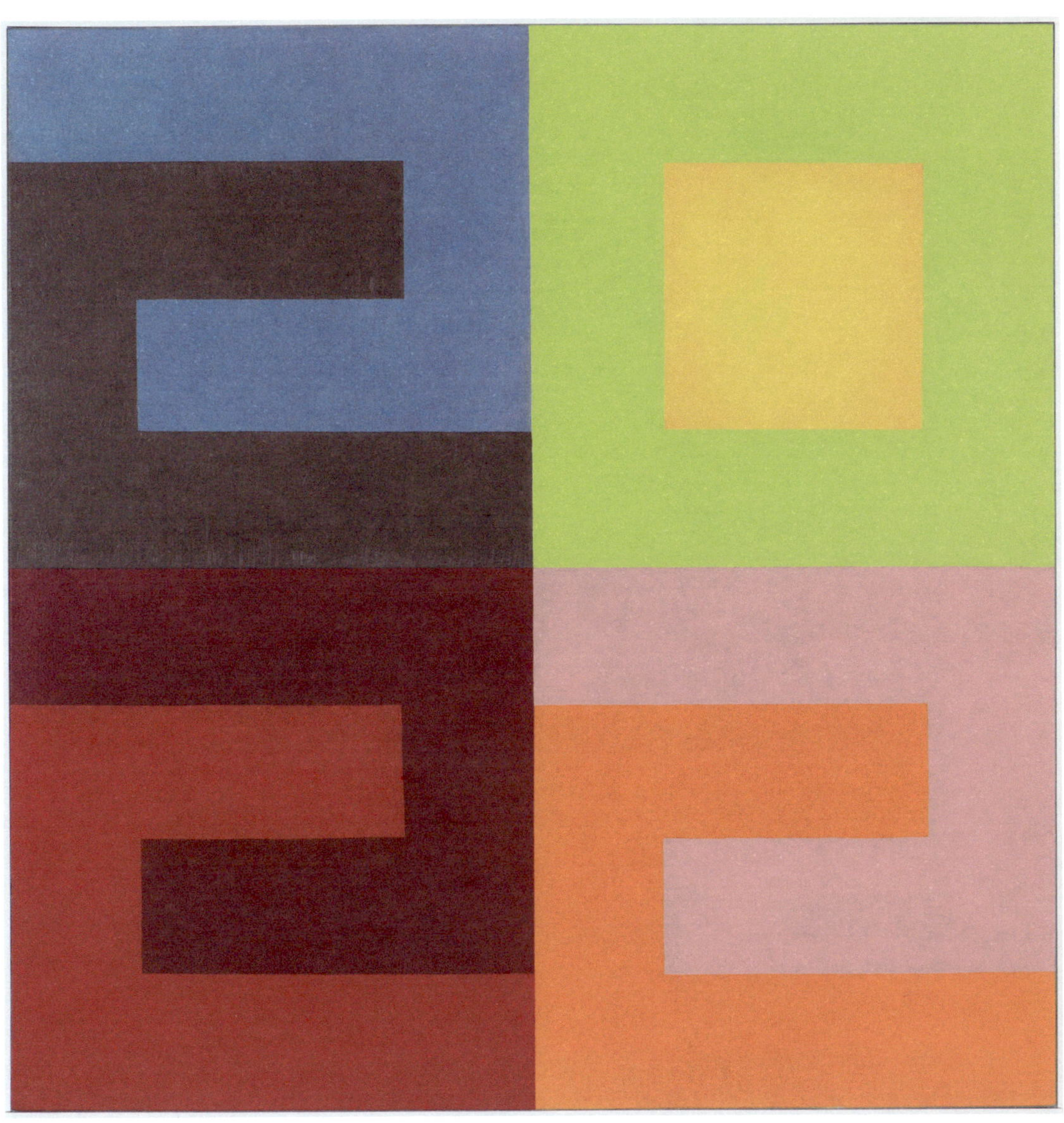

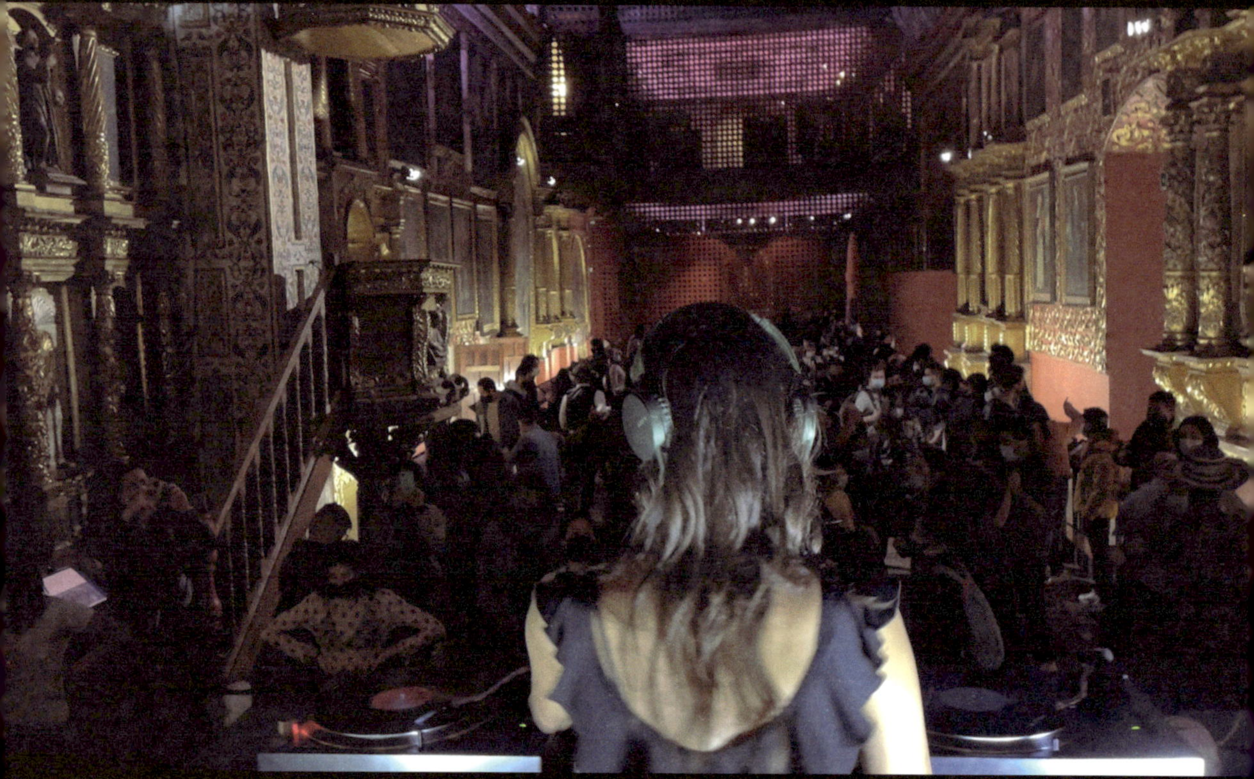

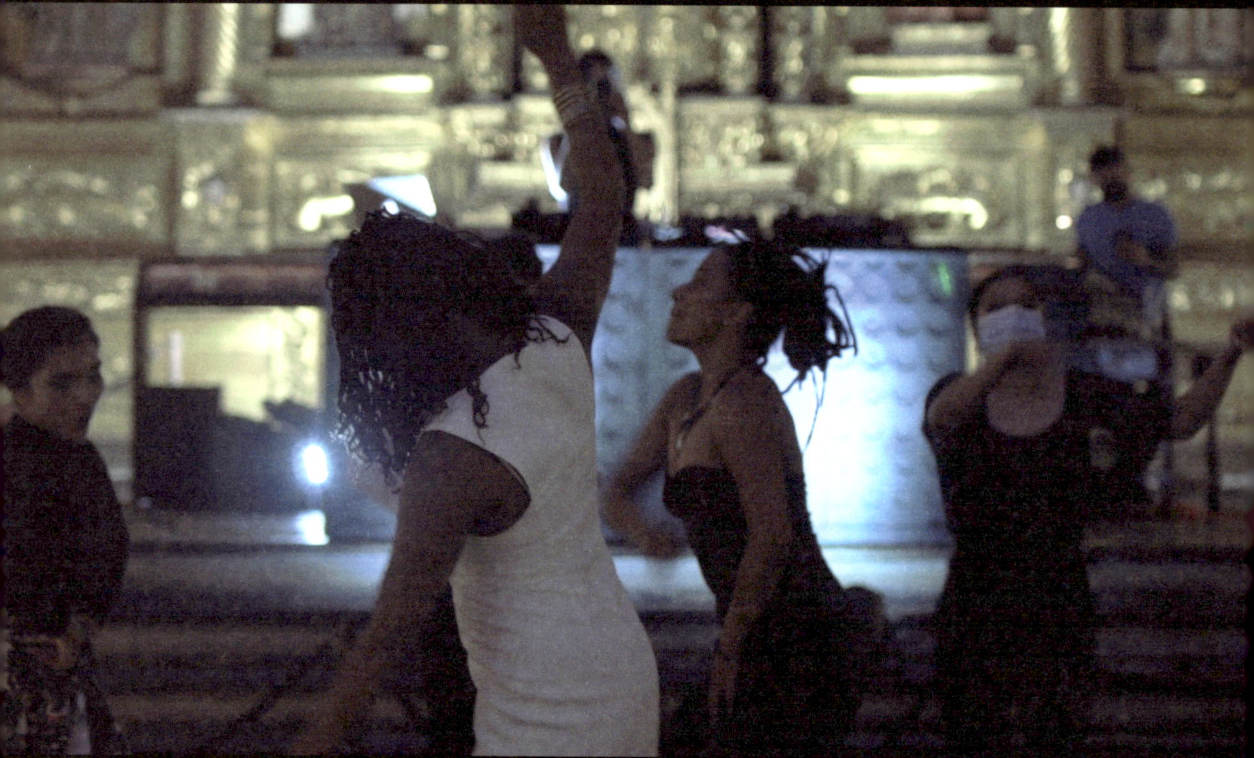

La plaga: A Public Dance with Pandemic Protocols, Bogotá, 2021

3-hr site-specific performance and video artwork,
single-channel, stereo, 7 min 19 sec

*La plaga*1 [The Plague] was a site-specific musical and social intervention by Pedro Lasch, held at the Santa Clara Museum in Bogotá on November 12, 2021, as part of the RƎEXISTENCIAS Biennial of Art and Decoloniality. Conceived as a public dance carried out under pandemic protocols, this new social artwork made use of the museum's splendid baroque architecture to craft a memorable and intense collective experience—one that allowed for the coexistence of joy and suffering, playfulness and gravity, creativity and critical reflection. Documentation of the event also became the source material for a video artwork by the same title, edited by Pedro Lasch and Michael Blair.

—

1   *La plaga* refers to a Spanish-language rock and roll song popularized in Mexico by Los Teen Tops in the early 1960s. Adapted from Little Richard's "Good Golly Miss Molly," the song became a widely recognized song in the *Rock en español* genre and circulated within Latin America. Lasch's piece resemanticizes the term *plague* within the context of the COVID-19 pandemic, when public health protocols—initially perceived as exceptional—were gradually normalized, and in some regions, selectively relaxed. By staging a choreographed public dance under pandemic measures, the work questions how collectivity, sociability, and even joy can be renegotiated in times of crisis.

Curated by David Arteaga and Adolfo Albán Achinte. Music and
DJ: Loa Malbec. Interlude: Divino Chibcha Selektor. Dancers:
Natalia Andrea Parada Casas, Alvaro Esteban Medina Ramírez,
Angie Lorena Cuesta Bautista, David Esteban Ruiz Hernández,
Mateo Popayán Cortés, Paula Popayán Cortés, Liza Bello, Esther
Asprilla, Alejandra Vargas, Laura Melo.

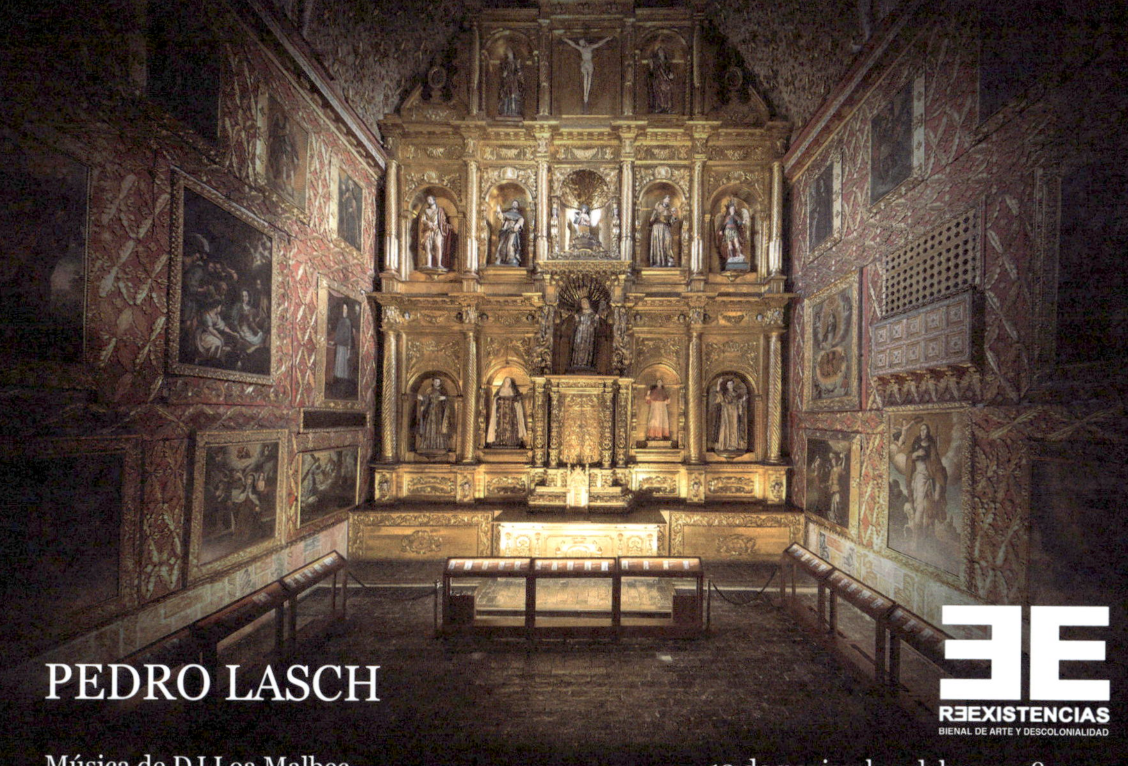

LA PLAGA
UN BAILE PUBLICO CON PROTOCOLO DE PANDEMIA
PEDRO LASCH
REEXISTENCIAS
BIENAL DE ARTE Y DESCOLONIALIDAD
Música de DJ Loa Malbec
Interludio de Divino Chibcha Selektor
12 de noviembre del 2021, 8-9pm
Museo Santa Clara, Carrera 8 No. 8 - 91, Bogotá
Organiza:
[Animal Simbólico]
Apoyan:
MUSEO SANTA CLARA
La cultura es de todos
Mincultura
SOCIAL PRACTICE
DUKE UNIVERSITY
FRANKLIN HUMANITIES INSTITUTE

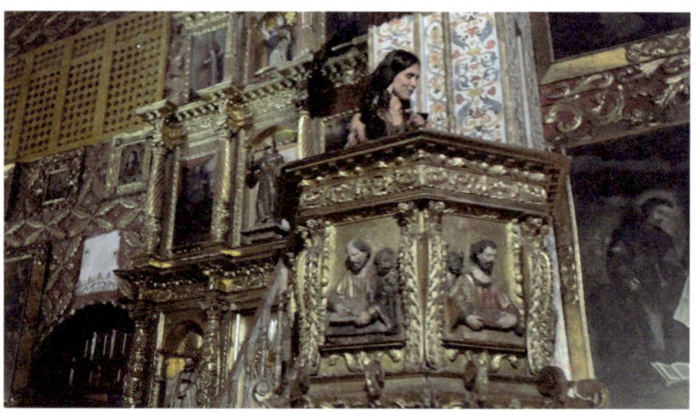
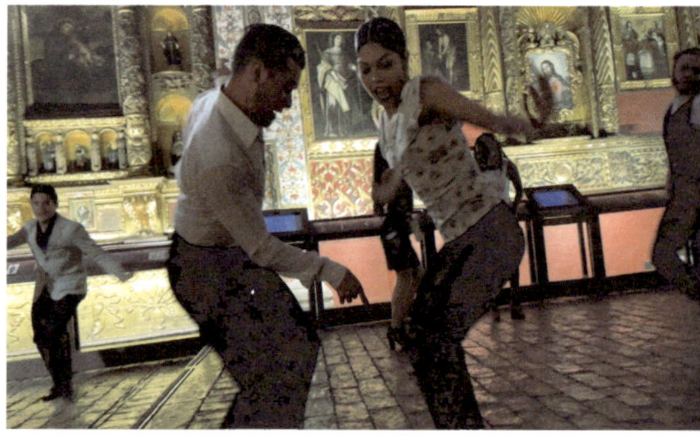
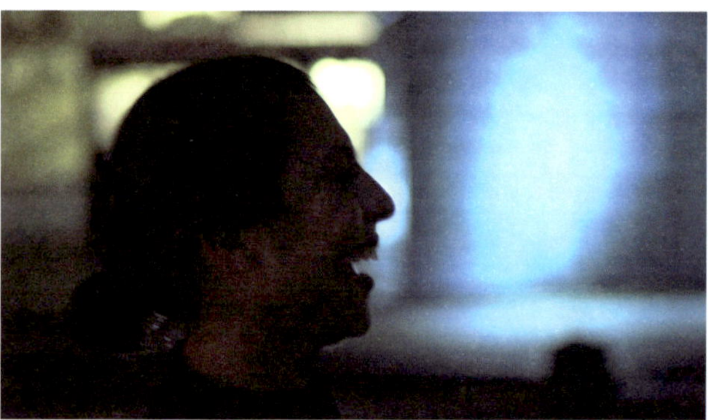
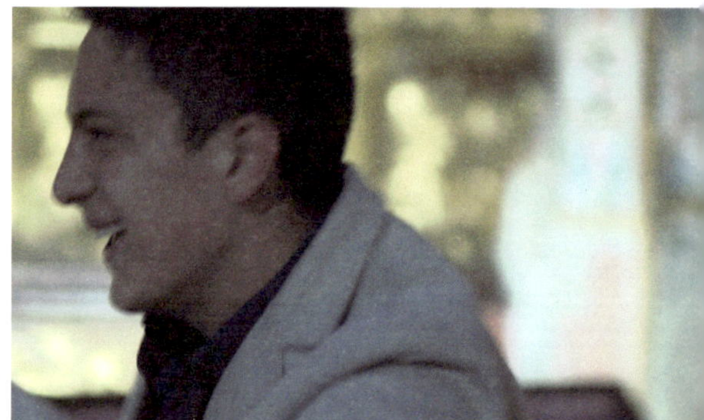
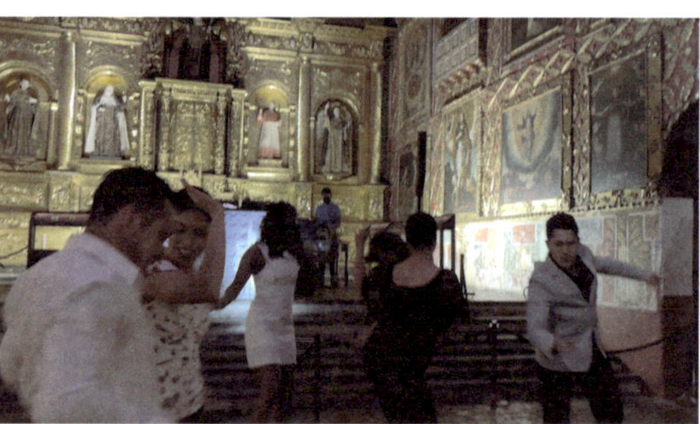
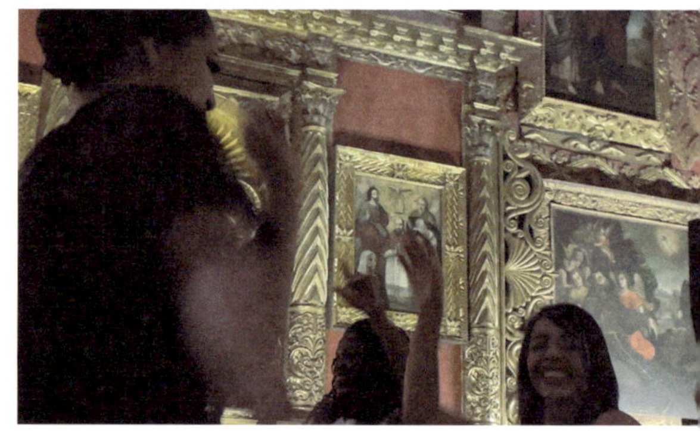
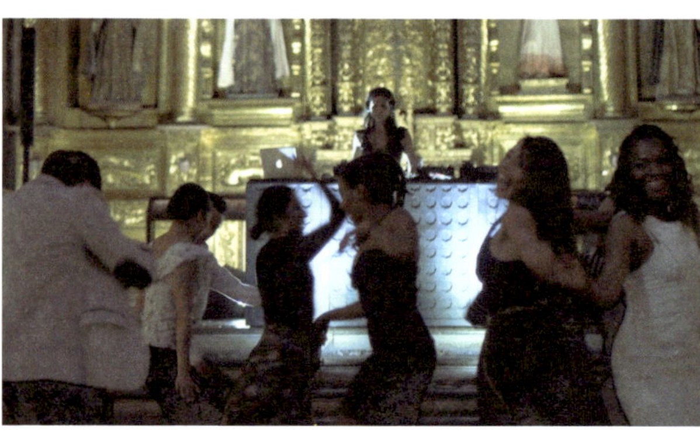
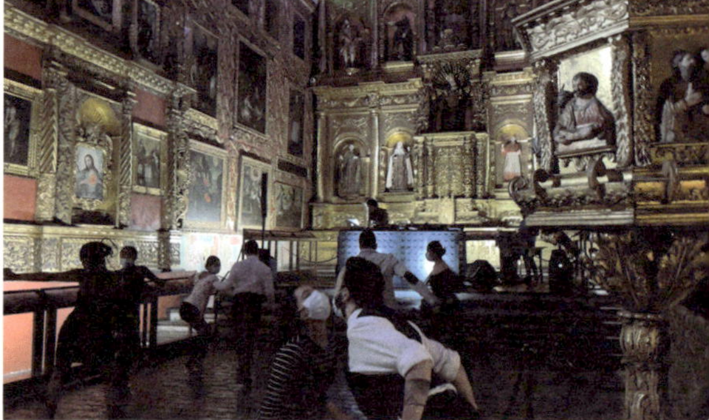

 La plaga, 2021. Social action and video stills. RƎEXISTENCIAS, Museo Santa Clara, Bogotá

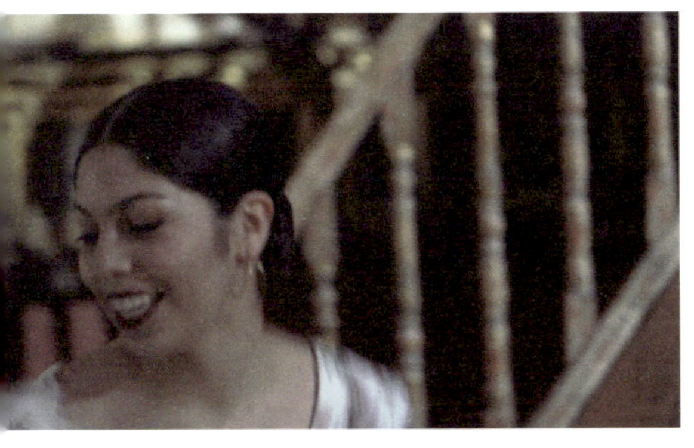
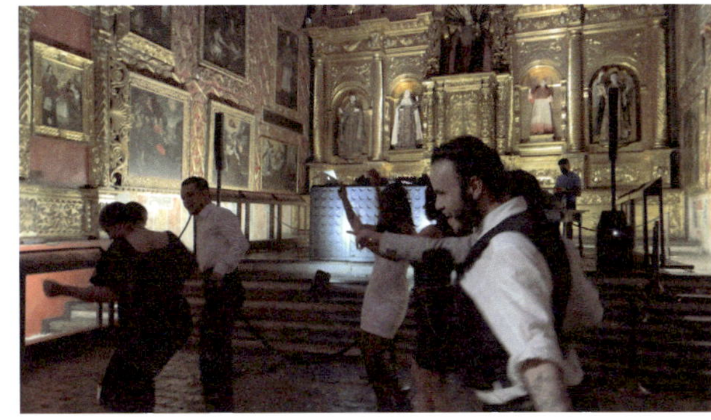
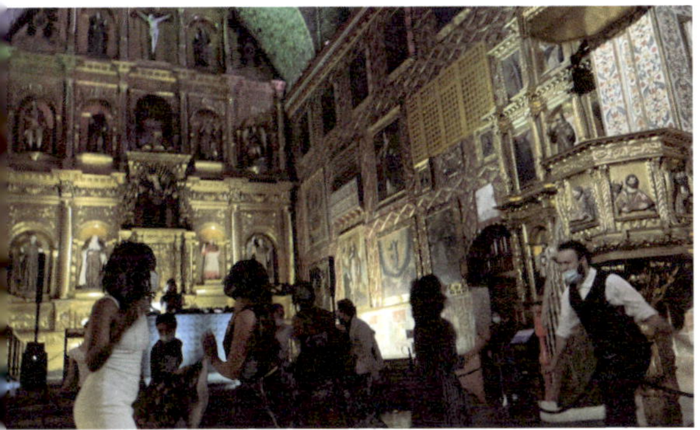
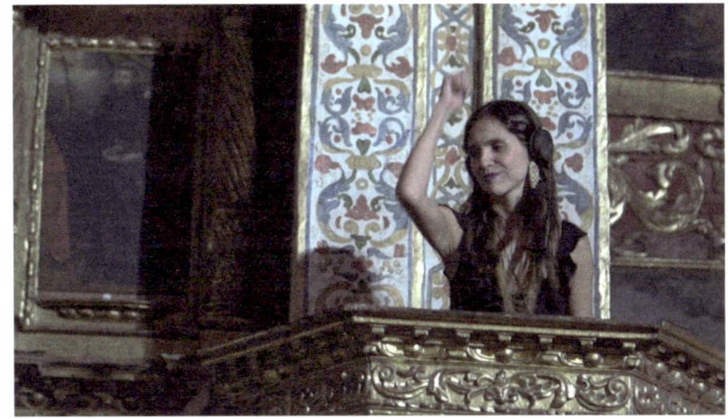
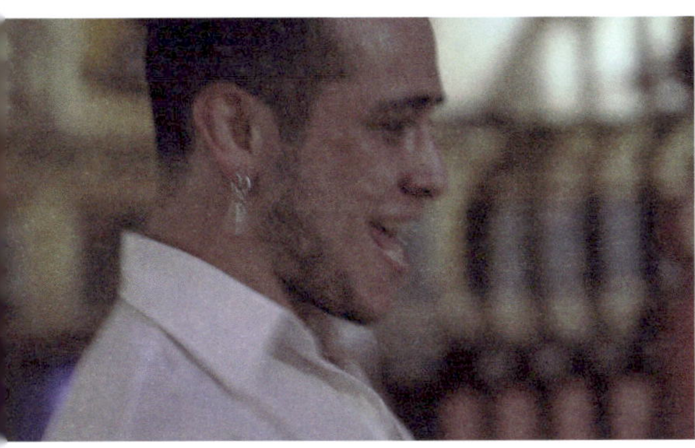
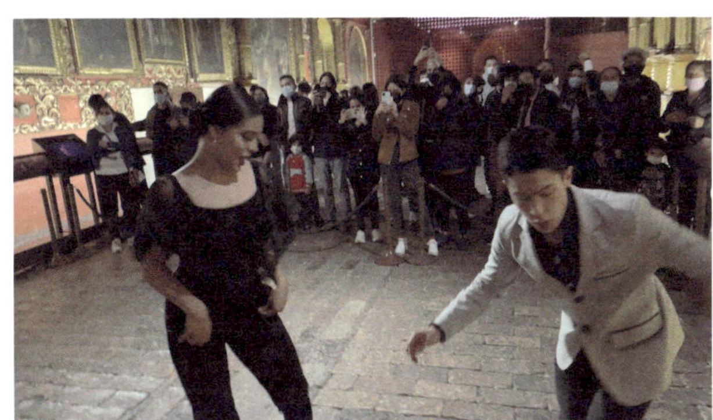
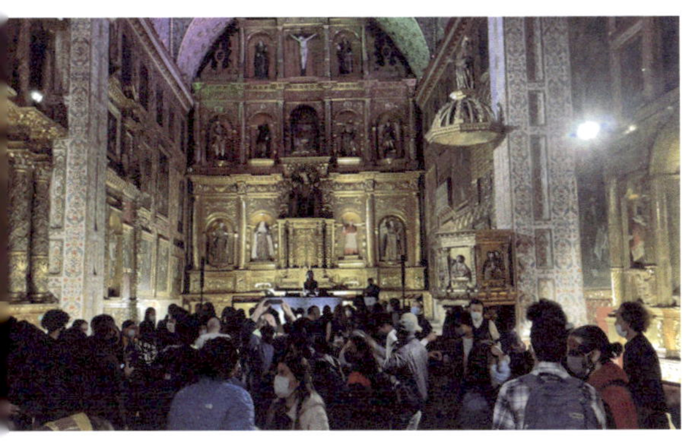
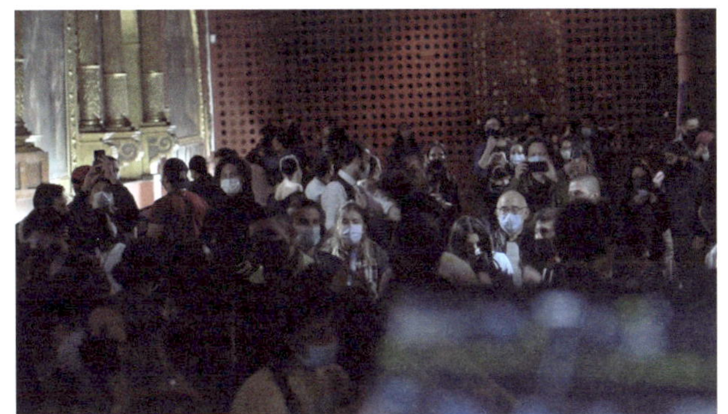

1986
HAVANA
FUKUSHIMA
2011

ISTANBUL
BHOPAL
2009 1984

Biennial Disaster Banners and Research Diagrams, 2010–2013

Physical and digital banners, installations, paintings, diagrams, collective research, and production workshops

These works are designed to take over large spaces as they provocatively pair well-known or deservedly memorable art events with global political, economic, or ecological disasters. Each banner offers a different challenge to viewers and participants, by the sheer specificity of its double naming. The banner "Venice / Chernobyl" triggers very different associations and significations than "Sharjah / Kanungu" or "Kassel / Banqiao." Additional layers of meaning appear through the physical and cultural context in which these seemingly celebratory corporate banners are placed. The banners also serve to initiate dialogues with local participants by means of workshops and public discussions. The banners are accompanied by research diagrams and a smaller print edition with notes. Some have been slightly adapted to later contexts, as was the case with the research diagram that became a central element of the series' presentation in Havana in 2015.

2002

KASSEL
BANQIAO

1975

SHARJAH
KANUNGU
2013   2000
SHARJAH
KANUNGU
2013   2000
SHARJAH
KANUNGU
2013   2000
SHARJAH
KANUNGU
2013   2000
SHARJAH
KANUNGU
2013   2000

1992

DAKART
LONDON

1952

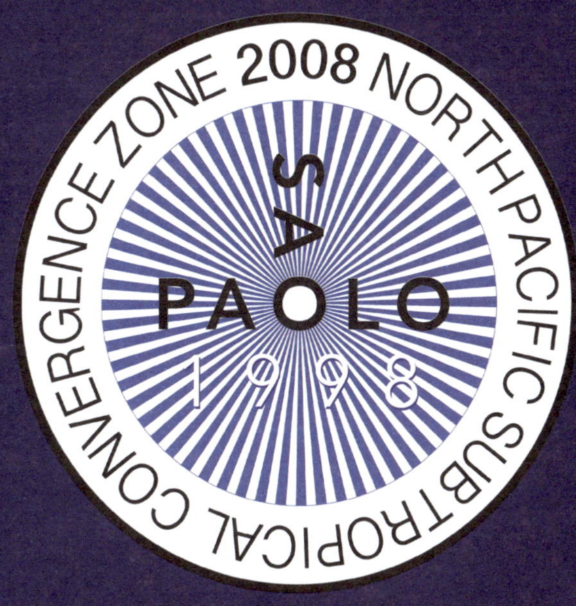

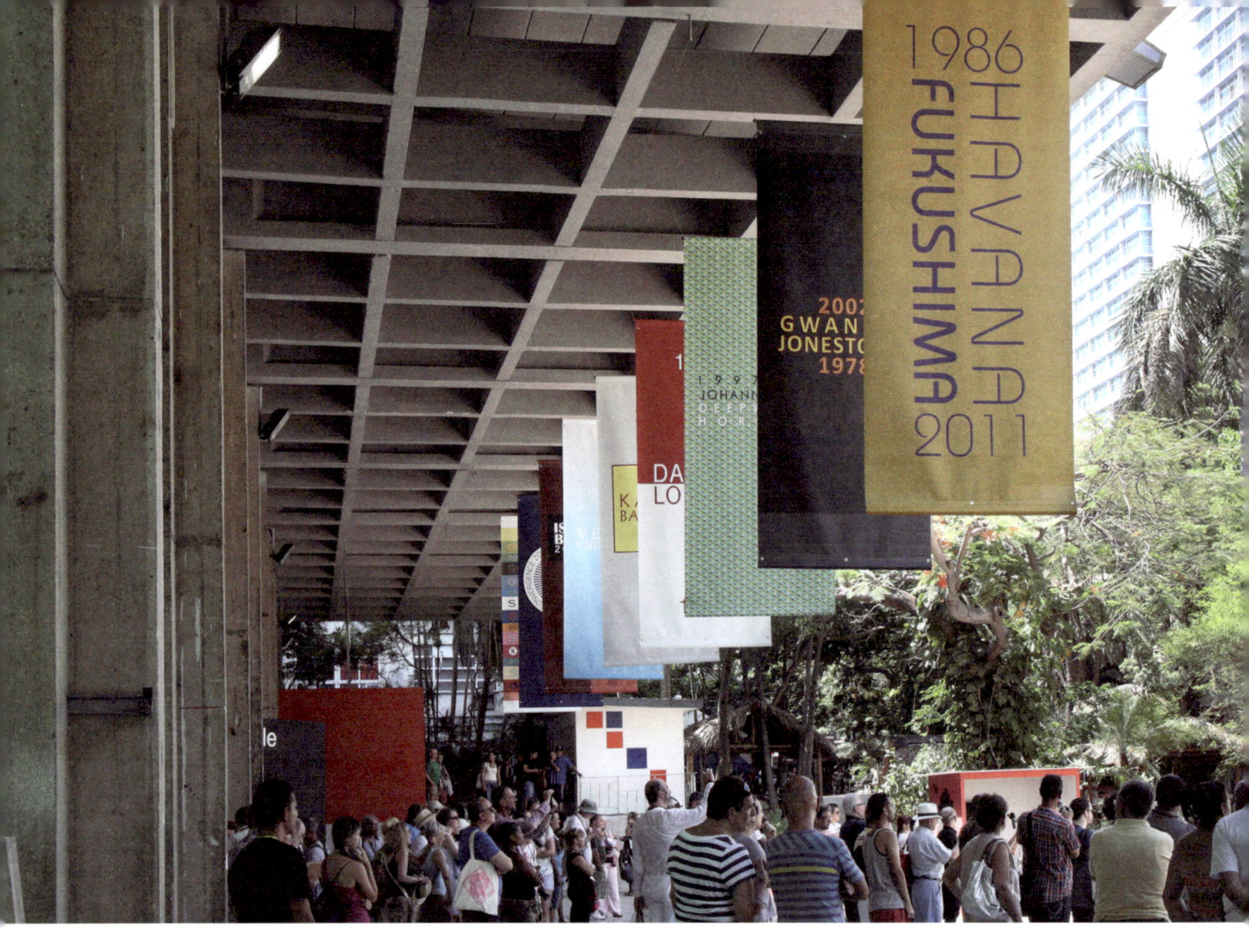

1986
HAVANA
FUKUSHIMA
2011
2002
GWAN
JONESTO
1978
1997
JOHANN
DEEP
HOR
DA
LO
KA
BA
ISTAN
B
VE
CH
S
K

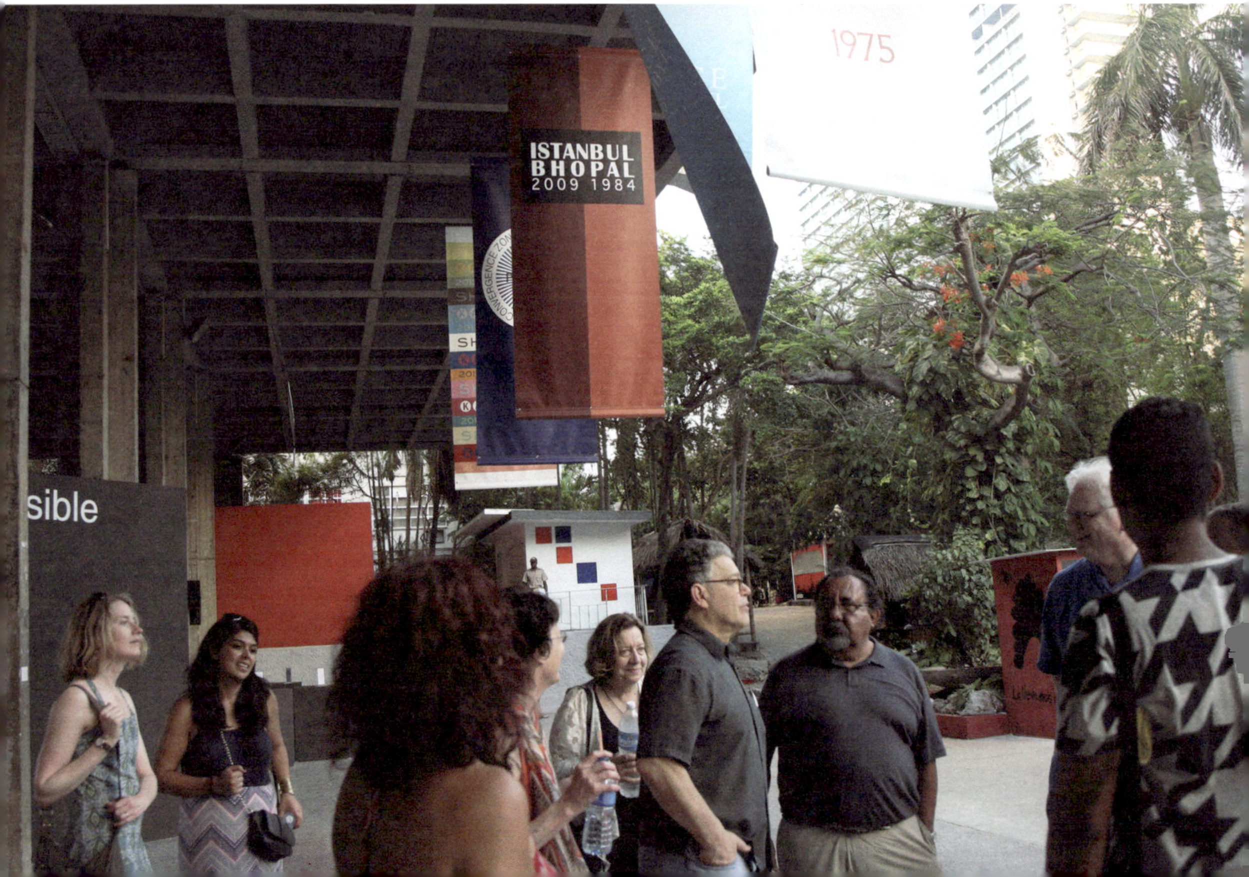

1975
ISTANBUL
BHOPAL
2009 1984
CONVERGENCE ZON
S
SH
KO
sible

Islands of Tragedy and Fantasy, Havana, 2015

Architectural banner installation, gallery display,
public archive, and workshop program

This work from the *Art Biennials and Other Global Disasters* series
was produced specifically for the 12th Bienal de la Habana (2015).
The open-air installation at Pabellón Cuba presented the series'
full edition of nine monumental banners, each pairing the name of
a well-known art event with that of a global political, economic, or
ecological disaster. This time, however, the row of banners opened
with a new addition, another banner showing what seemed to be
the hosts of the project welcoming us to Cuba. Featured here were
the images of the two main characters from the series *Fantasy
Island*: Tattoo, played by Hervé Villechaize, and Mr. Roarke, played
by Ricardo Montalbán—though in this version, Mr. Roarke had
been replaced by Joseph Goebbels, the Nazi Minister of Propaganda.
Goebbels and Villechaize shared a few things: Both committed
suicide by the age of fifty, both studied art before developing the
careers they are known for, Goebbels with a PhD in drama and
Villechaize with painting studies at the École des Beaux-Arts in
Paris. It is their roles in media history, however, that bring them
together as ideal hosts for *Islands of Tragedy and Fantasy*.

The world-famous series *Fantasy Island* (1977-84) is tightly linked
with forms of colonialism as old as Prospero and Caliban in

Shakespeare. The characters of Tattoo and Mr. Roarke presided over an imaginary world of leisure and pleasure that also marked the beginning of the neoliberal era that we so strongly associate with the phenomenon of art biennials. Joseph Goebbels, on the other hand, belongs to this project through his role of star curator—the term was of course not used at the time—of the famous 1937 *Entartete Kunst* [Degenerate Art] exhibition in Germany.[1] Many people consider the La Biennale di Venezia the birth of the "biennial phenomenon." But too many ignore the importance of the production mounted by Goebbels and Adolf Ziegler in the history of mega-exhibitions and their global impact. The over two million visitors their exhibition attracted made even the La Biennale di Venezia of its time seem like a provincial affair. Goebbels' face, towering over the modernist architecture of the Pabellón Cuba, kept that history in the foreground of collective workshops and conversations about exhibition-making, totalitarianism, and other man-made disasters.

A key part of the project centered on the formation of The Theater of Statistical Operations, a temporary research group that staged workshops and exchanges during the Biennial. Housed in a separate, indoor gallery, this element included the display of prints, maps, research diagrams, books, and other materials available for viewing and used during the workshops. Two unrealized productions by Lasch and The Theater of Statistical Operations were the insertion of the American TV series into the *paquete semanal,* an offline bundle of digital content; and the employment of Villechaize and Goebbels lookalikes as hosts of real-life biennial activities in Cuba.

—

[1] "Degenerate Art" [*Entartete Kunst*] was a term used by the Nazi regime to describe modernist and avant-garde artworks that they deemed un-German, subversive, or culturally corrupt. The infamous Degenerate Art exhibition (1937) in Munich showcased confiscated works from artists like Kandinsky, Picasso, and Klee, presenting them in a manner meant to ridicule and discredit modern art. This campaign was part of a broader effort to impose an ideologically controlled aesthetic aligned with Nazi ideology. See: *Degenerate Art: The Fate of the Avant-Garde in Nazi Germany* (exh. cat.), curated by Stephanie Barron (New York: Harry N. Abrams INC Publishers - Los Angeles County Museum of Art, 1991).

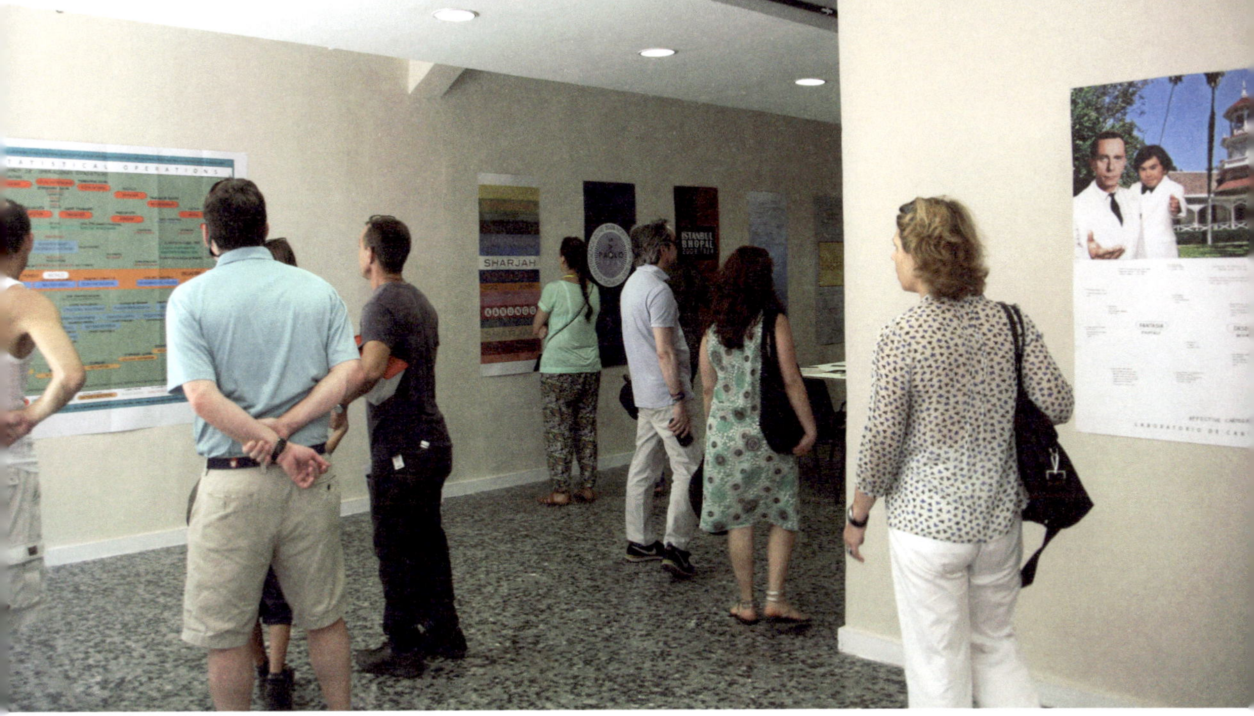
SHARJAH
ISTANBUL
BHOPAL
FANTASIA

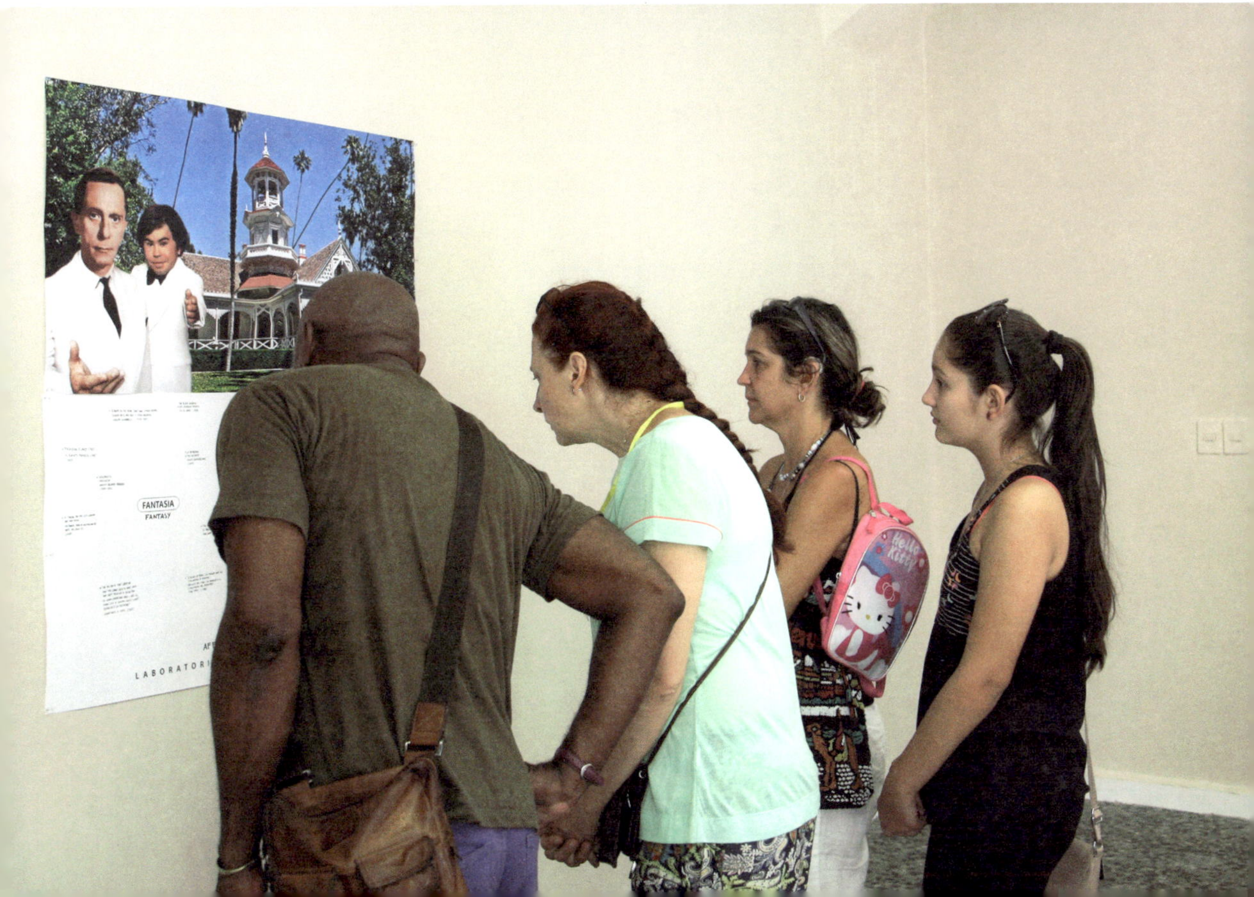
FANTASIA
FANTASY

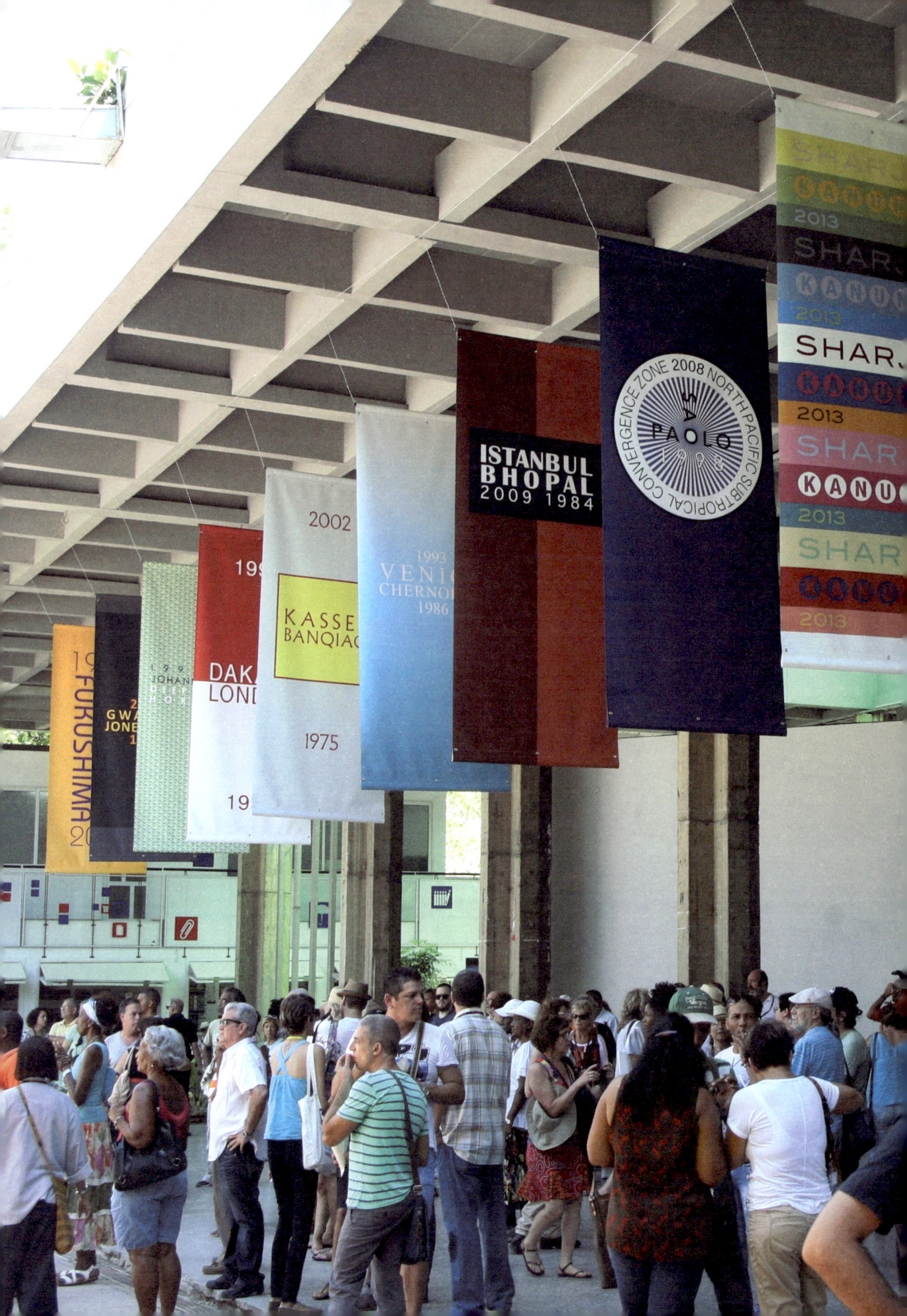

FUKUSHIMA
GWA
JONE
DEEP
HOR
DAK
LOND
2002
KASSE
BANQIAO
1993
VENIC
CHERNO
1986
1975
ISTANBUL
BHOPAL
2009 1984
CONVERGENCE ZONE 2008 NORTH PACIFIC
SUBTROPICAL
PAOLO
SHARJ
2013
SHAR
KANU
2013
SHARJ
KANU
2013
SHAR
KANU
2013
SHAR
KANU
2013

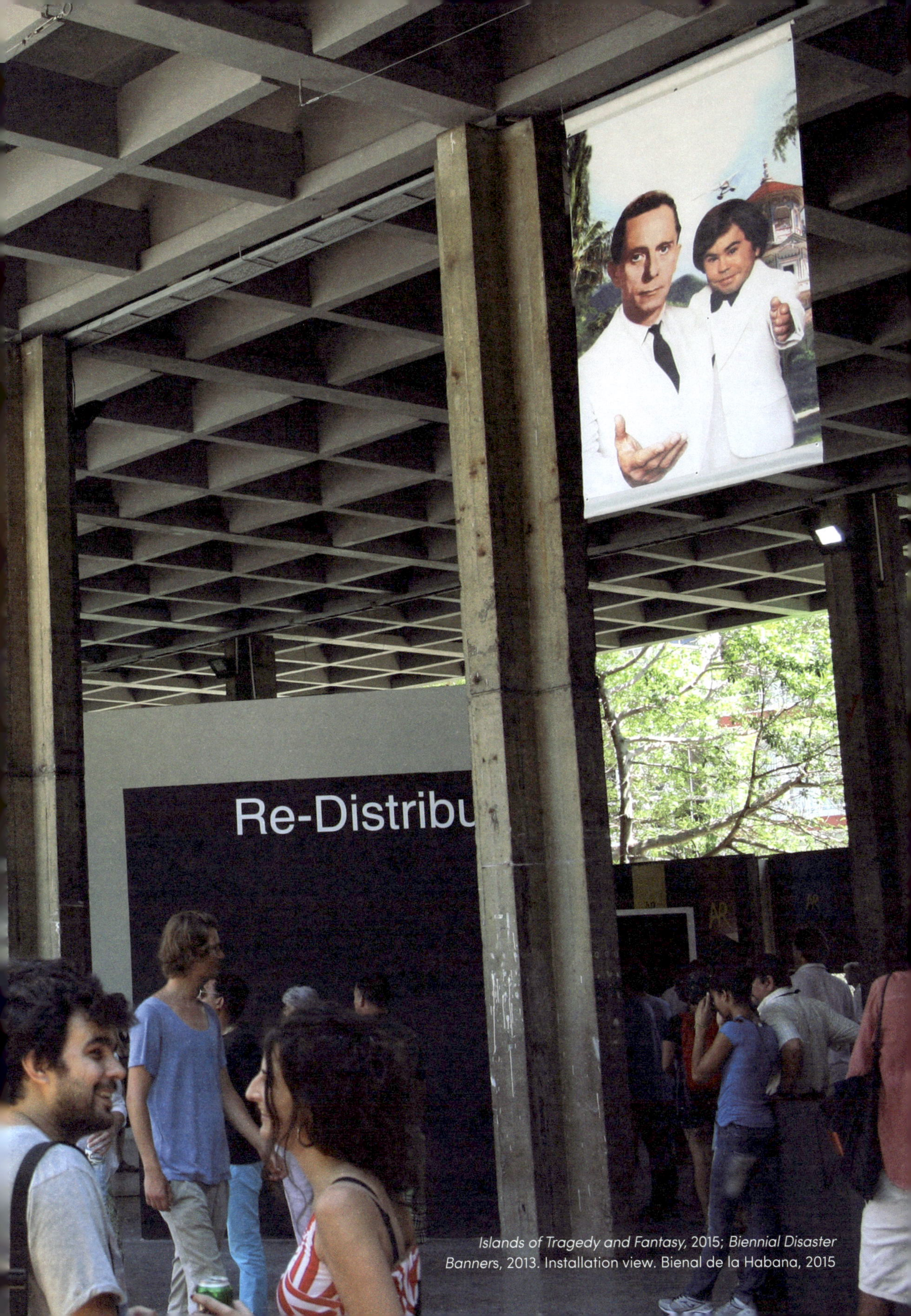

Islands of Tragedy and Fantasy, 2015; *Biennial Disaster Banners*, 2013. Installation view. Bienal de la Habana, 2015

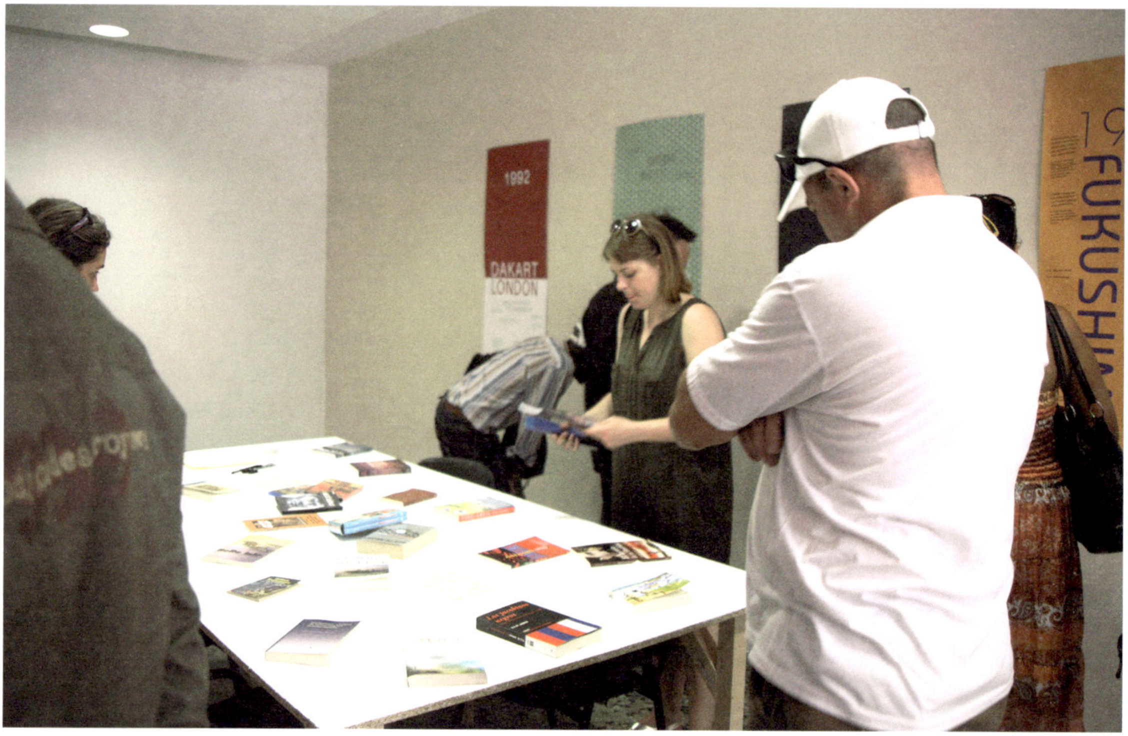

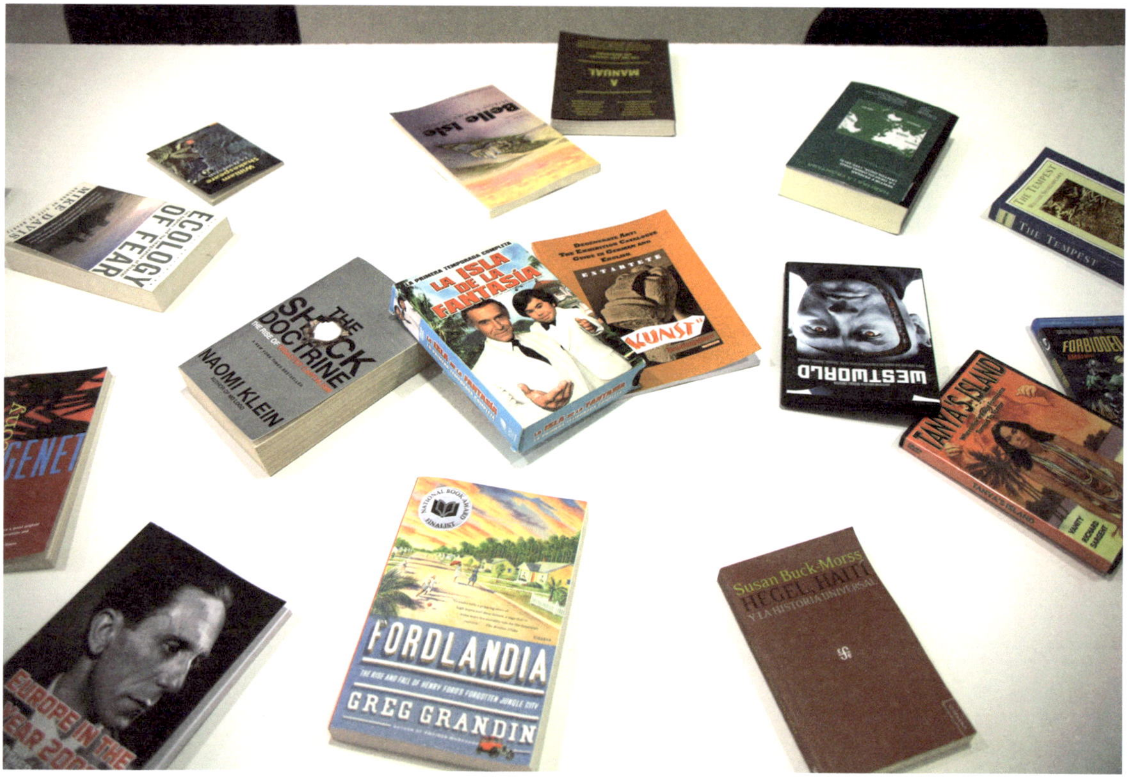

TOP: Viewers and workshop participants engaging with *Islands of Tragedy and Fantasy.* Bienal de La Habana, 2015

102   BOTTOM: Public access bibliography for *Islands of Tragedy and Fantasy.* Bienal de La Habana, 2015

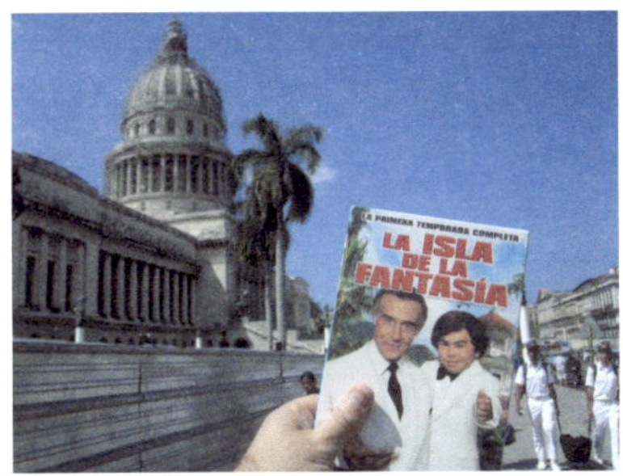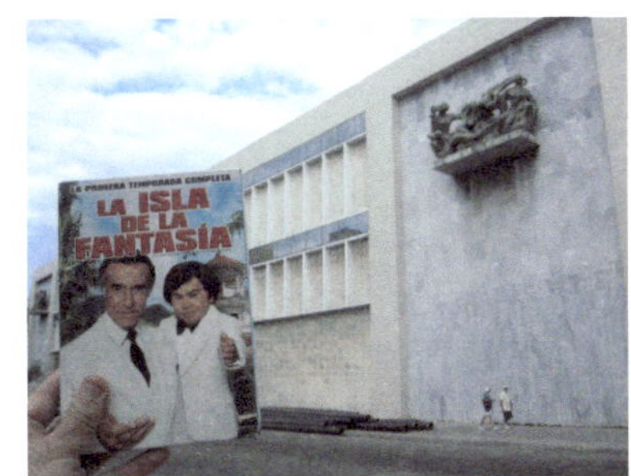
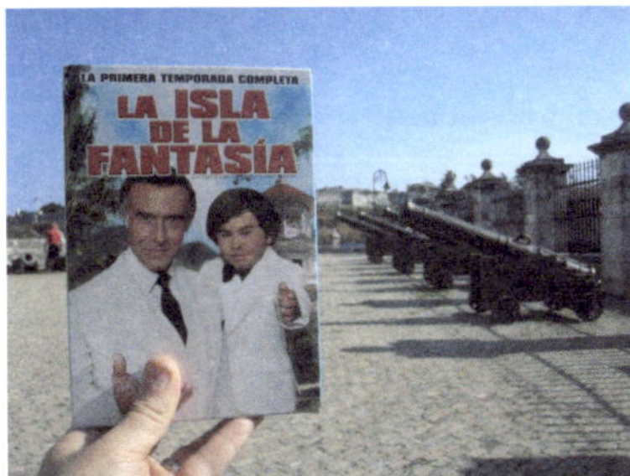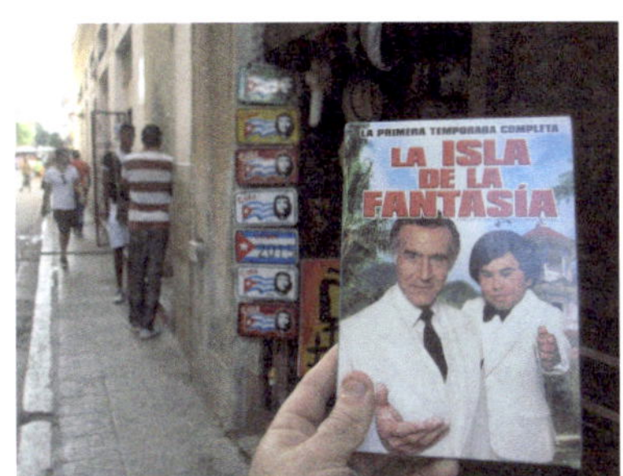
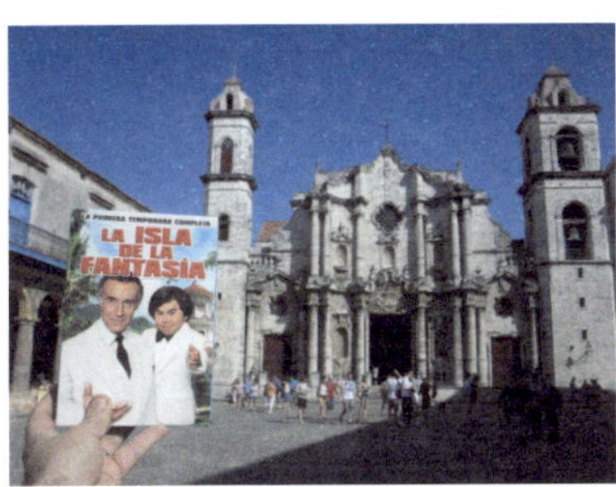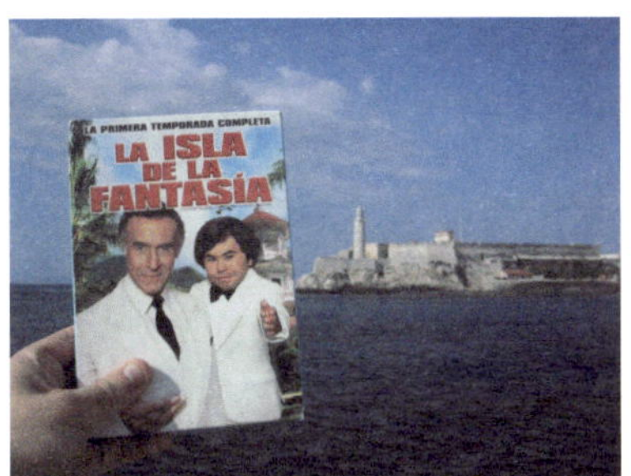
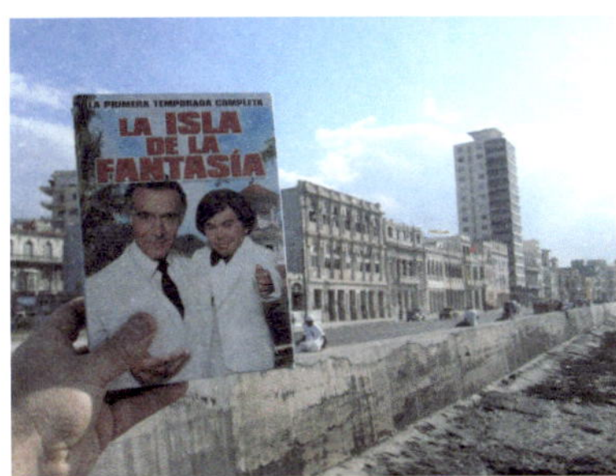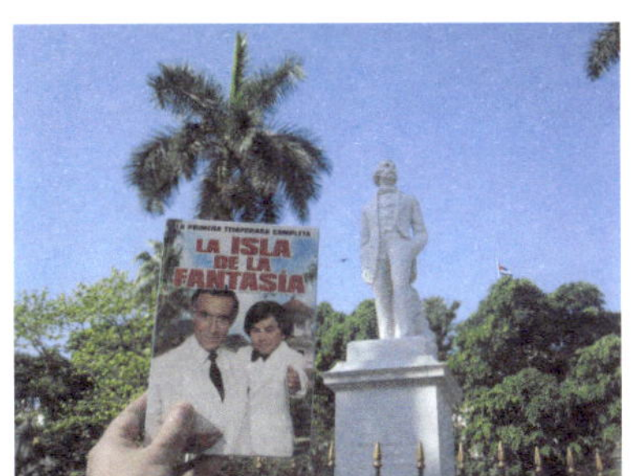
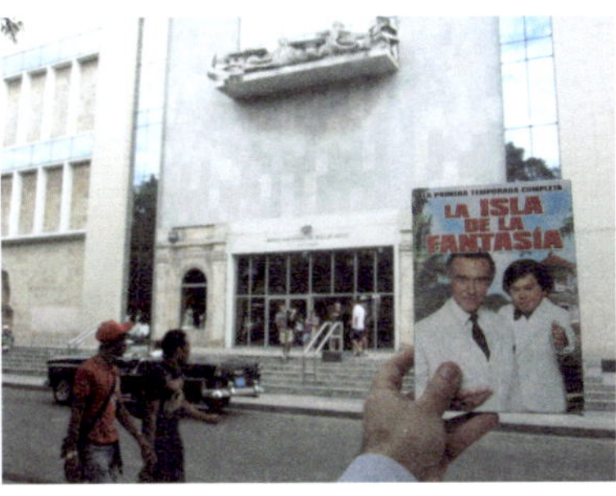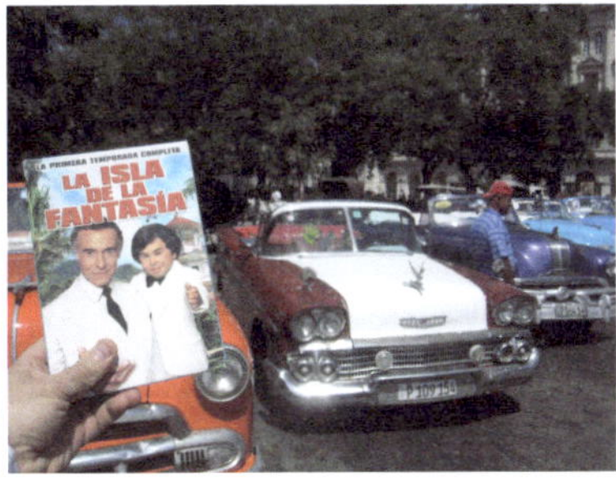

Snapshots documenting the use of the series *La isla de la fantasía* [Fantasy Island] as a conversational device with people in Havana for *Islands of Tragedy and Fantasy*. Bienal de La Habana, 2015

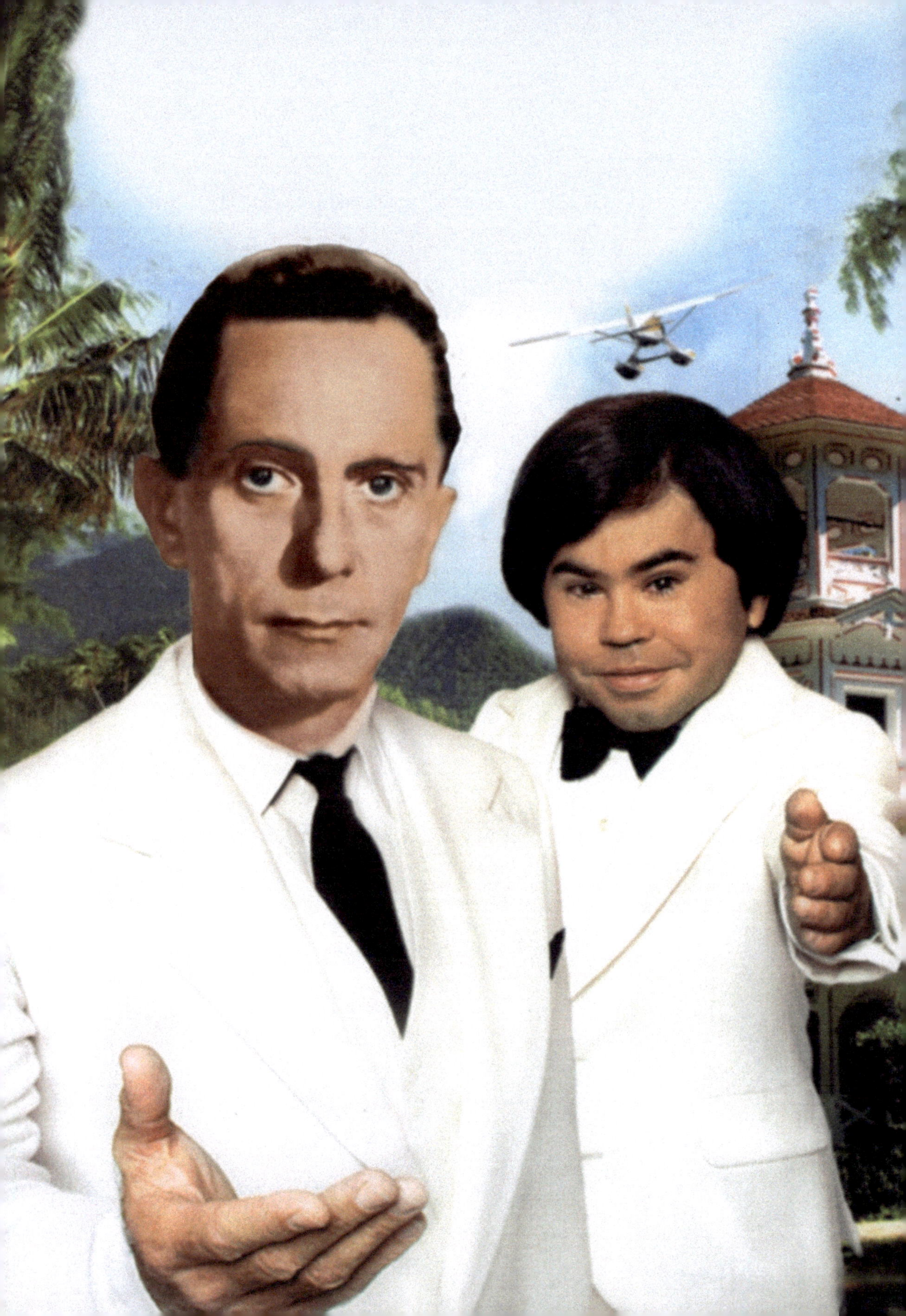

Dannys Montes de Oca Moreda
July 21, 2022

Pedro Lasch and the Intersection of Art, Politics, and Entertainment

I met Pedro Lasch in 2012 when, as organizer of the theory-focused events at the Bienal de La Habana, I invited the group Estéticas Decoloniales, led by Walter Mignolo at Duke University,[1] to participate in the biennial's eleventh edition. This allowed me the opportunity to come into contact with his work, and I came to understand the development of his practice as an essential path for thinking about contemporary art in its endeavor toward social transformation. What most impressed me, though, were his contributions to those mechanisms of artistry not found in the formal construction of poetics within the Western aesthetic tradition but that instead propose the creation of an alternative, parallel methodology capable of being put into action as part and parcel of our daily lives.

It's no coincidence, then, that Pedro Lasch was one of my guests at *Entre, dentro, fuera* [Between, Inside, Outside] (2015), an exhibition cocurated with the scholar Royce W. Smith for the twelfth Bienal de La Habana. The exhibition brought together Cuban and US artists from different backgrounds, whose work served as bridges of social

—

1   The panel took place at the Centro Teórico Cultural Criterios with the participation of Dalida María Benfield, Raúl Moarquech Ferrera Balanquet, Pedro Pablo Gómez Moreno, Pedro Lasch, Alanna Lockward, and Miguel Rojas-Sotelo. See: *Oncena Bienal de la Habana: Prácticas artísticas e imaginarios sociales* (Havana: Centro de Arte Contemporáneo Wilfredo Lam / Consejo Nacional de las Artes Plásticas, 2012).

intermediation—part of the general strategy around which the event was convened.[2] The space selected for the exhibition was the Cuban Pavilion, since it is well located within the city's urban fabric and widely accessible, as it's not only used for art exhibitions. This made it possible to create space for both the dialogue of the works and artists as well as for practices that developed inside and outside the artistic field itself.

Lasch's contribution, *Islas de tragedia y fantasía: las bienales de arte y otros desastres globales* [Islands of Tragedy and Fantasy: Art Biennials and Other Global Disasters], should be understood through the activation of its structural components and the unusual way they are articulated, if we take into account their frictions, unexpected twists, and complex intertextualities. It was a hybrid and transdisciplinary project made up of an installation of flags with the names of biennials, dates, and/or cities involved in disasters; a perfectly symmetrical and accurately proportioned diagram organizing the structure, components, and agents implicated in art biennials and situations that could be considered disasters; a kind of library or reference room of bibliographic and audiovisual materials; the rebroadcast on national television of the US series *Fantasy Island* (1977–1984),[3] along with its distribution on cassettes, CDs, and in the *paquete semanal*;[4] and the creation of a research group called the Teatro de Operaciones Estadísticas [Theater of Statistical Operations] for the purpose of generating discussion sessions.

—

2   *Entre, dentro, fuera. Entre la idea y la Experiencia. XII Bienal de la Habana*, curated by Dannys Montes de Oca Moreda and Royce W. Smith (Havana: Centro de Arte Contemporáneo Wilfredo Lam/Consejo Nacional de las Artes Plásticas, May 22, 2015–June 22, 2015). With the participation of: Agnes Chávez (Cuba–US), Pedro Lasch (Mexico–US), Elizabeth Stevenson (Canada–US), Levente Sulyok (Bulgaria–US), Stephanie Syjuco (Philippines–US), and the Cubans Susana Pilar Delahante Matienzo, Omar Estrada, Adonis Ferro, Levi Orta, Guillermo Ramírez Malberti, Glenda Salazar, and Harold Vázquez.

3   This action, despite being proposed as part of the project, wasn't carried out within the framework of the biennial.

4   The rebroadcast of *Fantasy Island*, despite being proposed as part of the project, wasn't carried out within the framework of the biennial. The *paquete semanal*, or "weekly packet," is an informal compilation of information, advertising, communication, connections, and alternative distribution that circulates throughout Cuba and collects audiovisual material of all kinds (with the exception of politics and pornography), based on theme and genre.

One the one hand, the work synthesized the artist's personal experience of the first edition of the Ghetto Biennale in Port-au-Prince at the end of 2009—an event that didn't have much impact in the media, in contrast to the coverage of the tragic events of the earthquake that would hit the city in January 2010. On the other hand, Lasch wondered about the accelerated growth of art biennials in the last decades in parallel with global disasters (natural or provoked by human action). How did the names of certain cities—those associated with catastrophes—serve as a facade for improving the places' economic conditions, even when structural conditions in them were not addressed between biennials? How, in the name of art, were projects being carried out that overran and failed to respect the infrastructure designed for daily life in many cities?

This dismantling intersected with the critical perspective presented in Naomi Klein's book, *The Shock Doctrine: The Rise of Disaster Capitalism*, which was included in the reference room along with other literary and essayistic works that, although published earlier, irrefutably document the marriage of disaster and coloniality, modernity and domination, nature and civilization. Works like *The Tempest* by William Shakespeare, *Heart of Darkness* by Joseph Conrad, *The Black Jacobins* by C. L. R. James, and *Caliban* by Roberto Fernández Retamar also made it possible to explore the relationship between concepts like utopia and control zones. This relationship was further evident in the series *Fantasy Island*, in which the protagonists were invited to satisfy their longings and ambitions only to later meet with the most unexpected vicissitudes.

Lasch brought together all possible variants of a contemporary situation in which art, culture, politics, and entertainment intersect. From the perspective of biennials and disasters, for example, he reminded us of the symbolic stunt staged by Joseph Goebbels, the Nazi minister of propaganda, and the regime's curator, Adolf Ziegler, and its possible impact on the history of global mega-exhibitions. Goebbels' face appeared on the poster that announced Lasch's work, tying together *Fantasy Island* with the *Entartete Kunst* [Degenerate Art] exhibition carried out in Germany in 1937, a maneuver that demonized avant-garde art, appealing to the conservative German art canon. By referring to this propagandist program, Lasch also hinted at the potential shock factor of many biennials and international events, veiled by the aura of neoliberal contemporaneity.

To the general questions posed by the project, we should add many others regarding the immediate context of Havana and its history of resistance and cultural production. Following that thread, the Teatro de Operaciones Estadísticas that Lasch activated proposed, for example, a discussion about the history of confrontations and attempts to "normalize" the relations between Cuba and the United States seen as a historic disaster wrapped in economic and political interests— one about television as a medium that links the artistic and cultural avant-garde with the entertainment industry, one about the *paquete semanal* as a strategy of cultural resistance against the limits of information circulation, and one about the Cuban Civil Defense's resources and strategies for the recovery of a country constantly hit by natural disasters like hurricanes. They also discussed economic strategies for implementing artistic education and making artistic life possible in Cuba, conditioned, as they are, by the arbitrary circumstances of the embargo, and, consequently, all of the related issues that could arise.

These workshops, along with the aforementioned books, diagrams, and historical recontextualizations of biennials and disasters, established tangential links between the themes and subthemes proposed by the artist. In a way, his strategy was connected to the experience of postdramatic theater, a kind of interweaving of installation, performance, intellectual *dérive*, and even a debate carried out as a happening, shifting attention from the piece to the quotidian situations and historical events that the participants brought to the space; as a result, a space of political consciousness emerged.

The shock effect created by the interconnected components of the work itself led us to the need to unravel both its participatory typology and those events, occurrences, and conditions of disasters that were either intended to be hidden or that we had never before seen through this prism. As an artist who defends the stances promoted by decolonial aesthetics and is active in biennials and peripheral art events, Lasch established a connection with the set of affects fostered by the exhibition, although it was really a set of historic, generational, and global responsibilities. Seen from a distance, Pedro Lasch has been, time and again, consistent in his own trajectory full of geopolitical implications and critical gazes—a path that started with the collective experience of 16 Beaver Group[5] and that he currently com-

—

5   Pedro Lasch was an active member of 16 Beaver Group, an artist-run
     space at 16 Beaver Street in New York from 1999. The collective has

plements with his work as a professor, theorist, and collaborator with organizations of immigrants, Indigenous groups, and international workers. This quality comes through not so much in activism that could end up encapsulated in his work but rather in a set of tools that he has been able to place at the borders between art and politics, not only because of his ability to create narratives and symbolic links that are effective with audiences but because of his drive to broaden and expand artistic practices that are, ultimately, the lookout point from which he sends out his lights to us.

—

functioned as a meeting space for people involved in art, politics, and education, promoting the exchange of research, concerns, and strategies for collective action.

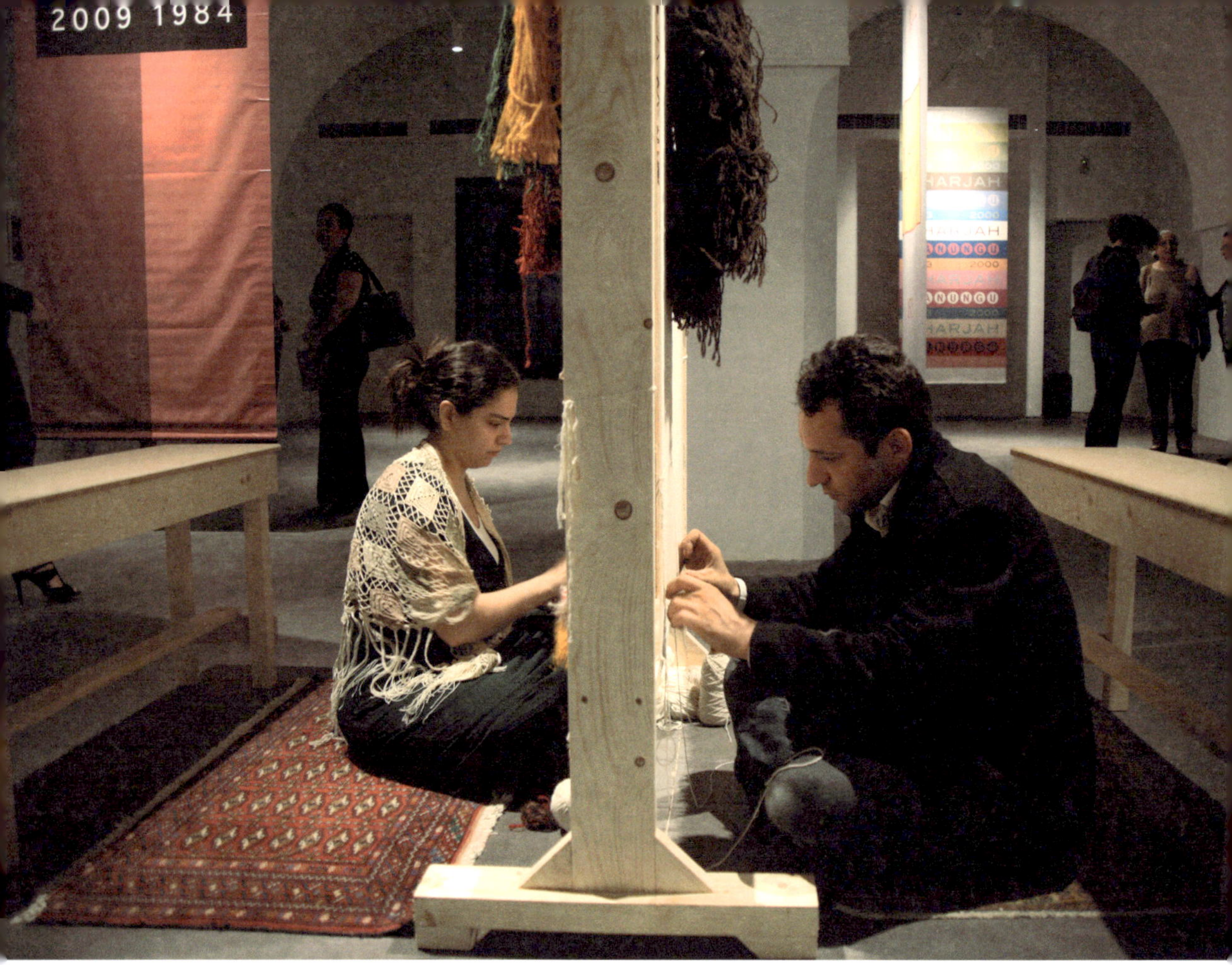

2009 1984
SHARJAH
KANUNGU
2000

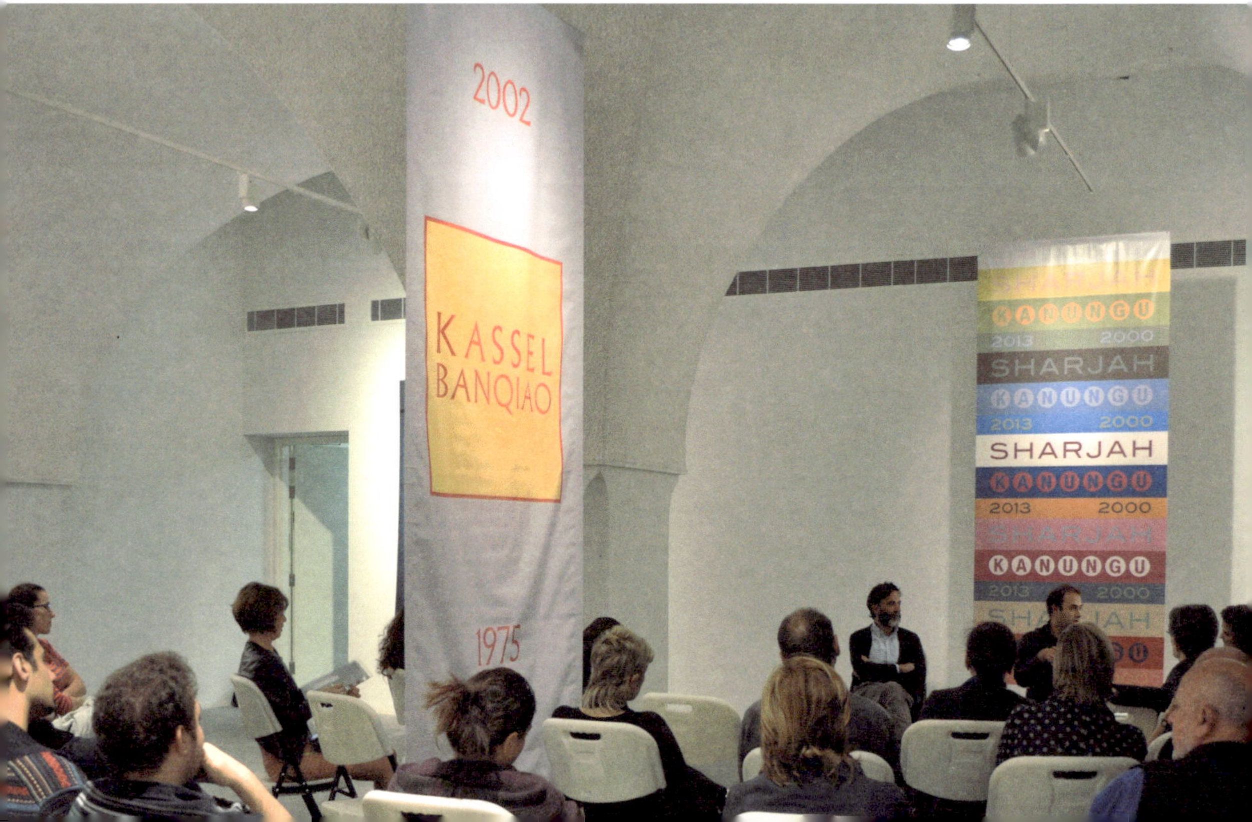

2002
KASSEL
BANQIAO
1975
KANUNGU
2013 2000
SHARJAH
KANUNGU
2013 2000
SHARJAH
KANUNGU
2013 2000
SHARJAH

Art World Disaster, Beirut, 2013

Banner installation, gallery display,
public archive, and workshop program

This work was produced for the AUB Byblos Bank Art Gallery in Beirut, Lebanon (2013). The seemingly celebratory corporate banners were used to initiate dialogues with local participants by means of a series of workshops and public discussions. They also served as the artistic and conceptual core for an exhibition and public program that included local artists, students, curators, activists, and scholars.

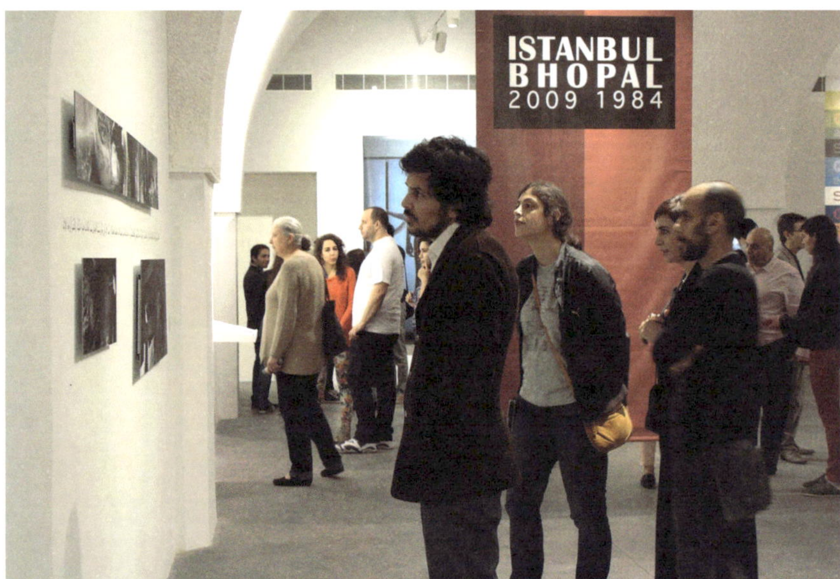

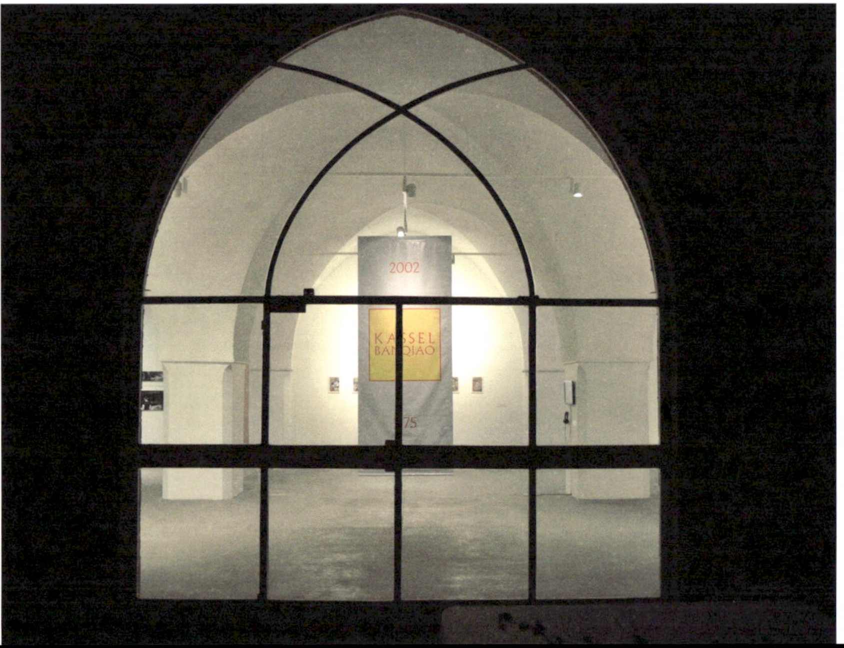

Biennial Disaster Banners, 2013. Installation views. *Art World Disaster*, AUB Byblos Bank Art Gallery, Beirut, 2013

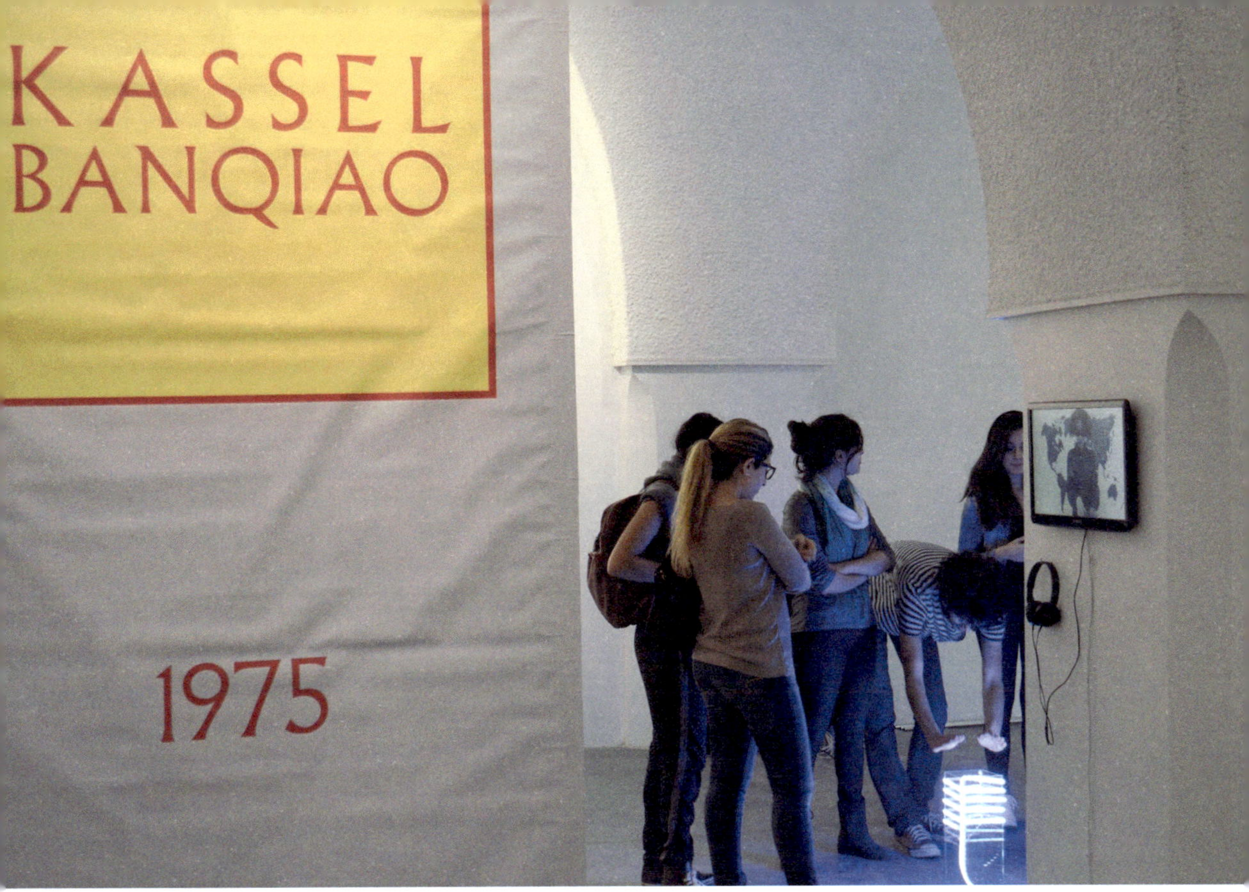

KASSEL
BANQIAO
1975

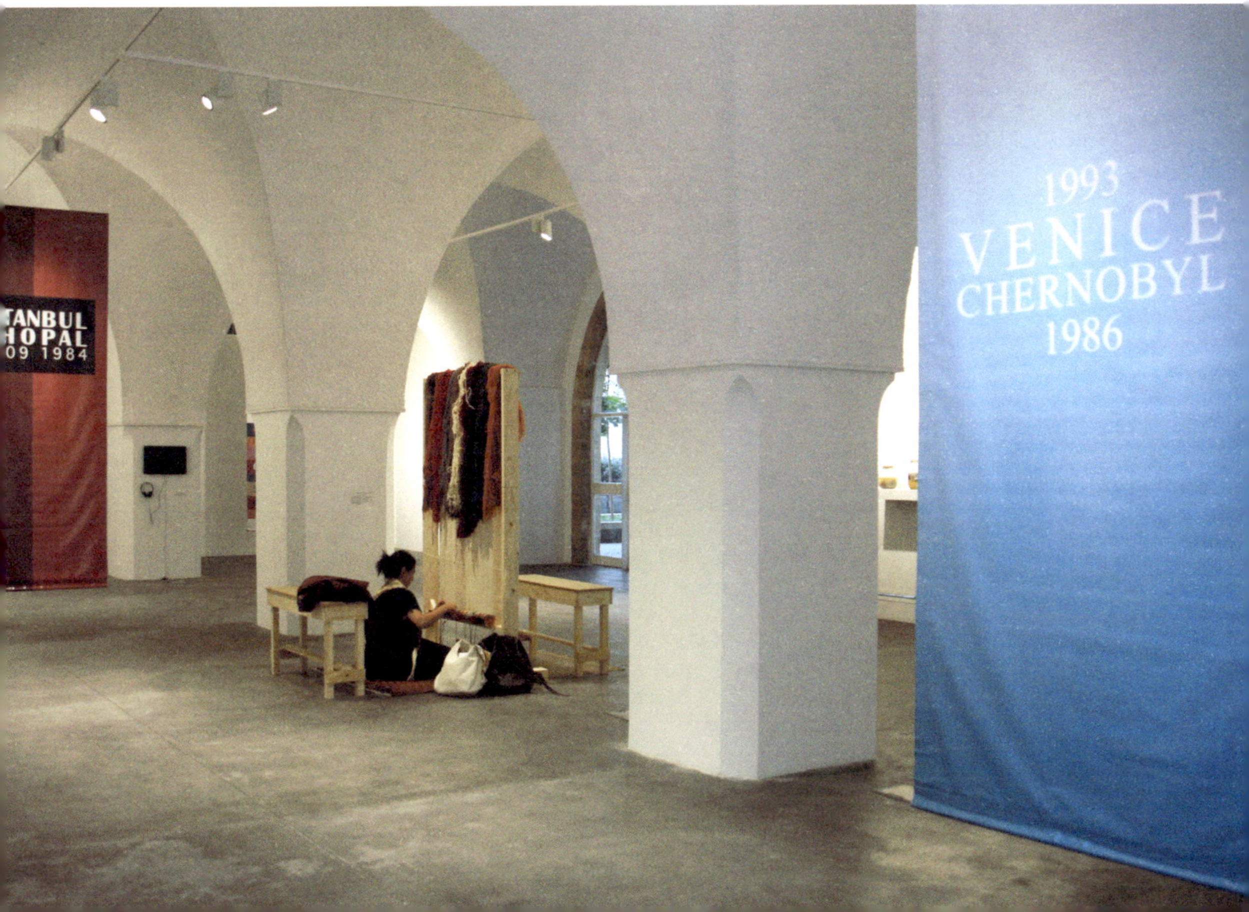

TANBUL
HOPAL
09 1984
1993
VENICE
CHERNOBYL
1986

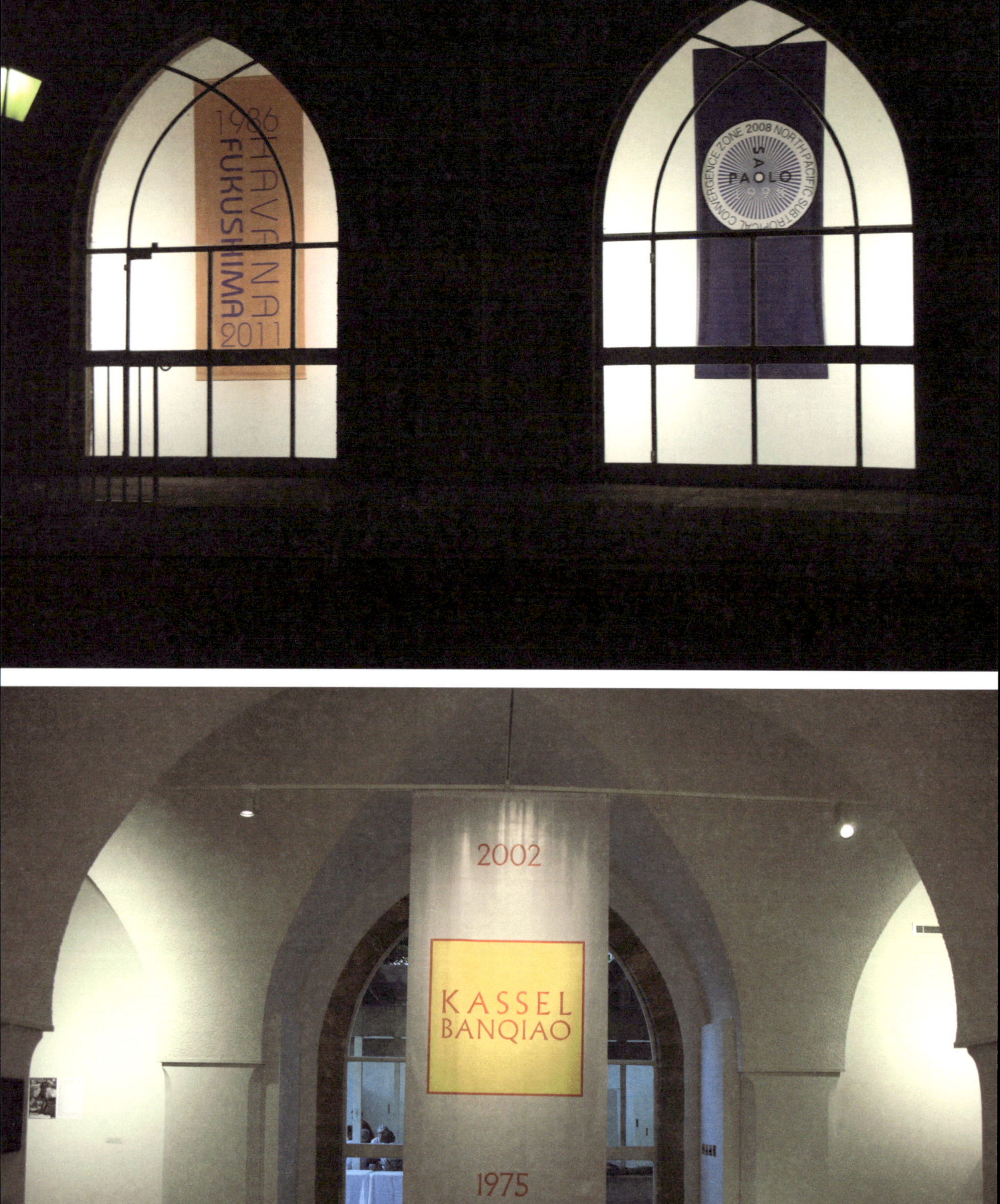

1986
HAVANA
FUKUSHIMA
2011

CONVERGENCE ZONE 2008 NORTH PACIFIC SUBTROPICAL
A
PAOLO

2002
KASSEL
BANQIAO
1975

Octavian Esanu
July 9, 2022

Art and Disaster

In 2013, the American University of Beirut (AUB) Art Galleries hosted a project by Pedro Lasch, which incorporated research, pedagogy, activism, and art for social change. Lasch proposed an exhibition-workshop-course called *Art World Disaster* that he carried out together with AUB art instructor Kasper Kovitz and students from the Concept 1 course. During the semester—and long before the online teaching of the pandemic—Lasch lectured and conducted studio visits and critique sessions over the internet. Lasch and Kovitz worked together with individual students, helping them methodically advance from their initial ideas to the final stage of production and display. The closing phase of the project, which Lasch carried out in Beirut, involved teaching the last sessions in person, organizing a workshop and a few discussions, and assisting the students and participating local artists with the installation of their works.[1]

In his exhibition text, Lasch explained that the idea for this project came shortly after his participation in the Ghetto Biennale in Port-au-Prince in 2009. He recalls that this biennale in Haiti was memorable in many ways, but despite the organizers' and artists' attempts to

———

1   Artists included Magali Claude, Dima Hajjar, Sandra Issa, Nayla Kronfol, Sana'a Mouhaidli, Edwina Nassar, Ghassan Nassar, Georges Rabbath, Christopher Rizkallah, Saba Seyedeh Sadr, Nataly Sarkis, Lara Tabet, Karen Zeidan. A public conversation between Lasch and artist Walid Sadek was also part of the exhibition's program.

bring it to the attention of international art and culture audiences, there was hardly any interest in the "marginal event." One month later, however, a major disaster struck Haiti. The January 2010 earthquake brought not only suffering and death to the island but also the attention of the international media. All of a sudden, American journalists, policy experts, art lovers, and cultural critics "discovered" art in the western side of the island of Hispaniola. In light of this eye-opening Caribbean experience, Lasch also produced a series of banners in which he paired "sites of culture" with "sites of disaster" (for example, "Venice / Chernobyl," "Sharjah / Kanungu," and "Kassel / Banqiao"). By hanging these banners in the gallery among the works of students and local artists, he invited the audience to reflect on the controversial mechanisms of cultural legitimation in our age.

Those committed to a materialist historiography have known all along that every site of culture is at the same time a site of devastation. In thesis VII of the "Theses on Philosophy of History," Walter Benjamin[2] underscores the link between culture and barbarism. One might interpret his thesis by saying that works of art do not only express, represent, and convey the harmonious, the beautiful, the majestic, the sublime, or whatever, but they also—and at the same time—conceal contradictions and conflicts: the exploitation of labor, the toil of the enslaved person, the sweat of the oppressed. To read Lasch's banners through Benjamin's thesis, for every edition of the La Biennale di Venezia to display the most beautiful and truthful—or both—it must also conceal the ugliest and the falsest. The delightful fruit of artistic genius is also the product of those who work in shifts to clean, maintain, or supervise a culture whose expressive pleasures they cannot savor, or for which they are not acknowledged except as sold wage labor.

And in Kassel, every documenta that showcases the triumph of Western democracy through what is called "contemporary art" must also conceal the dubious relationship that this democracy—and its art—maintains with the forces of the market, and, in today's world, with tyrannical and genocidal practices, as well as with coercive apparatuses that silence those who still believe in the values this democracy only formally upholds.

—

2   Walter Benjamin, "On the Concept of History," trans. Dennis Redmond, in Marxist Internet Archive (1940). Accessed on May 12, 2025, at: https://www.marxists.org/reference/archive/benjamin/1940/history.htm.

Truth and untruth, democracy and market, freedom and repression, beauty and ugliness, education and ignorance, labor and capital, culture and barbarism, art and disaster—they all fold into each other, constituting a rich drapery whose folded splendor reveals as much as the reverse side conceals.

In his banner series Lasch placed art and disaster, or culture and barbarism, in a wider global context by pairing sites of symbolic and material accumulation of capital (Kassel, Venice, Sharjah) with sites of economic or political devastation historically constituted by colonial expansion, slavery, competitive modernization, and globalization.

But something else was also implied in the conceptualization of this event: Today our economic and cultural system leans more toward the barbarism or disaster side of the opposition. Naomi Klein[3] has written about the problem, suggesting that shock, terror, war, and natural disaster have become the fuel of choice for neoliberal capitalism. Economically, disaster has been used as an excuse, a pretext, or a treatment for what neoliberal discourse presents as the main problem of our age: the so-called inefficiency of the market. To solve it, disaster is offered as economic and aesthetic justification for transferring the resources of life from the poor to the rich—and in aesthetic terms, from the "ugly" to the "beautiful people," as the upper middle class has historically been called. As Klein's work demonstrates, this aesthetic-economic transference was first tested in Latin America and Eastern Europe during the 1980s and 1990s, before being implemented on a global scale. Disaster is the fuel that keeps the reactor of spectacle capitalism stable, and it is up to the corporate media to keep enriching this fuel by directing the world's attention to sites of major natural, cultural, political, or economic devastation—as exemplified by Pedro Lasch's testimony about the 2009 earthquake in Port-au-Prince.

Art and suffering (or misfortune) have always been close to each other. What has changed is the form in which this relationship occurs, or whose suffering art addresses. In the distant past, suffering, sorrow, despair, madness, and pain found expression, for example, in the ancient Greek tragedy. Yet back then not everyone was invited to express suffering in this elevated form. By providing collective relief

—

3   Naomi Klein, *The Shock Doctrine: The Rise of Disaster Capitalism*
     (New York: Picador, 2007).

and distraction, or educating the young through the actions of great characters, tragedy gained its force of conviction from the belief that only a chosen few knew how to properly suffer. It is one thing when misfortune happens to a prince, king, or demigod, and another when it occurs to a layperson. In accordance with classical definitions of tragedy, we agree to partake in the heroic suffering of the former, but will not consent to share in the distress of the latter. For the prince, suffering was part of the godly fate, and for the free laborer or enslaved person, it was just the misery of everyday life. With the disappearance in the modern age of kings and princes, of gods and rituals, of sacrifices and myth, tragedy—as an ennobled and elevated form of suffering—recedes into the background of what is now mass culture. This new reality, shaped by egalitarian, down-to-earth, materialist, and pragmatic values, focuses on the ordinary aspects of life and clashes with the ethos of classical tragedy, where the every-day realities of the salesman, lawyer, or clerk cannot relate. Tragedy, which was the superior and dominant form of human expression of sorrow for centuries, has been displaced by the thoughts and idioms of the common folk. What was once tragic became simply misery, misfortune, and disaster.

Today, the original sin of disaster culture is not only present in its themes and motives but also in its locations. Usually, a major disas-ter becomes a site of mass culture: The more odious the disaster, the larger the arena, the brighter the spotlight, and the greater its competitive arousal. This is obvious in our latest disaster: the war in Ukraine. As soon as Russia started the war, Hollywood and other Western political or cultural celebrities rushed to Ukraine to show their support—while simultaneously leveraging the opportunity to increase their visibility in global coverage of the conflict. They hurried to Ukraine and other war zones to step into the spotlight or position themselves against the backdrop of the disaster, harvesting cultural prestige and extracting symbolic currency by drawing on the intense energy accumulated through the collective grief and resilience of affected communities. The situation is not very different in the "art world." Today, the most well-known amphitheaters of contemporary art are also historical sites of major disasters. The history of the La Biennale di Venezia has been closely linked to Italy's late-nine-teenth-century colonial expansion into North Africa, and as far as Kassel is concerned, documenta was established in the aftermath of World War II as part of the denazification and self-purification car-ried out under the cold gaze of the victorious Allies. This connection between the site of art and the site of calamity, between culture and barbarism, can be extended to many other biennials and exhibitions that have proliferated in our world of disaster capitalism.

Like the economy, culture, and Hollywood, contemporary art today is a by-product of disaster. However, the process works differently in different places. In Western countries, the focus is often on distant historical disasters (slavery, colonialism, racism, fascism, Nazism, communism) that must be incessantly confronted to make our contemporary present appear happier, freer, or more prosperous. In contrast, non-Western countries often find themselves compelled to exploit their own disasters, which are usually more recent results of distant first-world disasters (like colonialism or slavery). To achieve success as an artist from the Global South, it is sometimes necessary—horrible as this may sound—to be "lucky" enough to be part of a calamity that resonates on a global scale. Examples abound: from the collapse of the Soviet Union to the Rwandan Genocide, the Lebanese Civil War, Chernobyl, and Fukushima; the list of artists associated with these disasters is extensive.

In Lebanon, where the *Art World Disaster* project took place, local critics and artists are often debating the relation between local disasters and the international successes of the Beiruti artistic scene. From the Lebanese Civil War to 9/11, and from Israel's invasion to the Beirut port explosion—this series of disasters has drawn significant international attention, generating venues and spotlight energy that both local and foreign artists and cultural workers have used as sources of artistic material and inspiration. In the aftermath of Israel's 2006 invasion, for example, numerous Western museums, American art journals, metropolitan critics, curators, and institutions seized upon the opportunity to launch exhibitions, art journal special issues, or curatorial and theoretical texts focused on Lebanon. This strategy worked in the long term, fueling Beirut's continuing role as a major cultural hub in the region. In the past, during its so-called "golden age," it was its geopolitical location, banking sector, and oil wealth that contributed to this status; after 1989, the prolonged Civil War became the main sources of cultural energy, controversy, inspiration, and artistic material. Artist communities that have not had a recent disaster must wait—like Syrian artists, who have only recently had the spotlight shone on them. Many others in the Global South will have to be patient until the next U.S., Israeli, Nazi, or Russian invasion produces new opportunities for art and disaster.

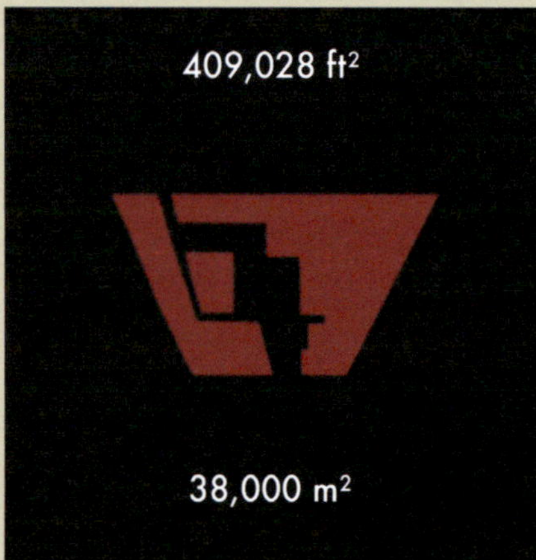

Sheikh Zayed Museum by Norman Foster

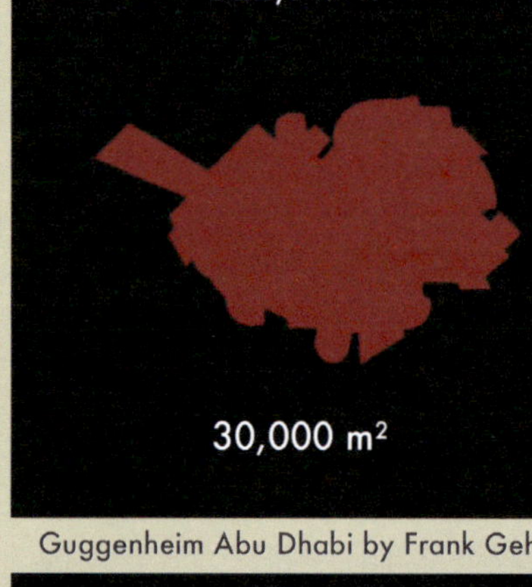

Guggenheim Abu Dhabi by Frank Gehry

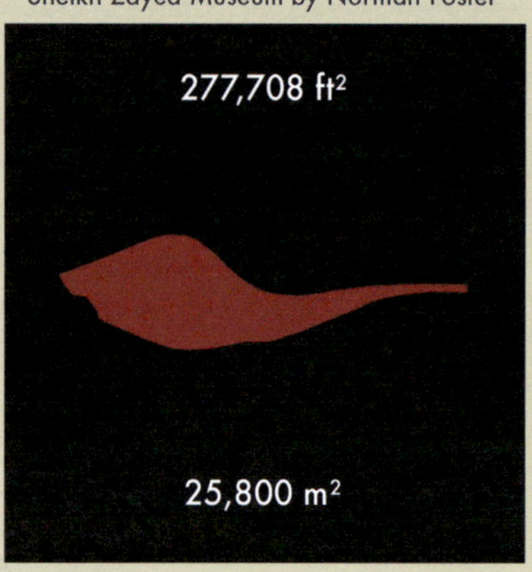

Performing Arts Center by Zaha Hadid

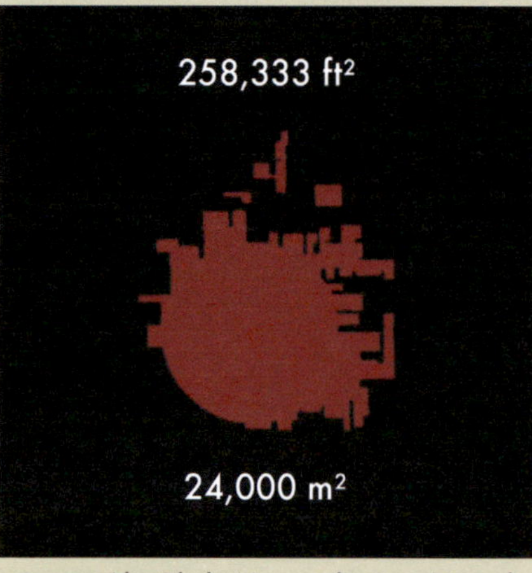

Louvre Abu Dhabi Museum by Jean Nouvel

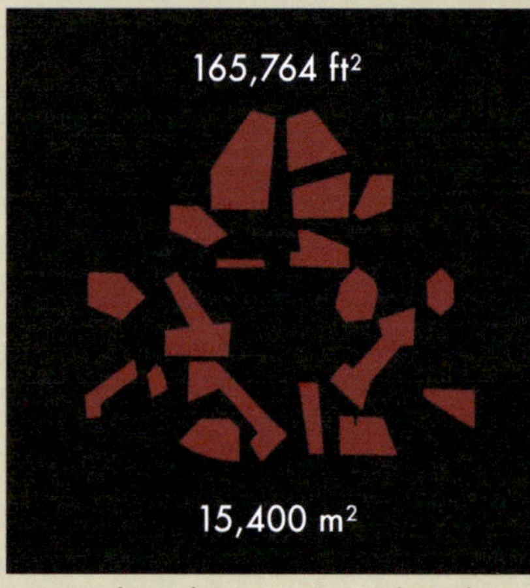

Biennale Park & International Pavilions

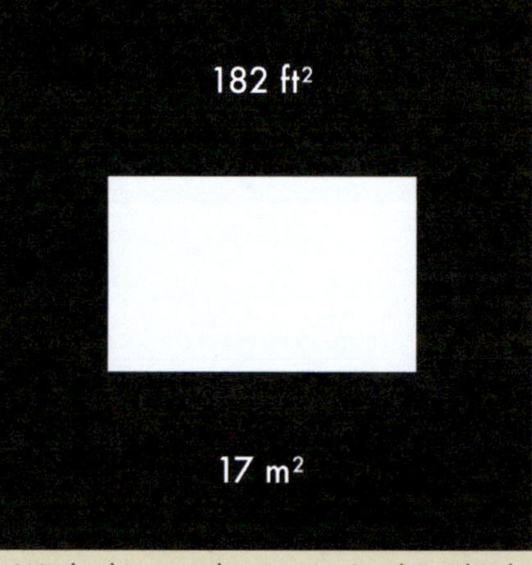

Windowless room housing ten Saadiyat Island construction workers, shared bathroom, no door

Of Saadiyat's Rectangles & Curves, or Santiago Sierra's One Sheikh, Two Museum Directors, Three Curators, One University President, Two Architects, and One Artist Remunerated to Sleep for 30 Days in 13 x 14 foot Windowless Room with Shared Bathroom and No Door (2013). From ART BIENNIALS & OTHER DISASTERS by Pedro Lasch.

Of Saadiyat's Rectangles & Curves or *Santiago Sierra's One Sheikh, Two Museum Directors, Three Curators, One University President, Two Architects, and One Artist Remunerated to Sleep for 30 Days in 13 × 14 foot Windowless Room with Shared Bathroom and No Door, 2013*

Digital campaign poster, unlimited edition print, and
set of six oil paintings on canvas, each 24 × 24 in

This artwork was Pedro Lasch's contribution to the international social justice campaign 52 Weeks of Gulf Labor, with the poster layout version released as Week 14, also included in the book *The Gulf: High Culture/Hard Labor*, edited by Andrew Ross.[1] Lasch's work and that of the fifty-two international artists in the campaign sought to bring attention to the unacceptable labor conditions in the construction of university campuses, art museums, and biennial grounds on Saadiyat Island in the U.A.E. Given that the institutions participating were all global in nature and claimed to represent the interests of art and learning, an international response seemed crucial. The poster shows the name of each building under the image that it represents in the set. The paintings only show the building area for each, with the name appearing on museum labels instead.

---

1   *The Gulf: High Culture/Hard Labor*, Andrew Ross (ed.), (New York: OR Books, 2015).

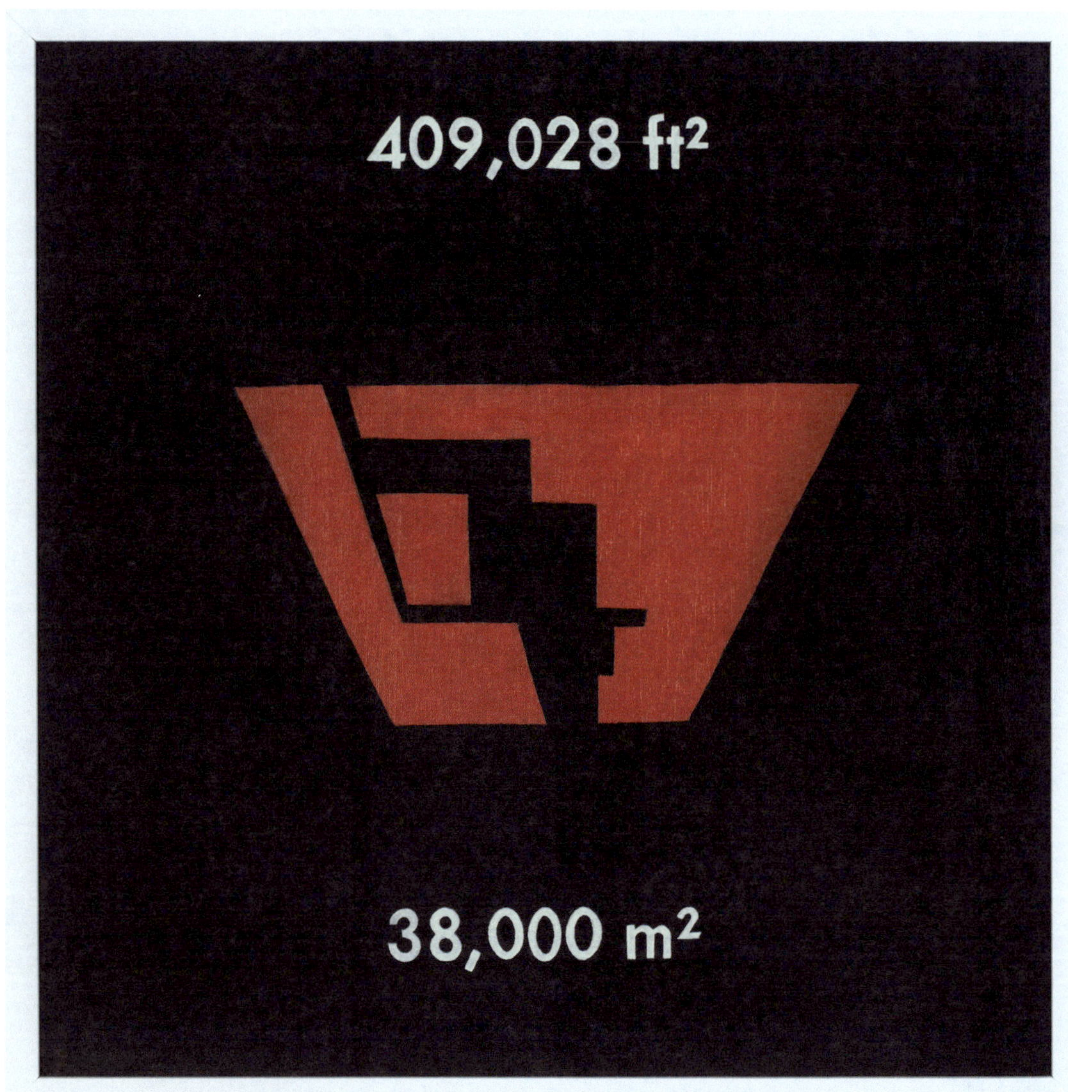

 Norman Foster, Sheikh Zayed Museum, 2013. Oil on canvas, 24 × 24 in

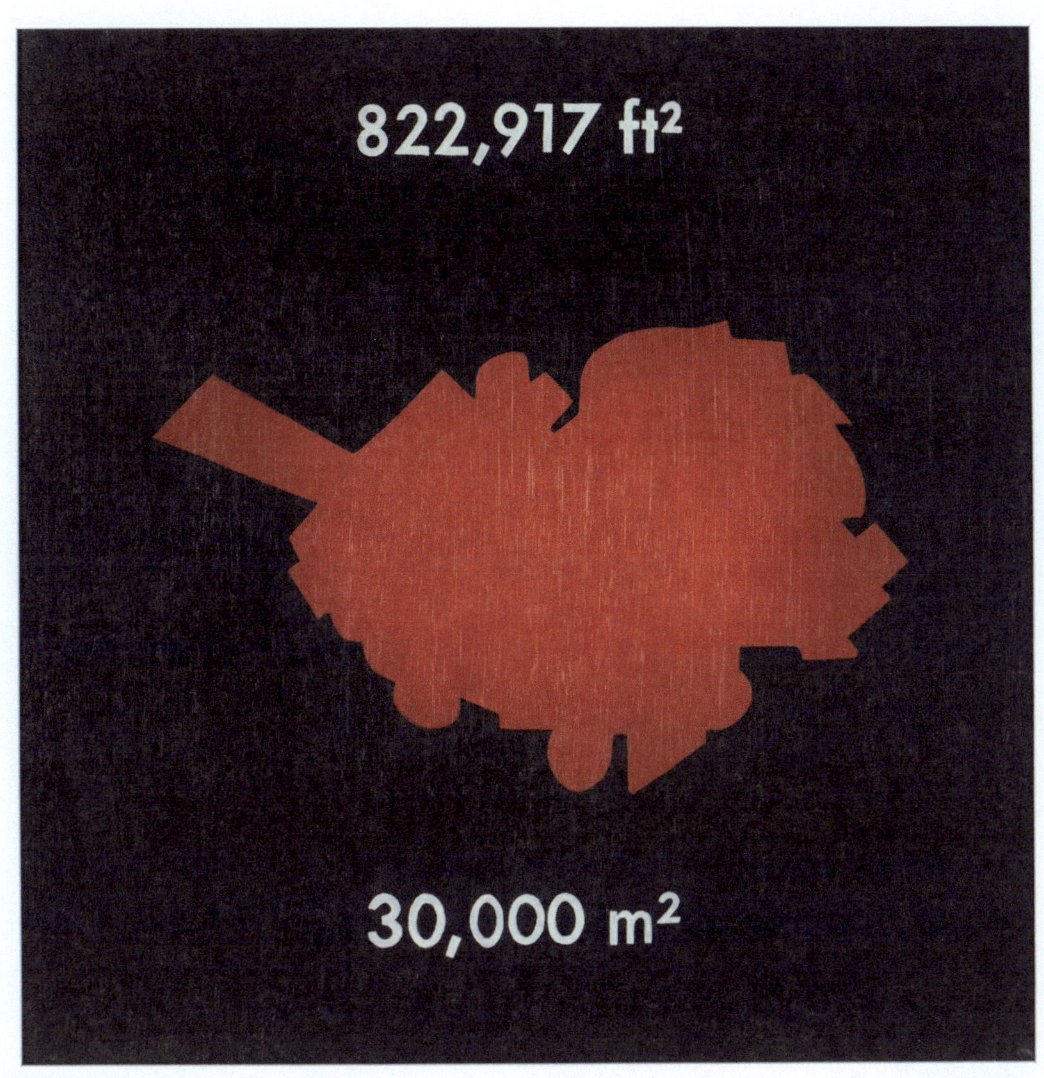

822,917 ft²
30,000 m²

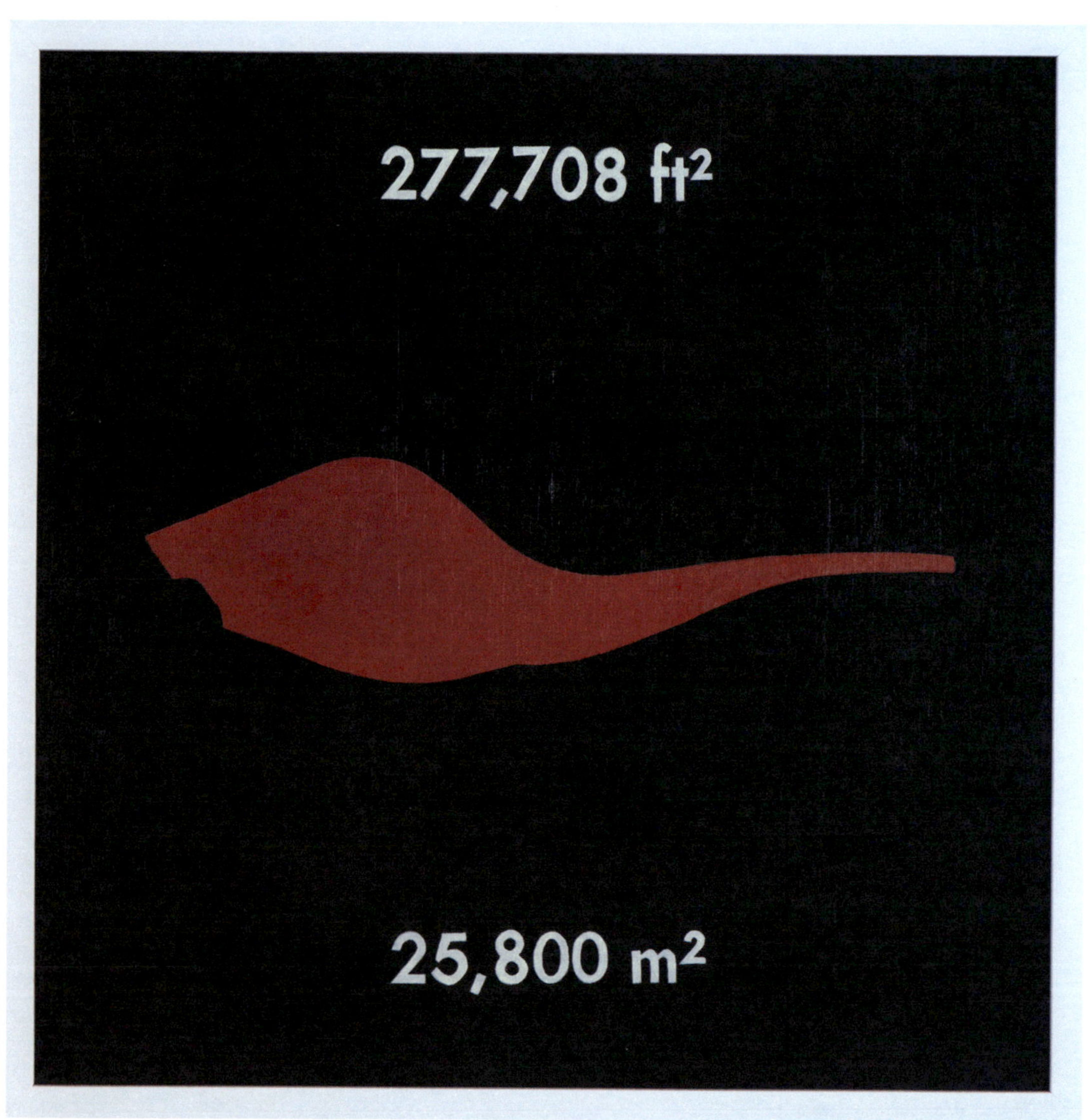

124   *Zaha Hadid, Performing Arts Center*, 2013. Oil on canvas, 24 × 24 in

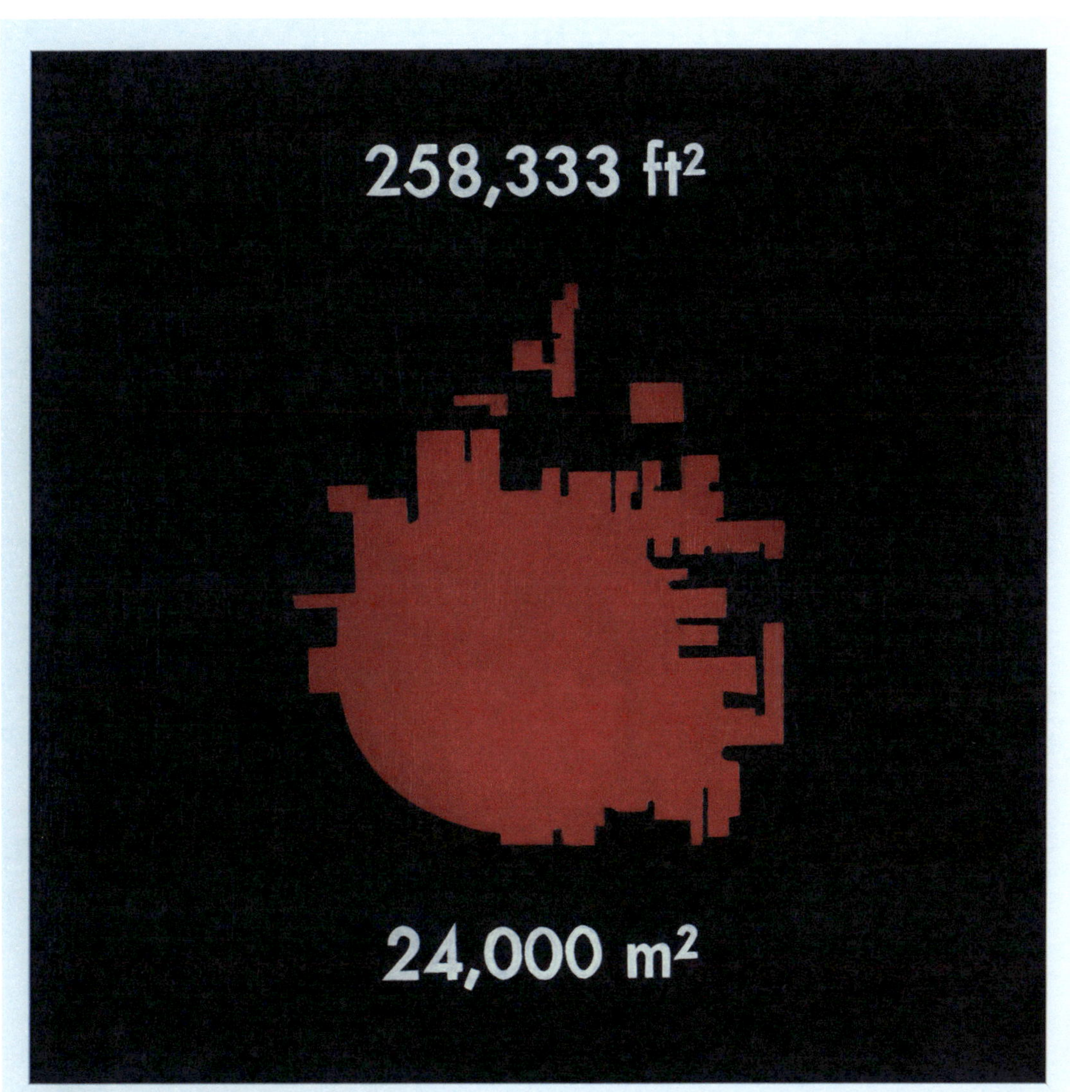

258,333 ft²
24,000 m²

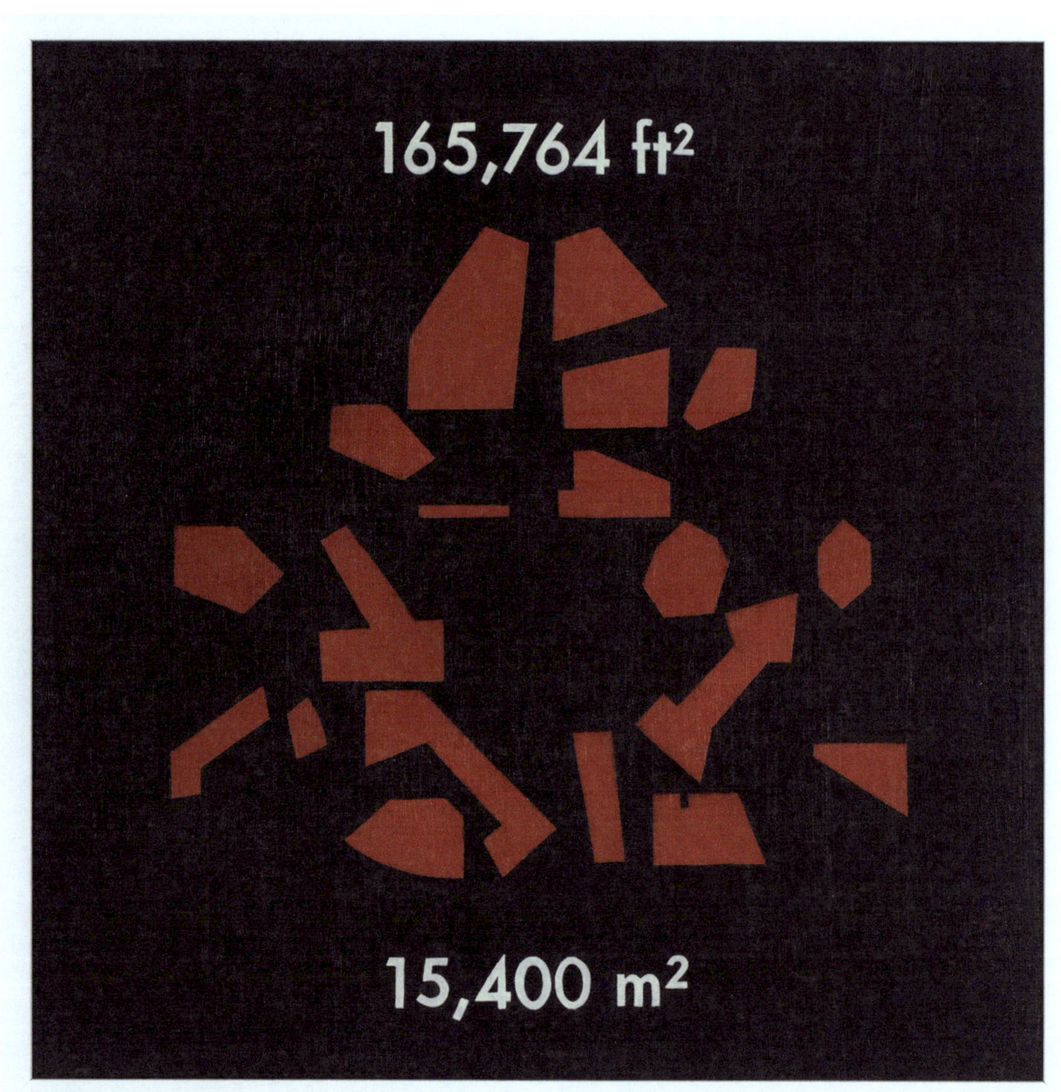

 Biennale Park & International Pavilions, 2013. Oil on canvas, 24 × 24 in

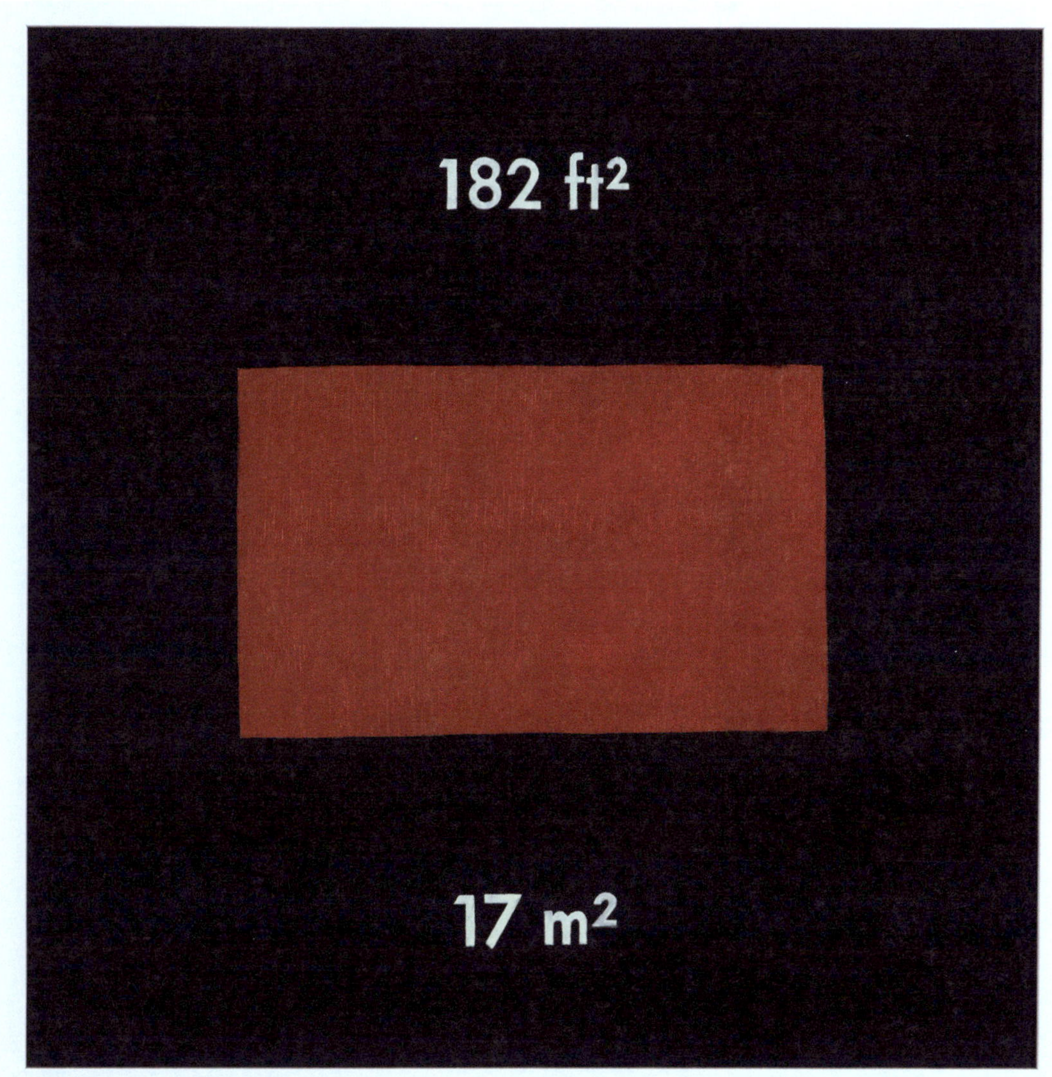

Windowless Room Housing Ten Saadiyat Island Construction Workers,
Shared Bathroom, No Door, 2013. Oil on canvas, 24 × 24 in   127

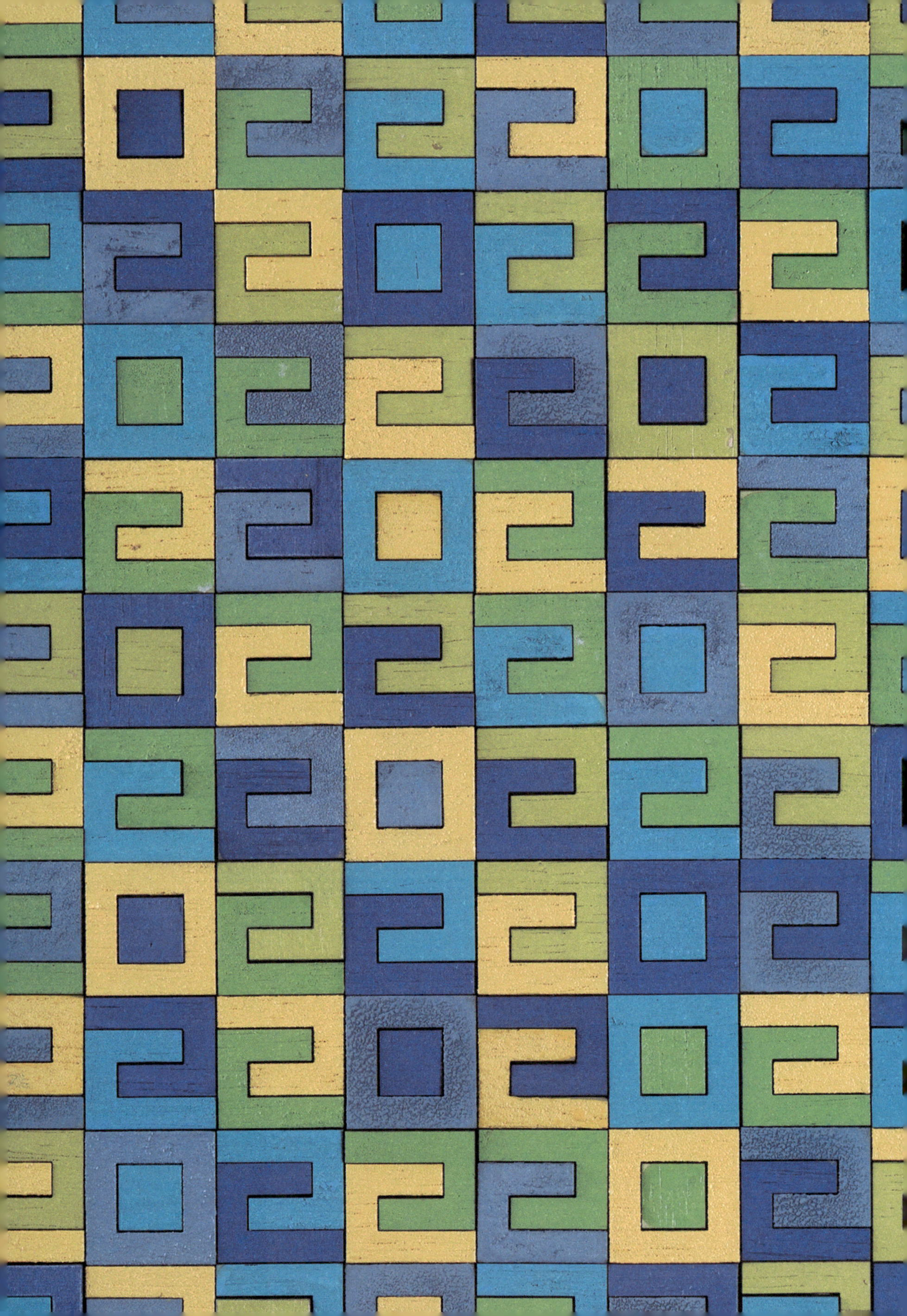

Biographies

(in order of appearance)

Pedro Lasch is a visual artist, a professor at Duke University, and the director of the Social Practice Lab at the John Hope Franklin Humanities Institute.

He has presented solo exhibitions and projects including *Open Routines* (Queens Museum), *Black Mirror* (Nasher Museum), *Abstract Nationalism* (The Phillips Collection), *Art of the MOOC* (Creative Time), *A Sculptural Proposal for the Zócalo* (Casa Wabi), and *Politics of Fiction* (Espacio México Montreal). His group exhibitions include MoMA PS1 (New York) MASS MoCA (North Adams); The Royal College of Art, Hayward Gallery (London), Baltic Centre for Contemporary Art (Gateshead); Centro Nacional de las Artes, Museo Universitario Arte Contemporáneo MUAC, and Galería Palacio Nacional (Mexico City); Prospect.4: New Orleans (2017), Gwangju Biennale (2006), Bienal de La Habana (2015), dOCUMENTA (13) (AND AND AND, Kassel, 2012), documenta fifteen (Atis Rezistans/Ghetto Biennale, Kassel, 2022), and the 56th La Biennale di Venezia (Creative Time Special Project, 2015).

Lasch is the author of six books, and his work has appeared in numerous catalogues and journals like *October*, *Saber Ver*, *Artforum*, *ARTnews*, *Cultural Studies*, *The New York Times*, and *La Jornada*. His online pedagogical artwork *ART of the MOOC* has had over 78,000 enrolled participants in 134 countries since it launched in 2015.

Cristina Paoli holds a master's degree in graphic design from the London College of Communication and a bachelor's degree in graphic design from the Universidad Iberoamericana. She is the author of the book *Mexican Blackletter* (2006). In 2011, she founded PERIFERIA, a design studio based in Mexico City focused on art book design and cultural graphic communication.

She has designed books and graphic materials for institutions such as SITE SANTA FE, Museo Tamayo Arte Contemporáneo, MUAC (Mexico City), Centro de Arte Dos de Mayo (Madrid), the Mexico Pavilion at the 53rd and 54th La Biennale di Venezia, the Chile Pavilion at the 15th Biennale Architettura; publishers including Alias

Blue/Green/Yellow Puzzle Variation, from the series 20 22 Painting Cycle, 2021. Industrial enamel on interchangeable wood pieces, variable dimensions

(Mexico), Arquine (Mexico), Cosac Naify (Brazil), Hatje Cantz (Germany), Electa (Italy), Editorial RM (Mexico–Spain), Turner (Mexico–Spain), Buchhandlung Walther König (Germany); and artists including Francis Alÿs, Teresa Margolles, and Melanie Smith, among others.

In 2014, she received an Honorable Mention in the Collection category at the first Latin American Editorial Design Awards (Buenos Aires) for the design of the Folios MUAC collection, as well as the DAM Architectural Book Award granted by the Deutsches Architekturmuseum and the Frankfurt Book Fair for the book *Talca: Cuestión de educación*.

André Eugène cocurated Atis Rezistans/ Ghetto Biennale's contribution for documenta fifteen at St. Kunigunde Church of Kassel with Leah Gordon. He was born in downtown Port-au-Prince in 1959 and is a leading figure in the artist collective known as Atis Rezistans and a broader movement known as the Sculptors of Grand Rue.

In 2006 André Eugène contributed to a large-scale collective sculptural work, which is on permanent exhibition at the International Slavery Museum in Liverpool. He is the codirector of the Ghetto Biennale, which has been held in Port-au-Prince since 2009. His work has been shown at the Musée d'ethnographie de Genève, the Parc de la Villette and the Grand Palais (Paris), the Fowler Museum at UCLA (Los Ángeles), the Frost Science Museum (Miami), Pioneer Works (New York), and MOCA North Miami; Nottingham Contemporary, and Triennale Milano. His work was included in the Haitian Pavilion at the 54th La Biennale di Venezia.

Leah Gordon cocurated Atis Rezistans/ Ghetto Biennale's contribution for documenta fifteen at St. Kunigunde Church of Kassel. She is an artist, curator, and writer. Her work explores the intersectional histories of the Caribbean plantation system, the Enclosure acts, and the creation of the British working class.

Gordon's work has been exhibited internationally, including at the Museum of Contemporary Art Australia (Sydney), the Dak'art Biennale (Dakar), the National Portrait Gallery (London), and the Norton Museum of Art (West Palm Beach). She is the codirector of the Ghetto Biennale in Port-au-Prince, was cocurator of *Kafou: Haiti, Art and Vodou* at Nottingham Contemporary; and *PÒTOPRENS: The Urban Artists of Port-au-Prince* at Pioneer Works (New York).

Gordon's book *Kanaval* was published in 2021 and 2022, her award-winning feature-length documentary *Kanaval: A People's History of Haiti in Six Chapters* was screened in cinemas and on BBC Four's Arena. Her work has also been shown at MOCA North Miami and Haus der Kulturen der Welt (Berlin).

Atis Rezistans created the works for St. Kunigunde Church of Kasse at documenta fifteen, along with their international collaborators from the Ghetto Biennale group. Atis Rezistans is a dynamic, majority-class group of artists working in the Grand Rue neighborhood of downtown Port-au-Prince, Haiti, often in harsh and difficult conditions.

It is a shifting community made up of experienced, mature artists, and a range of younger emerging artists. In 2009, Atis Rezistans hosted the 1st Ghetto Biennale and in the twelve years since they have hosted over three hundred international artists and formed many strong collaborative bonds. Participating members in documenta fifteen were Katelyn Alexis, Wesner Bazile, Adriana Benjamin, Jerry Reginald

Chery a.k.a. Twoket, Patrick Elie a.k.a. Kombatan, André Eugène, Londel Innocent, Louis Kervans a.k.a. Bakari, Jean Jonas Labaze, Michel Lafleur, Jean Muller Milord a.k.a. Soso, Jean Robert Palenquet, Herold Pierre-Louis, Mario Pierre-Louis a.k.a. Prela, Evel Romain, Jean-Claude Saintilus, Reginald Sénatus, and Wilerme Tegenis, all from Haiti.

Ghetto Biennale created all the works for St. Kunigundis Church of Kassel, Germany for documenta fifteen, along with their collaborators from Atis Rezistans. It is a group of international artists that emerged over more than a decade of collaborative productions with Atis Rezistans in Port-Au-Prince. Ghetto Biennale includes artists from many generations, working in a wide range of media, all of whom are committed to supporting Haitian artists and their communities and celebrating the global importance of Haitian history and culture.

Participating members in documenta fifteen were Cat Barich (Germany), Simon Benjamin (Jamaica/United States), Tom Bogaert (Belgium), Demar Brackenridge (Jamaica), Nanne Buurman (Germany), Vivian Chan (United Kingdom), Camille Chedda (Jamaica), John Cussans (United Kingdom), Edouard Duval-Carrié (Haiti/United States) Leah Gordon (United Kingdom), Sheldon Green (Jamaica), Bastian Hagedorn (Germany), Jean-Louis Huhta (Sweden), Laura Heyman (United States), L (United States), Pedro Lasch (Mexico/United States), Henrike Naumann (Germany), Carima Neusser (Sweden), Roberto N Peyre (Sweden), Martina Vanin (Italy), Elizabeth Woodroffe (Barbados/United Kingdom).

ruangrupa is a Jakarta-based collective, established in 2000, whose members—Ajeng Nurul Aini, farid rakun, Iswanto Hartono, Mirwan Andan, Indra Ameng, Ade Darmawan, Daniella Fitria Praptono, Julia

Sarisetiati, and Reza Afisina—served as the artistic directors of documenta fifteen. As an artist collective, ruangrupa has been involved in many collaborative and exchange projects, including participating in large exhibitions such as Gwangju Biennale (2002 and 2018), İstanbul Bienali (2005), Asia Pacific Triennial of Contemporary Art (Brisbane, 2012), Singapore Biennale (2011), Bienal de São Paulo (2014), Aichi Triennale (Nagoya, 2016), and *Cosmopolis* at Centre Pompidou (Paris, 2017).

In 2016, ruangrupa curated *Sonsbeek '16: transACTION* in Arnhem, the Netherlands. Between 2015 and 2018, ruangrupa co-developed the cultural platform Gudang Sarinah Ekosistem at the Gudang Sarinah warehouse in Pancoran, South Jakarta, together with several Jakarta-based artist collectives. In 2018, ruangrupa also co-initiated Gudskul, a public learning space established to practice an expanded understanding of collective values, such as equality, sharing, solidarity, friendship, and togetherness.

Hoor Al-Qasimi is the president and director of Sharjah Art Foundation (SAF) as a catalyst and advocate for the arts in Sharjah, as well as regionally and internationally, founded in 2009. Al-Qasimi has continuously expanded the scope of the foundation over its ten-year history to include major exhibitions that have toured internationally, artist and curator residencies in visual art, film and music, commissions and production grants for emerging artists, and a wide range of educational programming.

In 2003, Al-Qasimi cocurated Sharjah Biennial 6 and has since continued as biennial director. She was elected as president of the International Biennial Association (IBA) in 2017, an appointment that transferred IBA's headquarters to Sharjah. She also serves as the president of The Africa Institute and chair of the board for the

Sharjah Architecture Triennial. In 2020, Al-Qasimi served as curator of the second Lahore Biennale in Pakistan.

Carolyn Christov-Bakargiev is the director of Castello di Rivoli Museo d'Arte Contemporanea and Fondazione Francesco Fedcrico Cerruti in Turin. She is the recipient of the 2019 Audrey Irmas Award for Curatorial Excellence. She was Edith Kreeger Wolf Distinguished Visiting Professor in art theory and practice at Northwestern University (2013-2019).

Christov-Bakargiev began her career in the arts writing reviews for the magazine *Reporter* and for the newspaper *Il Sole 24 Ore*. Friendships with artists in Italy and internationally, including William Kentridge, Alighiero Boetti, Pierre Huyghe, Francis Alÿs, Mario and Marisa Merz, and Jannis Kounellis, propelled her curatorial work. She curated summer exhibitions at the Villa Medici (1998-2000), and served as chief curator at MoMA PS1 in New York. In 2008 she curated the Biennale of Sydney, followed by dOCUMENTA (13) in 2012, and the 14th İstanbul Bienali in 2015. Amongst her many major publications is the monograph *Arte Povera* (Londres, Phaidon Press, 1999).

Andrea Giunta is a professor at the Universidad de Buenos Aires. She was founding director of the Center for Latin American Visual Studies at the University of Texas at Austin. She has been a visiting professor at Duke University, the Ecole des hautes études en sciences sociales, Columbia University, and Humboldt University, and has also received fellowships from the Guggenheim Foundation, the Getty Museum, the Rockefeller Foundation, and the Donald D. Harrington Fellows Program.

She was curator of León Ferrari's retrospective at Centro Cultural Recoleta in Buenos Aires, cocurator of *Verboamérica* in the permanent collection of Latin American Art at Museo de Arte Latinoamericcano de Buenos Aires (MALBA), and of *Radical Women: Latin American Art, 1960-1985* at the Hammer Museum, Brooklyn Museum, and Pinacoteca de São Paulo. Since 2020 she developed several projects responding to the COVID-19 pandemic context as head curator of Bienal do Mercosul 12: Feminine(s): Visualities, Actions, and Affects in Porto Alegre, and curator of *Rethink Everything*, Les Rencontres d'Arles, and *Cuando cambia el mundo. Preguntas sobre arte y feminismos* at the Centro Cultural Kirchner.

Yuko Hasegawa is the artistic director of the Museum of Contemporary Art Tokyo (2016–present) and a professor at the Graduate School of Global Arts at Tokyo University of the Arts (2016–present). She is also the director of the 21st Century Museum of Contemporary Art, Kanazawa, and artistic director of Inujima "Art House Project" (2011-present).

She has worked on numerous biennale projects, including: The 7th Moscow International Biennale of Contemporary Art: Clouds⇄Forests (2017-2018), the 2nd Beijing Photo Biennial: Unfamiliar Asia (2015), Sharjah Biennial 11: *Re:emerge, Towards a New Cultural Cartography* (2013), the 29th Bienal de São Paulo (2010), the 12th Biennale Architettura (2010), La Biennale di Venezia, Japan Pavilion (2003), Shanghai Biennale (2002-2003), and the 7th International İstanbul Bienali (2001).

Rujeko Hockley is an assistant curator at the Whitney Museum of American Art. She is the curator of the Julie Mehretu retrospective, and cocurated the 2019 Whitney Biennial. Additional projects at the Whitney include *Toyin Ojih Odutola: To Wander Determined* (2017) and *An Incomplete History of Protest: Selections from the Whitney's Collection, 1940-2017* (2017).

Previously, she was assistant curator of contemporary art at the Brooklyn Museum, where she cocurated *Crossing Brooklyn: Art from Bushwick, Bed-Stuy, and Beyond* (2014) and worked on exhibitions featuring LaToya Ruby Frazier, the Bruce High Quality Foundation, Kehinde Wiley, Tom Sachs, as well as projects related to the museum's permanent collection. She is the cocurator of *We Wanted a Revolution: Black Radical Women, 1965-85* (2017), which originated at the Brooklyn Museum and travelled to three US venues in 2017-2018. She serves on the board of Art Matters, as well as the advisory board of Recess.

Candice Hopkins is a curator and writer of Tlingit descent. She is senior curator of the Toronto Biennial of Art and cocurator of the 2018 SITE SANTA FE Biennial. She was a part of the curatorial team for documenta 14 in Athens, Greece, and Kassel, Germany and a cocurator of the major exhibitions *Sakahàn: International Indigenous Art*, *Close Encounters: The Next 500 Years*, and *SITElines.14: Unsettled Landscapes* in Santa Fe, New Mexico. Her writings, essays, and presentations include "Outlawed Social Life" at *South as a State of Mind*, and "Sounding the Margins: A Choir of Minor Voices" at Small Projects in Tromsø, Norway.

She has lectured at FKA Witte de With, Tate Modern, Dak'Art, Artists Space, Tate Britain, and the University of British Columbia. She has received awards including the Hnatyshyn Foundation Visual Arts Award for Curatorial Excellence and the 2016 Prize for a Critical Essay on Contemporary ArtPrix from the Foundation Prince Pierre de Monaco. She is a citizen of the Carcross/Tagish First Nation.

Miguel A. López is a writer, researcher, and former codirector and chief curator of TEOR/éTica in San José, Costa Rica.

He has published in periodicals such as *Afterall, ramona, Manifesta Journal, e-flux journal, Art in America, Art Journal*, and *The Exhibitionist*, among others. His recent books as author and editor include *Robar la historia: Contrarrelatos y prácticas artísticas de oposición*; *The Words of Others: León Ferrari and Rhetoric in Times of War*; *Agítese antes de usar: Desplazamientos educativos, sociales y artísticos en América Latina*; *Alianças de Corpos Vulneráveis*; *The Obscene Death: Drawings 1982–1987: Sergio Zevallos*; and *A Wandering Body: Sergio Zevallos in the Grupo Chaclacayo (1982–1994)*. He has also curated *Social Energies / Vital Forces: Natalia Iguiñiz: Art, Activism, Feminism*; *Balance and Collapse, Patricia Belli: Works 1986-2016*; *Teresa Burga: Estructuras de aire* (with Agustín Pérez Rubio); and *God is Queer* for the 31st Bienal de São Paulo (2014). López is cofounder of the independent art space Bisagra in Lima, Peru.

Cuauhtémoc Medina is a critic, curator, art historian, and research fellow at Instituto de Investigaciones Estéticas at Universidad Nacional Autónoma de México (UNAM). He is chief curator of Museo Universitario Arte Contemporáneo at UNAM in Mexico City. He was the Tate Modern's first associate curator of Latin American Art (2002-2008) and head curator of Manifesta 9.

He was chief curator of the 12th Shanghai Biennale: *Proregress: Art in an Age of Historical Ambivalence*. In 2012 he became the sixth recipient of the Walter Hopps Award for Curatorial Achievement from the Menil Collection. Medina has also curated events and exhibitions like *Cuando la fe mueve montañas* by Francis Alÿs (Lima, 2001), *20 Million Mexicans Can't Be Wrong* (South London Gallery, 2002), and *La era de la discrepancia. Arte y Cultura Visual en México 1968-1997*. In 2009 he curated the project Teresa Margolles presented at the Mexican Pavilion at the La Biennale di Venezia.

Gabi Ngcobo is an artist, curator, and educator. Recent curatorial projects include *All in a Day's Eye: The Politics of Innocence in the Javett Family Collection* at the Javett Art Centre at the University of Pretoria, *Mating Birds* at the KZNSA Gallery (Durban). In 2018 she curated the 10th Berlin Biennale: *We Don't Need Another Hero* and was one of the cocurators of the 32nd Bienal de São Paulo (2016).

She is a founding member of the Johannesburg-based platform NGO–Nothing Gets Organised (2016) and Center for Historical Reenactments (2010–2014). Ngcobo's writing has been published in various publications including *Uneven Bodies (Reader)* (Govett-Brewster Art Gallery, 2021); *The Stronger We Become,* the catalogue of the South African Pavillion at La Biennale di Venezia (2019); *Public Intimacy: Art and Other Ordinary Acts in South Africa* (Yerba Buena Center for the Arts/SFMOMA, 2014); *We Are Many: Art, the Political and Multiple Truths,* Verbier Art Summit (2019), and *Texte Zur Kunst* (September 2017). In November 2020, Ngcobo was appointed curatorial director at the Javett-UP.

Lucia Pietroiusti is curator of General Ecology at Serpentine Galleries, London, as well as the curator of *Sun & Sea (Marina)* at the Lithuanian Pavilion at the 58th La Biennale di Venezia. She is the curator of POWER NIGHT at E-WERK Luckenwalde (2021) and cocurator of the 2020-2021 Shanghai Biennale.

Her projects include the recurring festival on consciousness across species, The Shape of a Circle in the Mind of a Fish, the publication *More-than-Human* and the publication and research project *Microhabitable.* At Serpentine, Pietroiusti founded and runs General Ecology, a strategic effort to embed environmental subjects and methods throughout the galleries' outputs and networks, as well as Back to Earth, gathering over 65 artist campaigns for the environment. The General Ecology Network, currently in development, convenes more than one hundred individuals and organizations across disciplines to prototype artist-led, environmentally driven systems change and bridge the knowledge/translation gap between culture, creativity, and ecology.

José Roca is a curator and artistic director of the 23rd Biennale of Sydney. He runs FLORA ars+natura, an independent space for contemporary art in Bogotá, and is the curator of the LARA collection in Singapore. He was the curator of Latin American art at Tate Britain (2012-2015) and managed the arts program at the Banco de la República in Bogotá for a decade. Roca was cocurator of the Poly/Graphic Triennial in San Juan, Puerto Rico (2004), the 27th Bienal de São Paulo (2006), and the Encuentro Internacional Medellín MDE07 (2007). He was artistic director of Philagrafika 2010 and served on the awards jury for the 52nd La Biennale de Venezia (2007). He was chief curator of the VIII Bienal do Mercosul. He is the author of *Transpolítico: Arte en Colombia 1992-2012* and *Waterweavers: A Chronicle of Rivers*, in conjunction with the homonymous exhibition. Roca was a Curatorial Fellow at the Whitney Independent Study Program, and a Whitney-Lauder Curatorial Fellow at the Institute of Contemporary Art in Philadelphia.

Ralph Rugoff was artistic director of the 2019 La Biennale de Venezia, and guest curator of the 13th Biennale de Lyon. He has been director of the Hayward Gallery in London since 2006, where he has curated numerous group shows including *The Painting of Modern Life: Paris in the Art of Manet and His Followers* (2007), *Psycho Buildings: Artists Take On Architecture* (2008), and *The Infinite Mix: Contemporary Sound and Image* (2016), as well as major retrospectives and solo exhibitions by Ed Ruscha, Jeremy Deller, Tracey Emin, and George Condo. He was also director of the California College of the Arts Wattis Institute in San Francisco.

Between 1985 and 2002 he wrote art and cultural criticism for numerous periodicals, publishing widely in art magazines as well as newspapers, including *Artforum*, *Artpresse*, *Flash Art*, *Frieze*, *Parkett*, *Grand Street*, *The Financial Times*, *The Los Angeles Times*, and *The Los Angeles Weekly*. His *Circus Americanus* (1995) is a collection of essays exploring the cultural phenomena of the American West. During this period he began working as an independent curator, organizing exhibitions such as *Just Pathetic* (1990) and *Scene of the Crime* (1997).

Trevor Schoonmaker is director at the Nasher Museum of Art at Duke University. Hired in 2006 as its first contemporary art curator, he has helped shape the museum's curatorial vision and contemporary art collection. Under his leadership, the museum has sought to recognize and support diverse artists who have been historically underrepresented.

Selected exhibitions at the Nasher include *Naama Tsabar: Composition 21* (2019); *People Get Ready: Building a Contemporary Collection* (2018); *John Akomfrah: Precarity* (2018); *Southern Accent: Seeking the American South in Contemporary Art* (2016); *Wangechi Mutu: A Fantastic Journey* (2013); *The Record: Contemporary Art and Vinyl* (2010); *Barkley L. Hendricks: Birth of the Cool* (2008); and *Street Level: Mark Bradford, William Cordova and Robin Rhode* (2007). He curated New Orleans Triennial, Prospect.4: *The Lotus in Spite of the Swamp* (2017), and *Black President: The Art and Legacy of Fela Anikulapo-Kuti* at the New Museum of Contemporary Art in New York (2003).

Schoonmaker served on the board of the Andy Warhol Foundation for the Visual Arts from 2010-2018.

Dannys Montes de Oca Moreda is a researcher, curator, and art critic based in Havana. She has been director general and curator of the Bienal de La Habana and director of Centro de Arte Contemporáneo Wifredo Lam in Havana. She is chief coordinator of the Biennial's theoretical event. She was also curator of the Bienal Internacional de Asunción, en Paraguay. She coauthored *Memoria: Cuban Art of the 20th Century* and cocurated *Doble Seducción* for Sala Amadís at INJUVE in Madrid.

Her international awards and fellowships include the Premio Nacional de Crítica de Arte Guy Pérez Cisneros from the Consejo de las Artes Plásticas (Havana), researcher in residence at Hunter College, (New York), researcher in residence at Ludwig Forum für Internationale Kunst (Aachen), researcher in residence at Digital Poetics and Politics Summer Institute at Department of Film and Media, Queen's University (Kingston, Ontario) curator in residence at Grand Water Research Institute (Hornby Island/Power Plant Contemporary Art Gallery, Toronto), and researcher in residence at Queen's University (Kingston, Ontario).

Octavian Esanu considers art history, criticism, exhibition-making, and art administration as part of his artistic practice. He was founding director and first curator of the Soros Center for Contemporary Art (Chișinău). Since 2012 he has been the founding director and curator of the American University of Beirut Art Galleries, and is associate professor in the Department of Art and Art History, where he teaches courses in art history, histories of exhibitions, and methods, practices, and theories of art and its modes of display.

He has degrees in studio arts, late socialist
agitprop and socialist realist representation,
capitalist design and interior architecture,
and a PhD in contemporary art history and
visual studies from Duke University. His
research activities, which combine theoretical and practical work, revolve around the
study of major transformation/transition
of art following the global processes of
modernization and neoliberalization. Since
2011 he has been part of the international
editorial collective of *ARTMargins Print*,
an MIT Press journal.

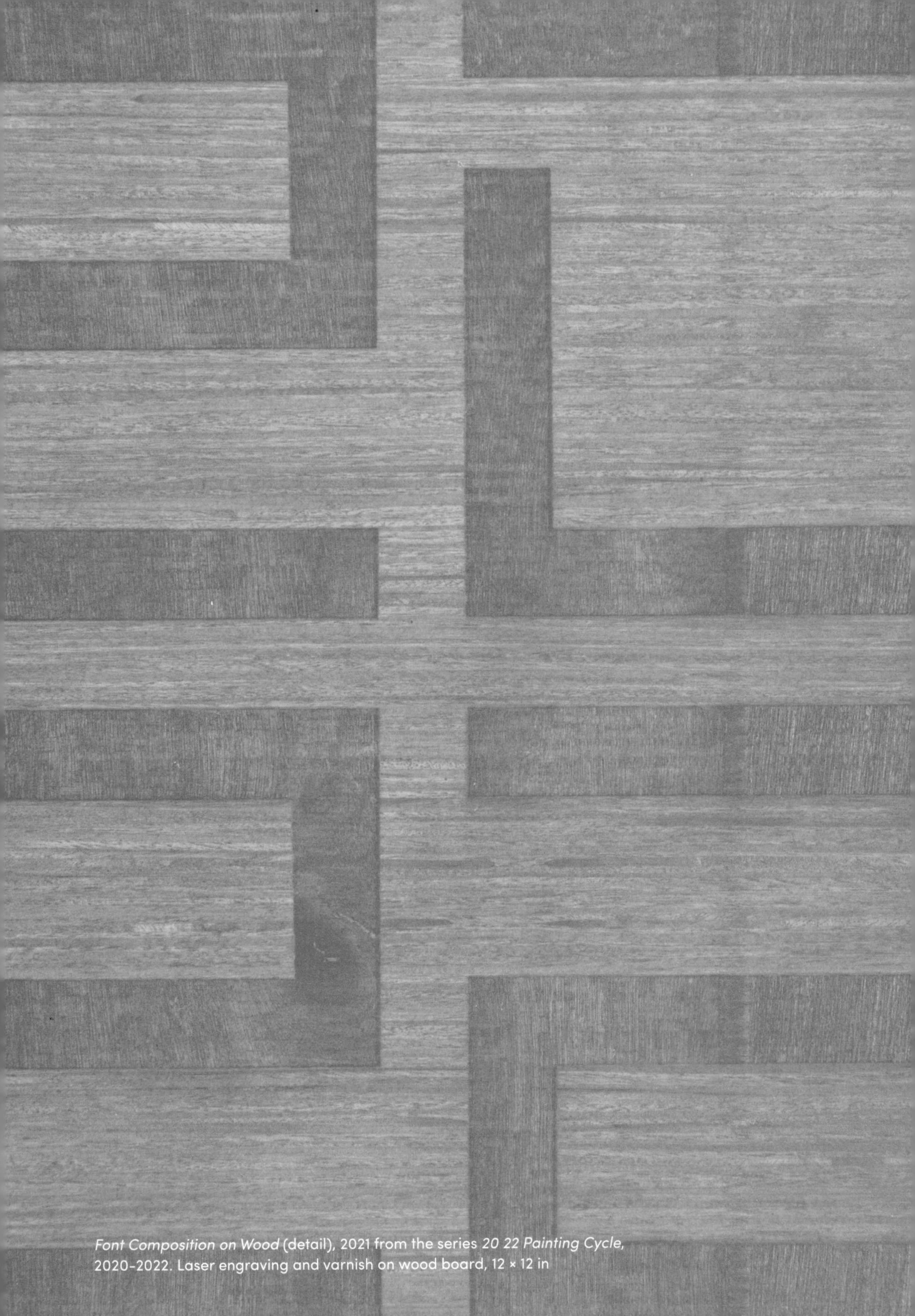

Font Composition on Wood (detail), 2021 from the series *20 22 Painting Cycle*,
2020–2022. Laser engraving and varnish on wood board, 12 × 12 in

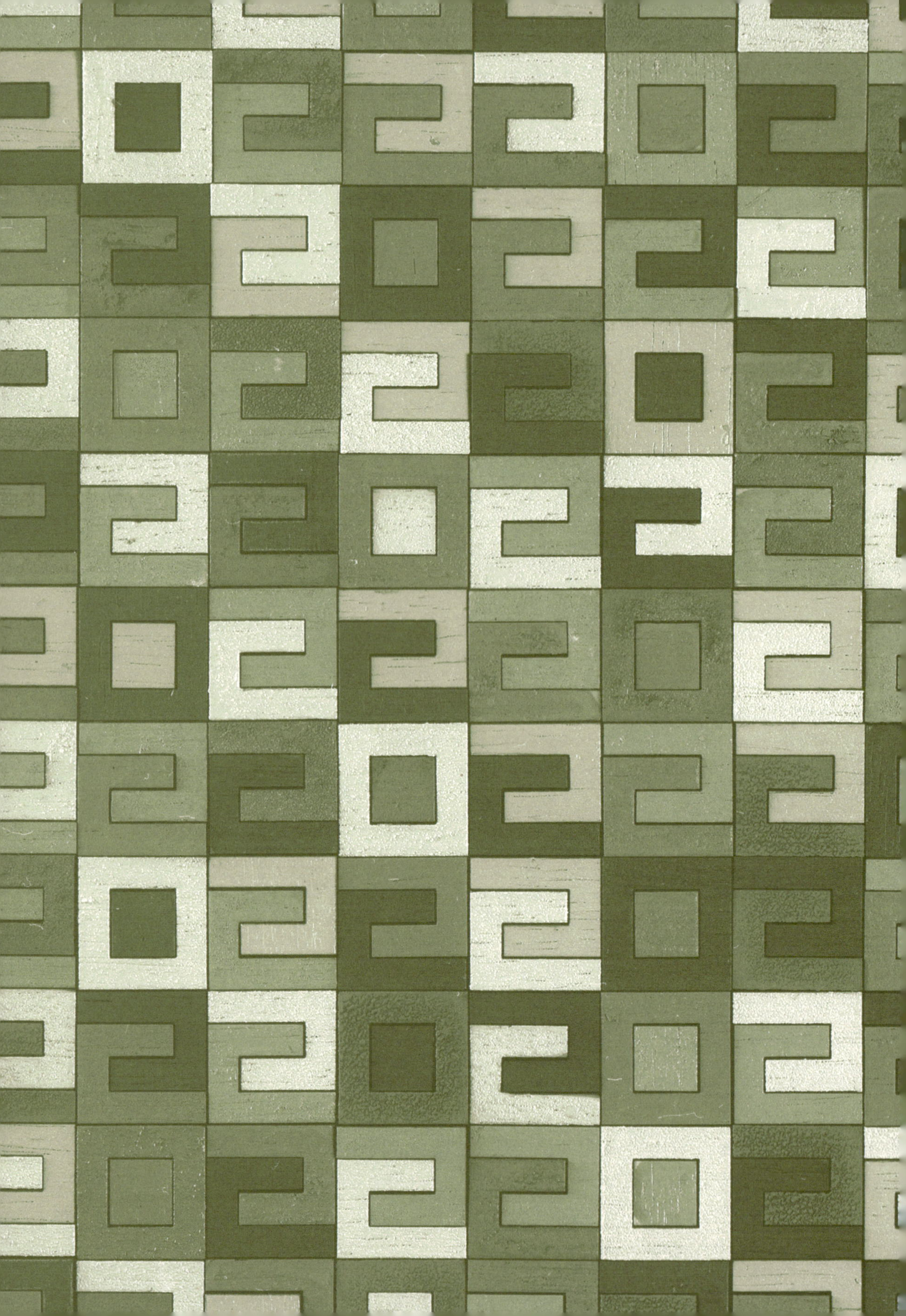

Spanish translation | **Traducción al español**

20 22: Introducción, presentación de artista

[p. 5]

A finales de 2009, trabajé con Leah Gordon, Andre Eugène y el colectivo Atis Rezistans de Puerto Príncipe, en la primera edición de la Ghetto Biennale (2009). En aquella época, produje dos proyectos en Haití: uno en colaboración con Miguel Rojas-Sotelo y otro con Esther Gabara, ambos referenciados más adelante en este libro. La Bienal fue verdaderamente memorable y exitosa en muchos sentidos; sin embargo, a pesar de nuestros numerosos esfuerzos por llamar la atención internacional sobre su relevancia, y sobre la de Haití mismo, los medios de arte y política ignoraron en gran medida el evento. A principios de enero de 2010, días después de haber abandonado Puerto Príncipe y de que la Ghetto Biennale hubiera terminado, Haití fue sacudido por uno de los terremotos más trágicos de la historia de la humanidad.[1] Murieron o desaparecieron miles de personas, entre ellas colaboradores con los que habíamos trabajado en la Bienal. Los mismos medios de comunicación internacionales que habían ignorado de manera sistemática esa tierra, se abalanzaron sobre ella, convirtiéndola en un evento mediático mundial durante muchos meses. Los comentaristas de noticias en la televisión y la radio comenzaron a describir la operación de ayuda humanitaria en Haití como un "tercer frente militar estadounidense", siendo los dos primeros, por supuesto, Afganistán e Irak. Los críticos de arte, que antes no mostraban ningún interés, estaban ahora ansiosos por acercarse al arte contemporáneo haitiano. Los mismos artistas que organizaron la Ghetto Biennale en 2009, ignorados en su mayoría en aquel momento, fueron celebrados en 2011 con la creación de un Pabellón de Haití, en nada menos que La Biennale di Venezia. Una conversación de 2009, antes del terremoto de Haití, resonó en mi mente en este nuevo contexto. Un hombre preguntó: "¿Sabes lo que esperan nuestros políticos?". Negué con la cabeza, sin saber la respuesta. "Otro desastre", respondió él.

La serie *Art Biennials and Other Global Disasters* [Bienales de arte y otros desastres globales] parte de esta experiencia personal, que obviamente no es exclusiva de

---

que comenzaron con la imposición de una deuda externa punitiva por parte de Francia, tras la Revolución haitiana, y la abolición de la esclavitud en 1804.

---

1 El terremoto que sacudió Puerto Príncipe en Haití el 12 de enero de 2010 registró una magnitud de siete en la escala de Richter y causó graves daños en la isla. El desastre causó la pérdida de más de 200,000 vidas y afectó a más de 2 millones de personas. La magnitud de la tragedia no se debió únicamente al fenómeno natural, sino a las vulnerabilidades económicas, sociales y urbanísticas subyacentes, así como a la fragilidad del Estado y a los siglos de políticas internacionales lesivas contra Haití,

Haití. En las últimas décadas, las bienales de arte parecen proliferar al mismo ritmo que los desastres globales. Este paralelismo recuerda al libro de Naomi Klein *La doctrina del shock: el auge del capitalismo del desastre*, en el que la autora expone la relación entre el capitalismo depredador y las catástrofes globales.[2] A partir del año 2010, mis primeras obras de la serie fueron un conjunto de diagramas de investigación en los que presentaba en términos racionales una analogía —en parte absurda— entre las mega exposiciones y los desastres, así como un conjunto de pancartas monumentales en las que juntaba de forma provocativa eventos artísticos conocidos con desastres políticos, económicos o ecológicos globales. Elaboradas mediante un proceso de dibujo, pintura y diseño digital, cada pancarta plantea un reto diferente a los espectadores y participantes, debido a la especificidad de su doble denominación. La pancarta "Venecia/Chernóbil" suscita asociaciones y significados muy diferentes a los de "Sharjah/Kanungu" o "Kassel/ Banqiao". Los lugares donde se exhiben estas pancartas aparentemente celebratorias revelan capas adicionales de significado gracias al contexto físico y cultural, ya sea en una galería de arte en Beirut (2013), en la Bienal de La Habana (2015) o en una muestra de arte en una estación de tren en Montevideo (2015).

En el marco de estas provocaciones, desarrollé otras obras a lo largo de los años para reflexionar colectivamente sobre preguntas como estas: ¿qué analogías se pueden trazar entre los eventos artísticos mundiales más destacados y las iniciativas de ayuda internacional, más allá de las costosas operaciones logísticas que implican la incursión temporal de cientos o miles de personas, tanto en bienales como en zonas

—

2   Naomi Klein, *El auge del capitalismo del desastre*, trad. Isabel Fuentes García, Albino Santos Mosquera, Remedios Diéguez Diéguez (Titivillus, 2006).

de desastre? ¿Qué constituye hoy en día un evento memorable, uno que involucre el arte pero que también vaya mucho más allá de él? ¿Qué categorías utilizamos para reconstituir los vínculos geográficos entre ciudades en medio de cambiantes estructuras culturales, comerciales y financieras? ¿De qué manera se ha utilizado el arte como mecanismo para legitimar a gran escala regímenes opresivos y sistemas económicos? ¿Pueden las zonas de desastre o conflicto armado ser también centros económicos y culturales, o son estos dos términos mutuamente excluyentes? Este libro reúne, por primera vez, el archivo de esta sostenida investigación artística de varios años, en el que cada capítulo aborda contextos específicos en los que se han escenificado y producido nuevas obras. Para abordar estas cuestiones, el libro incluye dos ensayos de los curadores Octavian Esanu y Dannys Montes de Oca, quienes llevaron la serie a contextos muy significativos en su fase inicial: el Líbano y Cuba, respectivamente.

El periodo comprendido entre 2020 y 2022, que da título a este libro, marca la fase más intensa y final de la serie. La documenta fifteen, de 2022, le brindó un cierre circular al proyecto: la presentación en la iglesia de St. Kunigundis en Kassel fue una oportunidad para retomar el origen haitiano desde un nuevo contexto cultural. Sobre todo, dada la emergente conexión de la contrabienal haitiana —un evento colectivo organizado por artistas— con una de las mega exposiciones más concurridas, respetadas por la crítica y mejor financiadas del mundo. Los acontecimientos globales terminaron de perfilar la discusión: un desastre medioambiental sin precedentes, una pandemia mundial como no habíamos visto desde la llegada del VIH/SIDA y el abrumador auge de nuevas formas de nacionalismo de derecha. Estos tres factores han planteado retos fundamentales para las reivindicaciones históricas y los mecanismos operativos de las bienales de arte internacionales y del neoliberalismo en general, por lo tanto, son una parte central de las obras más recientes de este libro.

Las obras presentadas en la documenta, junto con Ghetto Biennale y Atis Rezistans, aparecen bajo el nombre de *20 22: The Common Wind*, en referencia al año de la exposición, así como a los brillantes escritos del difunto historiador Julius S. Scott.[3] Los mismos números 20 y 22 —con un espacio entre ellos—, aparecen obsesivamente en cada uno de los cuadros en la serie pictórica que lleva ese nombre, todos pintados a lo largo de tres años y esbozados durante el peor periodo de confinamiento de la pandemia de COVID-19. Estas obras son un intento desesperado por aportar color a la monotonía gris de un periodo marcado por tanta muerte y duelo, pero también tratan de recordar acontecimientos y cifras en un momento en el que nuestra supervivencia individual y colectiva se convirtió en el frente universal que amenazaba con desaparecer todo lo demás. En este libro, las pinturas acompañan las ideas y frases de catorce destacados curadores, quienes participaron en una serie internacional de conversatorios en línea que también organicé durante el confinamiento de la primavera del 2021. *20 22 The Ongoing Biennial* [20 22 La bienal en curso] fue una serie de conversaciones semanales gratuitas a las que asistieron más de 3,000 espectadores durante catorce semanas consecutivas. Este fue un proyecto que abordó muchos de los temas mencionados anteriormente y además produjo un archivo permanente de ese momento excepcional.

Sería un error no abordar la actual documenta en relación con los desastres. Con el pasar de los años, la documenta fifteen de ruangrupa será considerada uno de los experimentos más audaces de su tipo, aún demasiado radical para ser aceptado

—

3 Julius S. Scott, *El viento común. Corrientes afroamericanas en la era de la Revolución haitiana* (Madrid: Traficantes de sueños, 2021).

por críticos, curadores y coleccionistas, muchos de los cuales se sintieron descolocados desde el principio por la deliberada falta de dependencia del colectivo respecto a la influencia y los recursos de la clase artística profesional, eludiendo los mecanismos tradicionales de validación y apoyo. La propia institución parece no haber estado preparada para hacer frente a la intensidad de los debates en torno a Palestina y el antisemitismo, que acapararon gran parte de la conversación durante los meses previos a la inauguración de la exposición y hasta sus últimas semanas. El antisemitismo global, la historia nazi y el Holocausto han formado parte de la serie presentada en este libro, desde la inclusión en los diagramas de investigación (2010) de la exposición nazi Arte degenerado [*Entartete Kunst*] y la figura de Goebbels en *Islas de tragedia y fantasía* en la Bienal de La Habana (2015). La historia de la supremacía blanca aparece de forma destacada en la manta colocada en la torre de la iglesia de St. Kunigundis, cuando se inauguró la documenta fifteen. La ocupación ilegal y violenta de los territorios palestinos por parte de Israel también se ha abordado en el *20 22 Painting Cycle* [20 22 Ciclo de pinturas], referenciando a Gaza en una de las pinturas. Entre amenazas semanales de censura, el evitable retiro de obras de arte y una tendencia creciente, tanto de las instituciones como de los artistas, a posar en lugar de negociar, cierro este escrito con gran tristeza y preocupación por el futuro de las exposiciones de arte. Parece que ha hecho falta un colectivo de Indonesia y un número sin precedentes de artistas racializados en la documenta para que los alemanes acepten que este evento internacional es también, ante todo, una exposición alemana. Por el bien del futuro de esta muestra y de otras exposiciones importantes a las que se dedica este libro, espero que estos sean sólo los dolorosos signos de un nuevo y mejor comienzo.

Pedro Lasch, 19 de septiembre de 2022, Kassel, Alemania

El viento común: de la Ghetto Biennale a la documenta fifteen

[p. 11]

Este capítulo de apertura presenta el entramado que conecta las obras realizadas en 2009 para la primera edición de la Ghetto Biennale en Puerto Príncipe, Haití, con aquellas producidas muchos años después por parte del colectivo durante su participación en la documenta fifteen en 2022. Las siguientes páginas incluyen textos descriptivos e imágenes sobre todas las piezas incluidas en ambas exposiciones. Los proyectos producidos en Haití, en 2009, fueron el resultado de una colaboración con Miguel Rojas-Sotelo, bajo el título *Bicentenario* y *Narcochingadazo*, así como talleres con máscaras de espejos, parte de la serie *Naturalizaciones*, realizados en colaboración con Esther Gabara. Ambos proyectos incluyeron la participación de miembros de Atis Rezistans, así como sucedió con los trabajos presentados en la documenta fifteen. Como se explica en la introducción, fue la experiencia trágica del terremoto de 2010 en Haití, y su respuesta internacional, lo que detonó el comienzo de la serie *Art Biennials and Other Global Disasters* [Las bienales de arte y otros desastres globales]. Sin embargo, es importante señalar que la pintura en un estandarte monumental, las instalaciones de vidrio de colores y los talleres de máscaras de espejos creados para Atis Rezistans en documenta no surgen como tal del desastre, sino todo lo opuesto. Pensados como un homenaje a los escritos lúcidos del difunto historiador Julius S. Scott en *El viento común*, las obras, los talleres y el marco colaborativo hacen eco de la apuesta de ese libro por los métodos informales de comunicación y las redes sociales transnacionales entre haitianos y no haitianos, empleados para amplificar el mensaje e impacto de la Revolución haitiana. Son un diálogo alegre de varias generaciones de artistas haitianos en este camino compartido entre Puerto Príncipe y Kassel, un camino que desborda la riqueza de una larga e inspiradora historia política.

Color Mask Prototypes no. 1-5 [Prototipos de máscaras de colores n. 1-5], 2010
Serie *Naturalizaciones*, 2022 – en curso
Instalación (prototipos de 30.5 × 30.5 × 0.6 cm, con soportes que varía dentro del rango de alturas humanas)
Hojas de acrílico pintadas y grabadas con láser, expuestas sobre soportes metálicos

Haciendo eco de los vitrales de St. Kunigundis en Kassel, estos prototipos experimentales incorporaron color a la serie de máscaras de espejo transparentes y reflejantes que el artista ha utilizado en varios contextos alrededor del mundo, incluyendo la primera edición de la Ghetto Biennale en Haití, en 2009. Cada prototipo es único, pero todos cambian drásticamente cuando la luz y el espectador se posicionan en frente, convirtiéndose en un rostro abstracto que dialoga con la audiencia y las esculturas exhibidas en Grand Rue.

The Common Wind y River and Bridge Mirror Mask Box Sets [Conjunto de máscaras espejos de El viento común y El río y el puente], Kassel, 2022
Serie *Naturalizaciones*, 2022 – en curso
Escultura interactiva, cajas de 31.8 × 40.6 × 26.7 cm, cada una con veinte máscaras de espejo grabadas de 21.6 × 27.9 cm

Estas máscaras fueron activadas en la documenta fifteen, retomando la manera en que se usaron durante la primera Ghetto Biennale en Puerto Príncipe, en 2009, como una especie de embajadoras de Atis Rezistans y la Ghetto Biennale, al salir del espacio expositivo hacia otros espacios de la bienal. La primera caja se centra en el impacto global de la Revolución haitiana y el trabajo del difunto historiador Julius S. Scott. Ésta incluye el título *The Common*

Wind [El viento común], en inglés en un lado, y en creol haitiano en el otro, *Van Momen An*. La segunda caja se centra en la metáfora de ruangrupa referida a que una exposición como documenta o la Ghetto Biennale es un puente que se extiende temporalmente sobre un pasado, presente y futuro mucho más complejo y continuo alrededor del ser colectivo, con la frase "El río y el puente": en indonesio, *Sungai dan jembatan*, y en alemán, *Die Brücke und der Fluss*. Los participantes de los talleres usaron estas máscaras para reflejar el arte de Atis Rezistans en sus rostros, tomando fotografías que fusionaron el cuerpo con las obras, así como palabras grabadas en el espejo seleccionadas según su relación con la emancipación racial y la organización colectiva. Facilitados por Pedro Lasch y un equipo de mediadores de arte (llamados *sobat-sobat*, por ruangrupa), estos talleres sucedieron semanalmente a lo largo de los 100 días que duró la documenta en la iglesia de St. Kunigundis, en el Fridericianum, en el espacio infantil RURUKIDS, y por toda Kassel y sus múltiples espacios de exposición.

Grand Rue y los talleres sobre Frantz Fanon, **Puerto Príncipe, 2009**
Serie *Naturalizaciones*, 2022 — en curso
Talleres comunitarios en el barrio Grand Rue y escuelas secundarias locales

Estos talleres de máscaras de espejo[4] fueron diseñados intencionalmente para dos contextos bastante diferentes. El primero sucedió durante la bellamente caótica apertura de la Ghetto Biennale en Grand Rue, con cientos de personas entrando y saliendo, usando las máscaras con muy

poca interacción verbal y de maneras bastante impredecibles. El segundo consistió en actividades más enfocadas con estudiantes de secundarias locales donde, sin ninguna prisa, pudimos experimentar con las máscaras tras haber revisado *Piel negra, máscaras blancas*, de Frantz Fanon (entre otros de sus escritos), la declaración de la Constitución haitiana de 1805 que decía: "Necesariamente debe cesar toda acepción de color [...]; a partir de ahora los haitianos sólo serán conocidos bajo la denominación genérica de negros",[5] así como las ideas y experiencias que los participantes trajeron a esta obra. Todas las imágenes de 2009 mostradas aquí pertenecen a estos talleres y fueron tomadas por Esther Gabara. Un ensayo visual titulado *Silent Absence* [Ausencia silenciosa],[6] que no se incluye en esta publicación, fue creado por Gabara y Lasch a partir de estas imágenes en 2010, con el fin de señalar el duelo y devastación causados por el terremoto sin precedentes de ese año.

documenta Wall Labels **[Cédulas a muro para documenta], Kassel, 2022**
Serie *Labels* [Cédulas], 2001 — en curso
Cédulas a muro convencionales con texto, dimensiones variables
Impresas en papel, adaptadas al espacio en cuanto a estilo y forma

Comenzando con cinco cédulas en el espacio expositivo de St. Kunigundis, esta nueva versión de la serie *Labels* fue instalada en Kassel bajo la forma de cédulas de museo colocadas de manera concisa, dispersas como textos poéticos que hablaban sobre

—

4   Para una bibliografía completa de los usos y métodos de la serie de *Naturalizaciones*, ver: Pedro Lasch, *What Are We Before We Are Naturalized?* (Washington: Provisions Library, 2015) y *Pedro Lasch: Entre líneas / Between the Lines* (cat. exp.), curada por Lucía Sanromán Aranda (Ciudad de México: Temblores Publicaciones-INBAL, 2024).

5   Constitución haitiana de 1805. Consultado el 4 de abril de 2025, en: https:// decolonialucr.wordpress.com/wp-content/uploads/2014/09/constitucion-imperial-de-haiti-1805-bilbioteca-ayacucho.pdf.

6   *Silent Absence* es una serie inédita de fotografías y textos a muro que Pedro Lasch fue invitado a realizar en 2009.

el arte y el entorno que les rodeaba, pero escritas de manera que pudieran escapar de su contexto original. Durante los 100 días que duró la documenta fifteen, otras cédulas aparecieron en los distintos espacios expositivos y plataformas colaborativas, a la manera de embajadoras de Atis Rezistans y la Ghetto Biennale.

Bicentenario y *Narcochingadazo*, Puerto Príncipe, 2009-2010
Talleres comunitarios y pintura mural en el espacio público

Desarrollado junto con Miguel Rojas-Sotelo, así como con individuos locales y organizaciones en cada uno de los sitios en que tuvo lugar, el proyecto *Narcochingadazo* surgió en el marco de la convocatoria "contra las oligarquías y sus celebraciones oficiales". La primera etapa de este proyecto se lanzó en mayo del 2009 en internet y con una serie de performances y acciones en español y maya yucateco, realizados en la ciudad de Mérida, Yucatán, durante Arte Nuevo InteractivA IV. Dedicado en su mayoría a establecer conexiones con individuos y grupos sociales que querían producir contra-narrativas de las innumerables celebraciones por el bicentenario de las independencias latinoamericanas, esta etapa concluyó con nuestras contribuciones para la primera Ghetto Biennale en Puerto Príncipe, en diciembre de 2009. El objetivo era colocar a Haití y al Caribe en el centro de los debates y la producción artística sobre los bicentenarios de 2010, especialmente en un contexto donde la Revolución haitiana había sido continuamente excluida de las narrativas oficiales, tanto hemisféricas como mundiales. Aquí, se reproducen imágenes del mural que Lasch y algunos colaboradores de Atis Rezistans pintaron durante un taller comunitario sobre una pared de gran formato en el barrio de Grand Rue. Para comenzar el taller, Lasch pintó los números 1810, 1910 y 2010 en la pared, con una fuente sencilla y cuadrada,

en referencia al *Proyecto 500* del artista colombiano Antonio Caro y a los diversos bicentenarios que se estaban preparando en las Américas en ese momento. Después de actividades comunitarias y discusiones sobre eventos relevantes que siguen siendo borrados de la memoria local y colectiva, algunos miembros del colectivo Atis Rezistans procedieron a pintar sobre el año 1810, reemplazándolo con el año 1804, asociado con la Revolución haitiana. El nuevo número se mantuvo visible durante el encuentro internacional, integrado visiblemente junto con otras actividades de la Ghetto Biennale que sucedieron al lado de dicha pared.

St. Kunigundis Common Wind Tower Painting [Pintura para la torre de St. Kunigundis "Viento común"], Kassel, 2022 Serie *Art Biennials and Other Global Disasters* [Bienales de arte y otros desastres], 2010-2022
Estandarte monumental colgado de la torre de la iglesia
Yeso y acrílico pintados a mano sobre tela de color, 10.40 x 1.20 m

Pintado a mano para la torre de la iglesia de St. Kunigundis en Kassel, este estandarte de gran formato sólo muestra números. Los años enlistados aluden a las historias que a muchos de nosotros nos han enseñado; las 36 fechas que ahí aparecen funcionan como un conjunto abstracto de preguntas visuales. Una declaración impresa del artista junto con una lista de eventos fueron distribuidas entre los participantes como puntos de partida para los talleres que tuvieron lugar durante los 100 días que duró la documenta. Al repensar la relevancia internacional de la Revolución haitiana en el contexto de la documenta, las fechas que aparecen en el estandarte también incluyen otros acontecimientos clave en la lucha mundial por la emancipación. Un conjunto de números contrastante pertenece a la expansión mundial de la supremacía blanca y la historia del comercio de esclavos euroamericano, la cual debería ser parte de nuestra memoria colectiva. Quizá menos esperadas, pero cruciales para el proyecto, son las fechas que cuentan la historia de las exposiciones internacionales, siendo estas las ferias mundiales, zoológicos humanos, bienales internacionales o muestras ideológicas como la exposición de Arte degenerado [*Entartete Kunst*], organizada por el partido Nazi en 1937. El acto de pintar fechas en el espacio público hace referencia a los talleres realizados por Lasch en la Ghetto Biennale en 2009.

Lista de eventos asociados con las fechas que se incluyen en la pintura:

2022: Atis Rezistans y la Ghetto Biennale en documenta fifteen, Kassel

2020: Pandemia global de COVID-19

2018: Publicación de *El viento común* de Julius S. Scott

2013: Establecimiento del Biennale Park en la isla Saadiyat en los Emiratos Árabes Unidos (EAU), en la isla artificial más grande del mundo

2010: Terremoto en Haití / Bicentenarios de independencia celebrados en las Américas

2009: Primera Ghetto Biennale. Mural inicial en honor a la Revolución haitiana

2005: El zoológico de Augsburgo presenta la exhibición *Afrika-Dorf* [Aldea Africana]

1994: Fin del apartheid en Sudáfrica

1993: Primera Sharjah Biennial

1987: Primera İstanbul Bienali

1984: Primera Bienal de La Habana

1981: Mauritania se convierte en el último país del mundo en abolir la esclavitud

1977: Yibuti se convierte en el último país africano en independizarse de colonizadores europeos

1964: Ley de Derechos Civiles en Estados Unidos

1958: La Exposición Universal de Bruselas incluye el "último" zoológico humano, una "aldea congoleña"

1955: Primera documenta en Kassel

1951: Primera Bienal de São Paulo

1942: Conferencia de Wannsee: los nazis coordinan la "Solución Final", plan de asesinato racializado, sostenido también por el trabajo forzado de judíos y de otras comunidades perseguidas.

1937: Exposición de Arte degenerado en Múnich; millones de personas visitan la exposición itinerante nazi

1904: La Exposición Universal de St. Louis organiza el mayor zoológico humano de la historia, con miles de personas exhibidas

1895: Primera La Biennale di Venezia

1888: Brasil se convierte en la última nación de las Américas en abolir la esclavitud

1886: Cuba se convierte en el último territorio español en abolir la esclavitud

1865: El Congreso de Estados Unidos abole la esclavitud con la Enmienda 13 / Se forma el Ku Klux Klan

1848: Segunda Ley de Abolición Francesa

1847: Liberia se convierte en el primer país africano en independizarse de colonizadores europeos

1825: Francia y Europa imponen a Haití una deuda extranjera exorbitante como compensación a los antiguos esclavistas

1810: Países americanos se independizan de España / México abole la esclavitud

1807: El Parlamento británico vota por abolir la trata de esclavos

1804: Se declara la independencia de Haití, primer país del mundo en prohibir permanentemente la esclavitud

1794: Primera Ley de Abolición Francesa, invalidada poco después por Napoleón

1791: Primera Exposición Universal en Praga / Ceremonia vudú en Bois Caïman enciende los levantamientos de esclavizados en Saint-Domingue

1619: Primera venta de esclavizados en colonias inglesas en Point Comfort, Virginia

1522: Primera gran sublevación de africanos esclavizados en las Américas, en la isla de La Española

1493: Colón transporta personas nativas esclavizadas; los primeros negros libres llegan a las Américas / Expulsión de judíos y moros de España

1441: A inicios del Renacimiento, Portugal comienza en África el comercio europeo de esclavos

20 22 The Ongoing Biennial Conversation and Painting Cycle [20 22 La bienal en curso, conversatorio y Ciclo de pinturas], 2020-2022

[p. 29]

Hoor Al-Qasimi, Carolyn Christov-Bakargiev, Andrea Giunta, Yuko Hasegawa, Rujeko Hockley, Candice Hopkins, Miguel A. López, Cuauhtémoc Medina, Gabi Ngcobo, Lucia Pietroiusti, farid rakun (ruangrupa), José Roca, Ralph Rugoff, Trevor Schoonmaker

En el contexto de una pandemia sin precedentes, confinamientos globales y la reformulación de cada aspecto del arte y la realización de exposiciones, las obras presentadas en esta sección se desarrollaron como dos series paralelas, aunque relacionadas entre sí: un ciclo de conversatorios público y semanal, con curadores internacionales y un conjunto de más de treinta pinturas de palabras abstractas referidas a eventos que tuvieron lugar en este marco temporal.

Organizado por Pedro Lasch y el Franklin Humanities Institute Social Practice Lab (SPL), junto con el apoyo de la FHI World Arts Initiative de Duke University, el ciclo de conversatorios *The Ongoing Biennial*

incluyó catorce curadores y profesionales de las artes de renombre internacional y más de 3,000 asistentes remotos provenientes de docenas de países entre enero y mayo de 2021. El FHI SPL ha preservado un archivo permanente de las conversaciones completas, el cual puede ser aún consultado por el público. Para esta publicación, hemos seleccionado una serie de frases de cada invitado en relación con los temas de las bienales, la realización de exposiciones internacionales y los retos que trajo este momento histórico.

La selección se muestra en orden alfabético, enlistando a cada curador por su nombre y acompañado por las pinturas que Lasch desarrolló durante ese periodo. Éstas fueron producidas a partir de un abanico de técnicas contemporáneas y tradicionales sobre lienzo, usando una tipografía especialmente diseñada para aumentar la tensión entre juegos visuales y legibilidad. Los números 20 y 22 aparecen de manera progresiva en cada pintura, con diferentes niveles de abstracción. Añadiendo color a un momento de monotonía gris y duelo, estas obras muestran nombres y acontecimientos de una época donde nuestra supervivencia individual y colectiva se convirtió en el trasfondo universal que amenazaba con borrar toda forma de memoria colectiva.

Hoor Al-Qasimi

"La primera Lahore Biennale se enfocó fuertemente en artistas de Asia del Sur. Así que cuando me invitaron a curar la segunda edición, querían que viera más allá de Asia Meridional, pero también que incluyera artistas de la región. Fue complejo, porque me interesaba invitar a artistas del llamado Sur Global y, con ello, abrir las discusiones alrededor del poscolonialismo y las historias compartidas que muchos de estos países estaban enfrentando. Fue una oportunidad para entablar conversaciones entre varios países y continentes".

"Al crecer como artista, muchas veces pensé en qué es lo que quería de una bienal. Crecí con la Sharjah Biennial, que empezó cuando tenía 13 años. Luego, en 2002, tomé la batuta, porque estaba intentando controlarlo todo y me dijeron: ¡hazlo tú misma! Entonces, se convirtió en mi trabajo. Pero, en el fondo, yo sólo era una artista joven que quería que pasaran cosas en Sharjah. No quería seguir huyendo a Berlín, Nueva York o Londres. Se volvió una suerte de responsabilidad para crear e inspirar a las siguientes generaciones. Ahora, han pasado casi 20 años desde que comencé a hacer esto y ha significado una gran diferencia para la escena del arte, no sólo en Sharjah, sino en toda la región: el Golfo, los EAU —todo está conectado".

"En 2002, cuando empecé a trabajar con la Sharjah Biennial, hacía muchas preguntas, ya que no estaba cómoda con la idea de representar países. Mucha gente viene de más que un sólo sitio; existen diásporas, personas de ascendencias mixtas y demás. Han habido tantos problemas alrededor de la nacionalidad y la identidad que me parecía que la idea de representar a un país era problemática; esa fue una de las primeras cosas que cambié".

"El pabellón de los EAU en Venecia fue realmente una exposición museística. Recuerdo que un curador me dijo: "Para Venecia necesitas hacer algo rápido, algo que la gente va a experimentar y luego pueda irse, algo como una experiencia llamativa". A lo que respondí: "Bueno, si la gente no tiene tiempo, no tiene que ver la exposición". Para mí era importante repensar la idea de la bienal como espectáculo, con gente que ve las obras de prisa; eso no debe ser un motivo para mostrar o no algo. Y porque trataba de hablar de los EAU, me interesaba hacer una exposición histórica, lo cual no fue fácil considerando el espacio y las condiciones".

"Nuestro foro March Meeting realizado en línea fue bien recibido. Se registraron más de 7,000 personas, asistieron 4,000 y el promedio de asistencia a las charlas fue de 200 a 300 personas; algo que no habría sucedido en nuestro espacio físico. Sin embargo, sí extrañamos esos momentos posteriores a cada charla para reunirnos. Para la siguiente ocasión, intentaremos combinar ambos formatos, porque es increíble tener gente de distintas partes del mundo escuchando y haciendo preguntas. Así que buscaremos la manera de hacer ambos".

"Para mí fue complejo pensar en opciones de realidad virtual, porque me rehúso a que nuestras exposiciones estén en línea. La gente está ocupada, les da pereza y dicen que vieron una exposición porque la vieron en línea. Necesitamos una audiencia. Necesitamos que la gente venga al museo. No es la misma experiencia. Pensaba en lo que hicimos en Lahore mientras hacía la presentación. No puedes recrear una exposición en línea. Simplemente no es posible".

Carolyn Christov-Bakargiev

"Fui nominada para curar la 16 Sydney Biennale en 2008. Decidí que esta giraría en torno al concepto *upside down* [lo invertido]. En cierto modo, aquello que retrocede, se repite, se revierte o gira y queda al revés. Fue básicamente una investigación centrada en la siguiente pregunta: ¿por qué los artistas que han sido revolucionarios en su práctica artística —en términos de materiales, forma, estructura y técnica—, y que han investigado formas relacionadas con la reversión, la inversión, la repetición, suelen haber sido también revolucionarios en lo político?"

"Hubo grandes precedentes para mi dOCUMENTA (13) del 2012 en lo que respecta a los artistas invitados. Supongo que soy un poco predecible, en el sentido de que, a lo largo de mi trayectoria, suelo invitar a los mismos artistas a distintas exposiciones—ya que hemos vivido una vida en común. Realmente, se trata de la vida, no sólo de la exposición. Es la forma de transitar treinta, cuarenta, cincuenta o sesenta años conversando y comprendiendo el mundo cambiante con las mismas personas y, a la vez, seguir abierto a conocer nuevos artistas. En todas las exposiciones que he realizado, he contado con artistas que me acompañan desde antes y con algunos nuevos".

"Sabes, la razón por la cual realicé de esta manera esta edición de documenta fue para detener algo que se estaba convirtiendo en una opinión generalizada que yo no compartía. Las bienales estaban siendo criticadas como trampas turísticas —formas en que las ciudades buscaban legitimarse mediante el turismo— y el sistema artístico se estaba desplazando hacia las casas de subastas y las ferias de arte. Fue el ascenso de Art Basel y el declive del sistema de las bienales. La razón es que la feria de arte, estructuralmente, se asemeja más al internet. El internet, en su estructura de sitios en red, se acerca más al modelo de feria de arte que al de bienal. Entonces, en ese momento necesitaba demostrar que la exposición internacional periódica todavía importaba, y ¡creo que lo logré!"

"Creo que el peligro principal ahora mismo es la sobredigitalización. Se observa claramente si rastreamos el flujo del dinero. De esto se trata siempre: de seguir el dinero, y hoy todo está en lo digital. La digitalización ciertamente ayudó durante la pandemia — no sólo para comprar cosas, sino también para experimentar eventos y actividades en línea. Gracias a internet, ciertos grupos marginados han podido avanzar al frente. No me opongo al pensamiento de alguien como Legacy Russell, ni al de las generaciones jóvenes que ven esto como una oportunidad emancipadora. Sin embargo,

creo que hay un riesgo: que en el futuro los movimientos ecológicos y la hiperdigitalización formen una alianza para salvar al planeta —manteniendo a la gente en casa y en línea todo el tiempo. Un peligro de tipo Matrix".

Andrea Giunta

"Creo que el arte debe ocupar un espacio cada vez que tiene la posibilidad. Para mí, lo verdaderamente retador no tiene que ver con criticar una bienal, sino ver aquello que una bienal me permite criticar —o cambiar— respecto al mundo. Jamás usaría el espacio de una bienal para hacer una crítica vacía del sistema. Quiero que sea una celebración del arte porque creo que éste tiene la oportunidad de hacer intervenciones poderosas".

"Cuando llegué a São Paulo al final de la exposición *Radical Women* [Mujeres radicales], Bolsonaro ascendió al poder. Lo mismo pasó en los Estados Unidos, porque cuando la exposición fue inaugurada en el Hammer Museum, Trump ascendió al poder. Entonces, una exposición que se concibió en un contexto particular puede volverse bastante radical en otro. Esto es importante porque quizás puedes tener una idea sobre el propósito, pero es el contexto lo que le da la chispa".

"Es responsabilidad de la exhibición histórica tener un concepto, comprender el contexto y trabajar con responsabilidad en la investigación durante ese periodo. En cierto modo, una exposición histórica es como una especie de corsé —sólo que más estructurada. Creo que la bienal te da más libertad, pero la responsabilidad que uno tiene al realizar una exposición histórica te hace repensar la contemporaneidad. Y si quieres presentar obras del pasado para reactivarlas en el presente, entonces no haces una exposición histórica sólo para encajonar el pasado".

"Muchos colegas decidieron que, cuando los museos estaban cerrados, no debíamos hacer nada, porque el arte debería experimentarse como algo esencial: la experiencia de estar en contacto directo con una obra de arte no puede sustituirse por ninguna otra. Pero, al mismo tiempo, creo que teníamos una enorme responsabilidad, porque lo primero que vimos durante la pandemia, cuando todo cerró, fue que muchos museos decidieron despedir a una parte importante de su personal, sobre todo educativo. Se desmantelaron departamentos y muchas instituciones centrales tomaron esas decisiones. Creo que tenemos que comprometernos más con la educación, porque en todo el mundo se cerraron escuelas. ¿Qué va a pasar, entonces, con la educación?"

"Respecto a la Bienal do Mercosul, que tuvo lugar justo al comienzo de la pandemia, su versión en línea no fue capaz de proponer las mejores soluciones, pues estábamos en medio de dos espacios: el físico y el digital. Teniendo que hacer estos cambios en menos de un mes, realmente hicimos lo mejor que pudimos. El equipo curatorial estaba en medio de una crisis porque, desde luego, en una situación tan extrema, cada quien sentía y actuaba de acuerdo con sus capacidades. Escribí una carta a los artistas, sólo para preguntarles cómo estaban. Después de 10 días sin saber qué hacer, las respuestas empezaron a llegar y fueron muy emotivas. Necesitaban estar en contacto, así que les propuse que enviaran un cortometraje hecho con un teléfono móvil. Esa se convirtió en nuestra primera actividad".

Yuko Hasegawa

"El rol del curador es cada vez más vital porque las personas anhelan narrativas. Una narrativa provee una especie de familiaridad, especialmente en relación con experiencias sensoriales únicas. Eso la hace sustancial; cuando uno se enfrenta únicamente a grandes volúmenes de datos, a menudo no puede comprometerse realmente con ellos. Sin embargo, algunos artistas poseen la capacidad de crear visualizaciones poderosas que facilitan ese tipo de conexión".

"Algunos curadores realizan bienales sin anclarlas a un marco conceptual concreto, simplemente seleccionan artistas y presentan sus obras. Para mí, en cambio, el tema o concepto funcionan como una herramienta crucial. Me ayuda a trazar una trayectoria, establecer una especie de coherencia. Mi primera bienal, en Estambul en 2001, coincidió con el inicio del siglo XXI, un periodo marcado por la incertidumbre e inestabilidad mundial. En ese momento, articulé un marco curatorial basado en lo que llamé las tres M y las tres C. Las tres M representan las fuerzas dominantes del siglo XX: 'los hombres', que simbolizan el individualismo y actitud egoísta; 'el dinero', refiriendo a la riqueza y el capitalismo; y finalmente, 'el materialismo'.[7] Estas fuerzas nos condujeron a un desarrollo inmenso que tuvo consecuencias profundas. Las tres C apelaron, por el contrario, a una suerte de proceso de enmienda en cara al siglo XXI: la coexistencia, la inteligencia colectiva y la conciencia".

"Para la 7 International İstanbul Bienali organice la exposición alrededor de las tres M y las tres C, en conjunto con mi investigación sobre la búsqueda de lenguajes sensoriales. Nombré aquella edición como *Egofugal*, un neologismo imposible de encontrar en los diccionarios. Significa moverse desde el centro hacia la periferia, volar hacia el exterior, porque eso conlleva apartarte totalmente de tu propio ego. Es un enfoque que te lleva a cuidar de los otros a tu alrededor tanto como te cuidas a ti mismo. Es una combinación entre el individualismo occidental y la colectividad del este".

—

7   Nota de la traductora: En la versión en inglés, la autora refiere a los términos men, money y materialism. De ahí que el concepto curatorial aborde tres M.

"Viajé al desierto de Taklamakán para investigar la frontera entre Oriente y Occidente. Puede haber sido un empeño algo caprichoso: simplemente quería localizar ese límite, literalmente el punto donde termina 'Occidente' y comienza el 'Oriente'. La propia Estambul funciona como una frontera geopolítica y se convirtió en un lugar fascinante para explorar la noción de lo *egofugal* dentro de un espacio híbrido, una zona de comunicación intercultural entre Este y Oeste".

"Mi mentor, Uzawa Hirofumi, un economista matemático, enfatizó la importancia del capital social común. En un tiempo en el que muchos hablaban del fin del capitalismo, él me recordó que el capitalismo nunca realmente termina; más bien, debemos repensar cómo el capital puede ser generado en formas novedosas. De acuerdo a Uzawa, el capital social común proporciona a los miembros de la sociedad servicios esenciales y estructuras institucionales que sostienen la vida humana y cultural. Se compone de tres categorías: capital natural, infraestructura social y capital institucional. El capital natural incluye el medio ambiente y los recursos naturales, como la atmósfera de la Tierra; infraestructura social, que abarca carreteras, puentes, sistemas de transporte público y servicios básicos; y capital institucional, que comprende hospitales, instituciones educativas, sistemas judiciales y policiales, administración pública, instituciones financieras y monetarias, así como el capital cultural. Dentro de este marco, la práctica curatorial puede activar y regenerar localmente estas formas de capital social común, fomentando programas e iniciativas que construyan confianza y participación en la comunidad. Este proceso constituye la base de mi enfoque curatorial".

Rujeko Hockley

"Como curadora, me gusta la idea de hablar desde mi propia experiencia, desde mi propia identidad. No se trata de que un sólo grupo, idea, artista o enfoque sea más valioso que otro, sino que cada persona merece su propia perspectiva, a través de un lente específico. Así que, sean cuales sean las obras, los artistas o las ideas que uno elija presentar al mundo desde la curaduría, la responsabilidad está en encontrar esa especificidad, ese lente; en compartir claramente con las audiencias para que, independientemente de su propia identidad, intereses, formación, educación o conocimientos, puedan acceder a la subjetividad de otra persona o de otro grupo".

"Cuando pienso en mi propia práctica como curadora, intento hacer exposiciones y trabajar con artistas que considero verdaderamente importantes, creando conversaciones que los lleven a un mundo más amplio a través de este espacio. Soy yo quien tiene que resultar convincente. Soy yo quien tiene que creer en ello. Tengo que entrar a salas en donde nadie se ve como yo y donde quizás la gente no crea que tenemos algo en común. Pero no se trata de hacerme agradable o legible para que se puedan sentir los puntos en común; se trata de ser entusiasta, sincera y tan seria respecto a lo que expongo, que otras personas puedan sentir que esto también es para ellas".

"¿Acaso ya no tenemos un público como el que llegamos a tener históricamente? En el futuro, ¿continuaremos viajando por todo el mundo para ver exposiciones y dar charlas? ¿O lo seguiremos haciendo así, en Zoom? Mucha más gente puede asistir de esta manera. No deberíamos renunciar a esto. No por el número de asistentes, sino porque así personas de todo el mundo pueden participar y escuchar a pensadores y creadores increíbles de una forma que, de otro modo, no sería posible. Están también las preguntas por la accesibilidad para quienes están físicamente aquí pero no pueden asistir, o quienes, por la razón que sea, no pueden asistir a un museo. Muchas de estas cuestiones, que han sido enunciadas por activistas de los derechos de la discapacidad, se vuelven de pronto posibles. Eso, para mí, es una gran ventaja".

"En cuanto a los movimientos por la justicia social, creo que esa cara del asunto, tristemente, no carece de precedentes. Tenemos actos de brutalidad policial alrededor del mundo, no sólo en los Estados Unidos. Tenemos décadas de activismo, agitación, cooptación y represión por parte del Estado. Este es un ciclo que vemos repetirse una y otra vez a nivel global. Lo que ha sido interesante es ver cómo el mundo del arte en general ha llegado a los mismos intereses con los que yo crecí y para los cuales desarrollé un estado de conciencia similar. Pienso en instituciones —sólo he sido una curadora desde la institución, así que no puedo hablar de la curaduría independiente—, y creo que van a verse muy diferentes. Algunas de ellas no sobrevivirán a la pandemia, principalmente por las presiones financieras, pero también porque lo que el público demanda de nosotras ha cambiado. Y tienen toda la razón; así que, si no podemos adaptarnos, es nuestra responsabilidad".

"Nos hemos estancado en los binarismos por muchas generaciones ya, especialmente en el contexto de la historia del arte negro, la producción cultural negra y la cultura visual. Se trata de imágenes positivas para elevar el espíritu, o bien de un profundo trauma, el peor —porque todo lo que nos pasa es terrible y traumático—, ¿no es así? Creo que los binarismos son completamente improductivos e inútiles, no sólo porque no son precisos, sino porque no dejan espacio para los matices ni las especificidades; puede haber alegría en circunstancias poco favorables o el trauma existe en situaciones que se supone que son positivas. La vida es más compleja".

Candice Hopkins

"Creo que durante un tiempo hubo una tendencia de las bienales a desmantelar por completo la exposición anterior o a hacer algo enteramente distinto. Parecía que, especialmente en los años noventa, las bienales eran en su mayoría vehículos del olvido, al tiempo que generaban nuevas ideas. En SITE SANTA FE, en cambio, pensábamos en cómo estas exposiciones recurrentes pueden trazar una continuidad, y eso dio forma al trabajo que hicimos. Me parece que hoy existe una reflexión más crítica sobre la estructura de las bienales: qué ofrecen y cómo pueden ser espacios de profunda investigación académica, no sólo vitrinas para lo novedoso, lo subrepresentado o lo desconocido".

"Para la exposición *Sakahàn: International Indigenous Art* [Sakahàn: Arte internacional indígena], me di cuenta de que existían muchas redes —visibles en los movimientos políticos de los pueblos indígenas— que no habían sido realmente representadas en exposiciones previas. A menudo, las muestras de arte indígena internacional se centraban en un sólo grupo lingüístico o en una relación específica con los colonizadores originales. Decidimos enfocarnos en artistas que hubieran tenido un impacto importante en sus comunidades, así como en quienes empezaban a tenerlo mediante su práctica".

"La riqueza de los pueblos indígenas alimentó el desarrollo del Renacimiento, aunque esto suele olvidarse [literalmente a través de la extracción de oro del Imperio inca y de otros territorios indígenas]. Otro ejemplo es cómo los surrealistas se interesaron por máscaras y otros objetos culturales de África, pero también observaron con detenimiento el arte de la costa noroeste de América del Norte y las máscaras inupiat. Me pareció una relación fascinante, porque demuestra lo importante que fue el arte indígena para el desarrollo del modernismo europeo. Vi una oportunidad para evidenciar estas conexiones. Se trataba más bien de crear vínculos, relaciones que flotaban bajo la superficie de la historia del arte".

"Como muchos saben, la documenta 14 fue criticada —especialmente en Atenas— por ser una forma de neocolonialismo. Fue una acusación difícil de escuchar, pero me hizo reflexionar sobre muchas cosas: no sólo sobre los derechos de las personas, sino también sobre los derechos de la tierra y sobre si las comunidades realmente quieren que estas grandes exposiciones se instalen en su territorio. Pensábamos mucho en el potencial de las resonancias —en si sería posible no sólo ejercer una escucha profunda, sino también escuchar *más allá*. ¿Cómo se escucha más allá de las resonancias coloniales para escuchar otra cosa? Esa orientación hacia el sonido, la resonancia y la escucha cambió mi manera de trabajar en esa exposición, y también transformó la forma en que muchos artistas la abordaron. Una de las preguntas en las que más pienso es: ¿cómo otorgamos agencia no sólo a las personas en un lugar, sino al lugar mismo?"

"Raven Chacon y yo co-escribimos una partitura titulada *Dispatch* [escrita en respuesta a los defensores del agua en Standing Rock], que se basaba en el análisis de quiénes estaban presentes, qué roles desempeñaban y en si esto podría convertirse en un marco para otros tipos de acciones. Fue una manera de reflexionar sobre el papel del arte, pero también sobre la función política del sonido —algo en lo que ambas hemos estado pensando mucho últimamente. Una de las posibles formas que puede tomar esa partitura es en fragmentos sonoros. Uno de los efectos más insidiosos de la supremacía blanca es dividirnos, ¿cierto? Y una de las maneras en que podemos resistir eso es uniéndonos. A eso lo llamo *sonorizar los márgenes* — reunir a personas que pudieron haber sido desposeídas por la fuerza, aún cuando no hayamos sido desposeídos en nuestras ideas".

Miguel A. López

"Para el equipo curatorial de la 31 Bienal de São Paulo era importante proponer una bienal que se enfrentara al conflicto o que se basara en él, entendiendo el conflicto no como un fracaso, sino como una condición productiva. Los conflictos son componentes integrales de un proyecto deomocrático; precisamente porque piensan en cómo las tensiones pueden enfrentarse o gestionarse sin que éstas desemboquen en violencia".

"Antes de la Bienal, ya venía trabajando con el grupo Red Conceptualismos del Sur, y más tarde en un proyecto titulado *Perder la forma humana* (2013-2014), una exposición que buscaba reunir a artistas y colectivos de los años ochenta que habían explorado la teatralidad de género y el travestismo en tensión con imaginarios políticos y religiosos dominantes. Para São Paulo me interesaba continuar esa reflexión pensando en una constelación de figuras específicas —Ocaña de Cataluña, Nahúm B. Zenil de México, Sergio Zevallos del Grupo Chaclacayo en Perú, y el dúo chileno Las Yeguas del Apocalipsis— que comenzaron a trabajar a finales de los setenta y durante los ochenta como respuesta a crisis, violencia o conflictos armados. En algunos casos fueron testigos de transiciones políticas de dictaduras militares a regímenes democráticos, como fue el caso de España y Chile. Su práctica canalizó de manera crítica esos contextos a través del travestismo como una forma de disrupción política y estética, revelando cómo también en las llamadas democracias los cuerpos no normativos seguían siendo perseguidos o vueltos ininteligibles. Eran figuras incómodas debido a su marginalidad deliberada y a una estética del exceso, pero también por las alianzas que establecieron con movimientos sociales y formas de activismo desde abajo. Me interesaba cómo cada uno de estos artistas había propuesto una intervención distinta en los imaginarios religiosos —Zenil, por ejemplo, imaginando formas de reconciliación entre el deseo homoerótico y la devoción espiritual—, y cómo su obra se entrelazaba profundamente con reflexiones sobre raza y nacionalismo".

"Al curar una sección para la Bienal de São Paulo, vi en el *Museo travesti del Perú* de Giuseppe Campuzano un marco radicalmente diferente para pensar la historia, la representación y el propio museo. La obra era un intento de deshacer las expectativas de verdad científica y legibilidad total que a menudo definían a los museos occidentales. En su lugar, el proyecto movilizaba estrategias experimentales a través de la narración, invocando conceptos como la terapia, la dualidad, la épica, el mestizaje y la coreografía, para proponer modos alternativos de organizar la historia. El *Museo Travesti* construyó un espacio que evitaba caer en la idea tradicional de formación de una comunidad basada en identidades fijas, y más bien operaba mediante una lógica promiscua, al tomar el cuerpo travesti como su *locus de enunciación*: un cuerpo falso, un cuerpo-prótesis, cuya naturaleza es la incertidumbre, como solía decir Giuseppe. Se oponía a una lógica de identidad estable, favoreciendo la ambigüedad y la contradicción sobre la coherencia, y abrazando un cuerpo inclasificable como el lugar desde el cual todas las historias podían ser desorganizadas".

"La Bienal de São Paulo fue controvertida, entre otras cosas, por su audaz y crítica aproximación a la religión. En los días previos a la inauguración, grupos religiosos organizaron una serie de protestas dirigidas a secciones específicas, en particular *Deus é bicha* [Dios es queer] (que incluía a Ocaña, Nahúm B. Zenil, Sergio Zevallos y Las Yeguas del Apocalipsis) y el *Museo Travesti*, junto con otros tres proyectos,

acusando a la Bienal de promover el aborto, la blasfemia y el sacrilegio. Estas reacciones, creo, pusieron en evidencia el deseo de la bienal de intervenir en la conversación pública y de entablar un diálogo crítico con ideas que configuran la vida social. En ese sentido, pienso que la bienal fue oportuna y valiente, al abordar cuestiones políticamente urgentes en medio de las elecciones presidenciales. También prefiguró trágicamente el ascenso del conservadurismo de ultraderecha en Brasil".

Cuauhtémoc Medina

"Una de las cosas que encuentro más extravagante es la manera en que muchos colegas hacen presentaciones expresando su descontento con la existencia misma de las bienales y explican todas las razones por las que no deberían hacerse. Estoy convencido, comprometido y totalmente entregado a la importancia de realizar bienales. Creo que la energía que siento al producirlas está directamente ligada a ese compromiso".

"El arte de la bienal produce algo muy potente: una tensión constante entre autonomía y circunstancia, especificidad y práctica individual. De algún modo, las polaridades bajo las cuales trabajamos son generadas por la propia situación de la bienal, de forma similar a cómo el arte del siglo XIX y XX fue moldeado por el espacio museístico".

"Mientras me preparaba para curar la 12 Shanghai Biennale, recordé esta palabra que inventó E.E. Cummings: *pro-regress* [pro-regresión]. Me pareció una idea muy interesante porque resume el presente como una ambivalencia profunda y una ambigüedad de valores y direcciones históricas. Así, organicé una exposición que intentaba cubrir cuatro áreas de ambivalencia: tiempo de guerra y tiempo de paz; nuestra comprensión de naturaleza y de cultura; la noción de libertad y la de control (la dificultad de separar lo liberal del lado dictatorial en nuestras estructuras de gobierno actuales); y, finalmente, entre cultura y arte, lo que a mi entender sugiere que siempre producimos desde una cierta visión de barbarie".

"Esto se vincula a un 'juego de producción de reputación' presente en una parte del sistema del arte contemporáneo que depende de las bienales y las instituciones. Una bienal que no se concibe en relación con impulsar la reputación y la relevancia de los artistas es una bienal mal ejecutada".

"Esperaba poder concentrarme en un sólo asunto: el derecho a respirar. Lo que estamos viviendo hoy no es sólo por la pandemia, sino también por las revoluciones políticas en Estados Unidos, en India, mientras intentamos no morir de esta enfermedad. Nuestras capacidades se han extendido a través de diversos medios de comunicación tecnológica y estamos creando un sistema social distinto y un modo diferente de producción a través de esta crisis. El movimiento Black Lives Matter, las protestas por George Floyd y la cuestión de la respiración —la forma en que morir y la imposibilidad de respirar adquieren múltiples connotaciones relacionadas con la salud, la ecología y la igualdad política— se han vuelto una obsesión para mí durante el último año".

Gabi Ngcobo

"Me parece bastante interesante que la Cape Africa Platform (CAPE) sucedió sólo dos veces, tal como la Johannesburg Bienniale. En el contexto de Sudáfrica, las cosas de alguna manera no duran demasiado. Algo puede suceder dos veces y es todo. Pero sí que dan forma a algo, dan cuenta de algo y ayudan a algunos artistas a entender sus gramáticas para ser en el mundo y, con ello, ya no ser tomados por

sentado, por decirlo de alguna manera. Personalmente, este evento dio forma a mi manera de pensar. Después de CAPE 07, pensaba que podría hacer lo que sea, aún cuando no tuviera nada, ya que lo único que se necesita son ideas".

"Algo que me interesa es cómo las cosas sucedieron en el pasado o en la historia. Si las señalas, parece que hablan del presente. De lo que realmente hablo es de esa espiral llamada historia. A veces se siente que uno sólo está dando vueltas en un mismo sitio, incapaz de librarse de una manera de pensar específica —o sobre cómo otros te piensan como sujeto".

"Recuerdo que en una charla pública, cuatro meses después de haber sido nombrada curadora de la Berlin Biennale, en la que el moderador me dijo: 'El tema de tu bienal es poscolonial, ¿verdad?'. Estas son situaciones en las que se da por sentado cómo se ve lo poscolonial para mí, pero no cómo se ve para los demás. Es importante, en este sentido, distribuir la responsabilidad, ya que todos somos poscoloniales y todos debemos hacernos cargo de este problema, pues no es la tarea de sólo algunas personas".

"Mi manera de trabajar es caótica. No me siento y hago listas, lo cual puede ser frustrante. Trabajo desde mi cuerpo y desde mi memoria. Tengo una manera de confiar en mí misma, de ahí que mi primera regla es: no te dejes en casa cuando necesitas ir a cualquier lado. Me tengo que llevar conmigo y tengo que ver las cosas desde mi propia perspectiva. Y si veo las cosas desde mi propia perspectiva, entonces quiero ver qué tipo de mundos uno puede crear. Me inspira el Combahee River Collective, y especialmente su convicción de que cuando las mujeres negras sean libres, eso significará que todo el mundo será libre. Me gusta pensar que lo que hago, como mujer negra, puede reflejar ese tipo de libertad para todo aquel que se sienta invitado en un lugar en el que antes no se sentía invitado".

"En cuanto a las críticas a la Berlin Biennale —y no precisamente todas, sino aquellas emitidas por hombres blancos que no se encontraron representados— estamos muy acostumbradas a ello en nuestro trabajo. Esta blanquitud y supremacía blanca, que es demasiado desgastante, nos frena y nos hace perder el tiempo. Tal como lo dijo Toni Morrison: 'La función más grave del racismo es la distracción. Te mantiene distraído de hacer tu trabajo'. Realmente queríamos hacer las cosas de una manera concreta y no abordar la blanquitud —que es un tema tan vasto, porque también existe dentro de muchas de nosotras. Estamos acostumbradas a mirar al mundo de una forma tan particular que, cuando se nos presenta de otra manera, una especie de desestabilidad ocurre dentro de nosotros. Y yo estaba bastante interesada en esa desestabilización de las cosas tal y como las conocemos".

Lucia Pietroiusti

"*General Ecology* [Ecología general] surgió después de pasar un buen tiempo en las Serpentine Galleries, marcharme por un año para tener un bebé y luego volver, habiendo aprendido todo tipo de rarezas sobre la existencia y sobre cómo mi propio cerebro había cambiado. Me formé en estudios de género. Antes de ello, fui curadora de programas públicos en la Serpentine. Así que, cuando volví, se me reveló esta misteriosa forma de comunicación de lo que se sentía como una comunicación interespecies a través del diálogo que sostuve con una cría y los métodos del cuidado, la responsabilidad y la obligación que ello conlleva —los cuales exceden al lenguaje. Esto trajo consigo una noción completamente nueva de la comunicación, la cual no tiene tanto que ver con la traducción. Comencé, entonces, a escribir un proyecto para la Serpentine, que

esencialmente necesitaría la transformación de esta labor: dedicarse obsesiva e infinitamente a la ecología".

"Todas las organizaciones mencionan en su declaración de principios algo relacionado con sostenibilidad y resiliencia. Sin embargo, cuando miras más de cerca, te das cuenta de que dichas palabras se refieren a la propia sustentabilidad y resiliencia de la organización. Así que me interesaba saber qué se puede incorporar a su propia estructura —algo que aún no esté hecho. Se trata de un trabajo en curso. No se trata sólo de una misión para presentar arte, sino que viene acompañada de una responsabilidad expandida y entrelazada, vinculada con la justicia planetaria; yo la llamaría más bien prosperidad, en lugar de sostenibilidad".

"En el contexto de la justicia y el equilibrio medioambiental, ¿podemos pensar en un enfoque que se desprenda del humano y que se centre, quizás, en algún antropomorfismo extraño y radical? Me refiero a que la distribución desigual de la crisis climática está realmente construida y levantada sobre las mismas líneas de violencia y extracción colonial: el mapeo es tan atinado. Así que, cuando hablamos de antropocentrismo, no estamos refiriéndonos a los humanos como especie, sino a un grupo bastante específico de humanos autoproclamados, cuyas consecuencias han sido realmente devastadoras. Los científicos dicen que no deberíamos antropomorfizar un árbol, pero a mí me parece mucho más estimulante pensar: ¿qué tal que un árbol sea capaz de amar, ser generoso, tener sentido del humor o incluso curar exposiciones? Digamos que el arte no trata de antropomorfizar al árbol, pero, quizás, ser antropocéntricos realmente significa asumir que el amor, la generosidad, el humor y el arte en los humanos son sólo manifestaciones de versiones planetarias de esas mismas cualidades".

"Tradicionalmente, el campo de la ecología y el activismo ecológico han tenido una serie de puntos ciegos, particularmente alrededor de la noción de conservación, pues adherida a ésta se encuentra la implicación de que algún tipo de tierra "intacta" existe. Pero, muchas veces, llamar a un territorio "intacto" supone un proyecto político de colonización —y con ello se niegan las previas existencia y coexistencia entre pueblos y especies más allá de lo humano que ahí se tejen. Soy también consciente del hecho de que, así como existe la extracción de materiales insólitos de la tierra, hay también un súbito surgimiento de discusiones en Sillicon Valley alrededor de las tradiciones y saberes indígenas. Tenemos que estar bastante conscientes de no hacer de las ideas lo mismo que hemos hecho a las montañas, tierras y ríos. Sería poco honesto hablar de ecología sin hablar de racismo, colonialismo, extractivismo, tierras indígenas, restitución y similares. Sería impreciso".

farid rakun (ruangrupa)

"ruangrupa fue fundado por seis artistas en Yakarta, en el 2000. No soy uno de los fundadores; los conocí alrededor del 2003, cuando era estudiante. Trabajé con ellos esporádicamente hasta el 2010. Entonces, volví a Yakarta y decidí quedarme; ruangrupa fue un factor importante en esa decisión. Yakarta es uno de los sitios más caros del país y muchos de nosotros no podíamos costearnos un estudio, así que la calle se volvió nuestro lienzo o, dicho de otra manera, nuestro espacio expositivo".

"Intentábamos acercarnos al videoarte, aunque ninguno de nosotros era experto, especialmente en el 2003. Por ello, usamos el formato del festival, pues era una oportunidad para convocar obras o personas que considerábamos interesantes de escuchar y de las que podíamos aprender para, luego, regalar obras de arte".

"En el 2007 se disparó una gran cantidad de invitaciones a bienales y construimos nuestra práctica artística de manera colectiva a través de la participación en estos espacios. Trabajar con locales se volvió nuestro *modus operandi*. Por ejemplo, para la Bienal de São Paulo, invitamos a colectivos locales a trabajar con nosotros y a usar el espacio que nos asignaron en el pabellón. Muchas de las obras, así como los talleres que se impartieron, eran de los propios paulistas. Varios proyectos fueron iniciados por ellos, pero trabajamos estrechamente durante un par de meses. Es por ello que algunos argumentan que nuestra práctica artística tiene cierta similitud con la práctica curatorial".

"En 2015, ruangrupa colaboró con otros colectivos en Yakarta. Se convirtió en un colectivo de colectivos y fue entonces cuando acuñamos el término *lumbung* para referirnos a nuestros procesos, una palabra coloquial que significa 'granero de arroz'. Se volvió un atajo para poder comunicar lo que estábamos intentando hacer en ese momento, es decir, una forma de gestión colectiva: cómo trabajar juntos. Justo esto es lo que hacíamos cuando documenta se interesó en nosotros".

"Estamos acostumbrados a un tipo de enfoque que es un tanto parasitario. Cuando éramos convocados por una institución de gran tamaño, el enfoque o postura por defecto consistía en preguntar: ¿qué podemos obtener de esta institución? Ahora estamos intentando hacer las cosas de otra manera. En lugar de tomar la puerta trasera y convertirnos en parásito, ¿qué tal si tomamos la puerta principal? Necesitamos volvernos transparentes. Eso es lo que estamos tratando de hacer en este momento".

"*Lumbung* es un método, no un concepto, ni tampoco un tema. No estamos intentando demostrar que *lumbung* es algo que conocemos del todo. Y si otros tienen otro tipo de métodos de gestión colectiva, combinémoslos. Esa es la razón principal por la que hacemos esto. También queremos celebrar el término agrícola 'cosecha'. Si este es un proceso de cosecha, creo que lo que hacemos —plantar, sembrar, cuidar, mantener, cosechar y, desde luego, comer— es, entonces, lo que somos. Es así como entendemos lo que hacemos en este momento, al tiempo que aprendemos de otros".

"El hipernacionalismo que sucede hoy —y que sabemos que puede suponer una amenaza— también ha fungido como salvación en ciertos momentos, por ejemplo, para este tipo de prácticas locales, incluidas las nuestras. Revisar el nacionalismo es una cosa y el colectivismo es otra. Ambos son el resultado de intentar hacer las cosas de manera diferente. Así que es interesante, por ahora, al menos para mí, pensar en cómo la división entre derecha, izquierda y centro —en el espectro político— ya no está tan marcada. Quizás podamos idear otro tipo de enfoque, sin verlo como algo binario. También podríamos tener otra respuesta, pero no queremos repetir los errores del pasado, desde luego. Así que es importante no caer en eso".

José Roca

"Creo que el modelo de la bienal tiene muchas posibilidades y algunos problemas. Uno de ellos es que, en algunos casos, las ciudades que sólo celebran la bienal terminan concentrando todos los recursos hacia un único acontecimiento espectacular de corta duración, y luego no les es posible financiar las artes durante el resto del periodo en que no hay bienal. Las bienales son recurrentes, pero también discontinuas. Entonces, ¿cómo conectamos lo que sucede dentro de una edición y la siguiente para que una ciudad no sufra la falta de programación entre una bienal y la que sigue? Creo que eso es lo que hemos intentado hacer con la Bienal do Mercosul".

"Veinticinco años después, me pidieron que organizara nuevamente la Bienal de Medellín. De alguna manera, dije: 'Bueno, quizás no es prudente hacerlo. Pensemos en otro proyecto, algo que realmente atienda las necesidades de Medellín'. Medellín se enorgullece de ser una ciudad bastante hospitalaria; ahora bien, si uno observa la programación de sus museos e instituciones, se da cuenta de que principalmente han mostrado al mismo grupo de artistas locales. El grupo canónico de artistas contemporáneos en Colombia nunca había sido exhibido ahí, por ejemplo. Pensé que esta noción alrededor de la hospitalidad podría ser un buen punto de partida. Decidimos no llamarlo bienal, porque el concepto mismo puede ser problemático y no queríamos atarlo a una regularidad específica. Así que se llamó Encuentro de Medellín, y su primera edición sucedió en 2007. Emplazamos varias ideas ahí. Una de ellas fue que el tema también sería una estrategia: ¿qué nos puede enseñar la hospitalidad y su tensión entre el anfitrión y el huésped dentro de la práctica museística? La otra fue que éste no iba a ser un evento de dos o tres meses, sino que sería algo extendido en el tiempo y el espacio. Estaba desplegado por todo Medellín, porque pensamos que no necesitábamos una activación extensa, sino algo que pudiera volver a tejer los hilos sueltos dentro de la comunidad artística que habían sido fuertemente afectados por el narcotráfico".

"Para la octava edición de la Bienal do Mercosul intenté trasladar todo lo que había aprendido en experiencias anteriores sobre geopolítica desde el punto de vista del arte. Así que desarrollamos algo que llamamos 'estrategias activadoras'. Éstas tenían el propósito de activar una escena, pero no necesariamente para terminar en una exposición. Luego, hicimos estrategias de exposición, que fungieron como el proyecto educativo propio de la Bienal. Un componente clave sucedió seis meses antes, cuando nueve artistas viajaron a través de la región, recorriendo las raíces históricas de la intrusión colonial en Rio Grande do Sul. Fue bastante efectiva en activar la región antes de que la Bienal sucediera".

"Para la 23 edición de la Biennale of Sydney, los ríos y otros cuerpos de agua tomaron un lugar importante. Los ríos son sólo un punto de partida; para continuar la metáfora, éstos componen una fuente que luego se enriquece con los afluentes. Todo lo que se encuentran en el camino los fortalece y los hace más diversos y, mientras se aproximan a la desembocadura, se ramifican en un delta de posibilidades. Entonces, éste fue el punto de partida y de lo que trató la Bienal. Aparte, exploramos muchos otros temas como los derechos de la naturaleza, las voces de la naturaleza. Si algunos ríos y otros cuerpos de agua han adquirido personalidad jurídica y pueden ser representados ante los tribunales, ¿pueden tener voz en una bienal, por ejemplo? Eso es algo que nos preguntamos. Esta bienal articula también relatos de creación de diversos grupos indígenas, ciencia especulativa, colaboraciones entre artistas y científicos, y un montón de otros temas".

"Una cosa que he aprendido al hacer estas distintas bienales, aquí y allá, es que no hay un modelo que funcione en todo lugar. Activar la escena local de Medellín, en 2007, tuvo un gran impacto, por ejemplo, pero hoy quizás ya no sea tan necesario, sabiendo que el Museo de Arte Moderno de Medellín ha resucitado con un programa increíble. Entonces, cada situación, en un tiempo y espacio específico, requiere un modelo diferente y hecho a la medida".

Ralph Rugoff

"Al organizar la 58 La Biennale di Venezia, reflexioné sobre la idea de que un hecho no es simplemente una relación existente en el mundo, sino que podrían existir hechos alternativos o paralelos. De forma paralela a esto, pensé en cómo nuestro discurso político se está "twitterizando": cada vez todo se está simplificando más. En mi percepción, el arte es uno de los últimos espacios culturales que permite un discurso complejo, con múltiples capas. Es lo opuesto a simplificar: conecta diferentes vías posibles del pensamiento. Para la Bienal, quería presentar menos artistas y destacar la forma en que estos creaban obras complejas, contradictorias y ambiguas: algo generativo, no algo que cerrara el significado".

"También siento que el arte depende mucho de su entorno físico y de cómo se instala. Pensé en este formato A y B para sugerir que se podría realizar una secuencia infinita de exposiciones con los mismos artistas. Así, presentar A y B en edificios distintos subrayaría que esos mismos artistas podrían hacer algo completamente diferente, y que la identidad del artista no está definida por un tipo particular de obra. Esperaba que los asistentes no se dieran cuenta —a menos que leyeran la cédula— de que se trataba de los mismos artistas en ambos espacios. Pero una vez que lo perciben, el reto es involucrarse con la reflexión subyacente a lo que superficialmente parecen ser tipos muy distintos de arte".

"La enorme mayoría de las bienales siguen formatos muy similares y suelen enfatizar una temática —y yo desconfío ligeramente de esas temáticas curatoriales. Me siento incómodo con esas declaraciones curatoriales grandilocuentes que parecen exigir que las obras las ilustren".

"Realmente pienso que el papel del curador es servir de puente entre el artista, la obra y el público. Se trata de encontrar maneras de hacer que todo sea lo más obvio, atractivo y seductor posible para los visitantes. Y si las personas pueden recorrer una exposición de distintas maneras, creo que eso también genera una sensación de descubrimiento y exploración. Por eso trato de encontrar formas de colocar al público en el mejor lugar, donde pueda involucrarse plenamente con la obra".

"Una de las cosas que ocurre cuando de repente no puedes ir a una galería o museo es que empiezas a pensar en todo lo que extrañas, y creo que uno de esos aspectos es la naturaleza pública de esa experiencia. No es lo mismo estar frente a tu computadora. Entonces comencé a fijarme en lo que había en la calle. Se volvió como una galería, y realmente lo disfruté. Considero que una parte importante de este momento de confinamiento fue encontrar formas de mantener una conversación pública continua".

"Dado que la Hayward Gallery no podía estar abierta, comisionamos a artistas para retratar a trabajadores esenciales que tuvieron que seguir trabajando durante la pandemia. Nunca antes había pensado en una exposición al aire libre, pero al final hicimos unas dieciséis obras visuales de gran escala y poemas de seis poetas, todos respondiendo a la pandemia. Eso inauguró una nueva línea de trabajo: hacer cosas al aire libre y colaborar con varios artistas que también son parte de nuestro propio barrio".

Trevor Schoonmaker

"Lo que hice en Prospect.4 fue, esencialmente, reunir artistas que no habían tenido una visibilidad significativa. Quise curar algo que, francamente, yo mismo desearía ver. Trabajar de nuevo con los mismos artistas forma parte de eso: es algo significativo para mí, porque se está construyendo una relación con ellos que siento de forma muy profunda. Para mí, curar es totalmente subjetivo e increíblemente personal. No es un proceso donde me distancie como investigador objetivo. Se trata de proyectar —no de reflejar. No me limito a espejear lo que sucede afuera; proyecto lo que quiero decir

desde un lugar más íntimo. Puedo mostrar mis intereses personales, pero también se trata de encontrar un nicho que tenga una inclinación activista. Me gusta destacar a artistas históricamente ignorados y marginados, pero esto también refleja mi propia experiencia. Y puede sonar extraño si me ves —hombre blanco y heterosexual—, pero mis pares, mi familia y mi recorrido no son lo que podrías anticipar".

"La curaduría es, para mí, un proceso creativo. No es estrictamente un proceso intelectual o de investigación. Es más bien la idea de producir algo creativo como encarnación de la esperanza, de alguna manera. Esperas hacer la diferencia. Esperas generar cambios. Esperas provocar diálogo. Y si tus ambiciones son grandes, tal vez termines moviendo la aguja del canon".

"Todo el mundo estaba en modo de crisis por la pandemia y sus riesgos sanitarios —pero también por un ajuste de cuentas racial. La pandemia realmente quitó la capa superficial y expuso todas las desigualdades de la sociedad estadounidense y del resto del mundo. El proyecto de Carrie Mae Weems deja dolorosamente claro que estas no son dos crisis distintas. Son dos caras de la misma moneda y lo ilustra de forma bellísima —y en ocasiones dolorosa. Muestra cómo el COVID-19 ha afectado de forma desproporcionada a comunidades racializadas y nos ha permitido buscar colaboraciones que ni siquiera sabíamos que eran posibles con organizaciones locales e individuos".

"La crisis pandémica reveló algunas cosas, como una mayor conectividad a través de plataformas virtuales forzadas como ésta. Más allá de nuestro entorno inmediato, me siento más conectado a nivel internacional y nacional —sin necesidad de subirme a un avión, quemar combustibles fósiles o gastar dinero. Eso, para mí, es positivo. Creo que los museos tuvieron dificultades al principio para redefinirse y adaptarse, mientras que las artes escénicas, el cine y los medios audiovisuales ya contaban con contenido listo. No podían simplemente decir: 'Mira, aquí está esta obra o esta película, disfrútala'. Creo que impulsar realmente el componente tecnológico —lo virtual— puede ayudar a complementar lo que hacemos en persona".

La plaga: A Public Dance with Pandemic Protocols [La plaga: una danza pública con protocolos pandémicos], Bogotá, 2021

[p. 87]

Performance de sitio específico, 3h, y videoarte, monocanal, estéreo, 7 min 19 s

La plaga[8] fue una intervención musical y social de sitio específico realizada por Pedro Lasch el 12 de noviembre de 2021, como parte de RƎEXISTENCIAS Bienal de Arte y Descolonialidad, en el Museo de Santa Clara de Bogotá. Pensada como una danza pública realizada bajo protocolos pandémicos, esta obra de arte social hizo uso de la espléndida arquitectura barroca

—

8   *La plaga* hace referencia a la canción de *rock-and-roll* en español del mismo nombre popularizada en México por el grupo musical Los Teen Tops al comienzo de los años sesenta. Adaptada de la canción "Good Golly Miss Molly", de Little Richard, la canción se volvió un referente del Rock en español y circuló a lo largo de Latinoamérica. La pieza de Lasch redimensiona el término *plaga*, dentro del contexto de la pandemia COVID-19, cuando los protocolos de salud pública —originalmente percibidos como extraordinarios— se fueron normalizando gradualmente y, en algunas regiones, se relajaron de forma selectiva. Por medio de la puesta en escena de una danza pública coreografiada bajo las medidas pandémicas, esta obra cuestiona cómo la colectividad, la sociabilidad e incluso la alegría pueden ser renegociadas en tiempos de crisis.

del recinto para configurar una experiencia colectiva memorable e intensa —donde alegría y sufrimiento, juego y gravedad, creatividad y reflexión crítica podían coexistir. La documentación del evento también se volvió la fuente material para la obra de video del mismo nombre, y fue editada por Pedro Lasch y Michael Blair.

Curaduría: David Arteaga y Adolfo Albán Achinte. Música y DJ: Loa Malbec. Interludio: Divino Chibcha Selektor. Bailarines: Natalia Andrea Parada Casas, Alvaro Esteban Medina Ramírez, Angie Lorena Cuesta Bautista, David Esteban Ruiz Hernández, Mateo Popayán Cortés, Paula Popayán Cortés, Liza Bello, Esther Asprilla, Alejandra Vargas, Laura Melo.

Biennial Disaster Banners and Research Diagrams [Pancartas de bienales y desastres y Diagramas de investigación], 2010-2013

[p. 93]

Pancartas físicas y digitales, instalaciones, pinturas, diagramas de investigación colectiva y talleres de producción

Estas obras son diseñadas para ocupar amplios espacios, pues combinan de manera provocativa eventos artísticos muy conocidos o memorables junto con desastres globales políticos, económicos o ecológicos. Cada cartel ofrece un reto distinto a quien observa y participa por la mera especificidad de su doble enunciación. La pancarta "Venecia / Chernóbil" detona asociaciones y significados completamente distintos a la de "Sharjah / Kanungu" o "Kassel / Banqiao". Capas adicionales de significado aparecen a través de los contextos físicos y culturales en donde estas pancartas, aparentemente celebratorias, son emplazadas. Las pancartas también sirven para iniciar diálogos con participantes locales por medio de talleres y conversatorios públicos. De igual manera, están acompañados de diagramas de investigación y una edición impresa de pequeño formato con notas. Algunos han sido adaptados a contextos posteriores, como fue el caso del diagrama de investigación que fungió como elemento central para la presentación de la serie en La Habana en 2015.

Islas de tragedia y fantasía, La Habana, 2015

[p. 97]

Instalación de pancartas, exposición en galería y programa de talleres

Esta pieza, que forma parte de la serie *Art Biennials and Other Global Disasters* [Bienales de arte y otros desastres globales], fue producida específicamente para la 12 Bienal de La Habana, en 2015. La instalación, colocada al aire libre en el Pabellón Cuba, presentó la serie completa de nueve pancartas monumentales, en donde cada una contraponía un evento artístico conocido junto con un desastre político, económico o ecológico internacional. Esta vez, sin embargo, la fila de carteles se inauguró con una nueva adición: una pancarta que mostraba lo que parecían ser los anfitriones del proyecto dándonos la bienvenida a Cuba. En ella se representaron dos de los personajes principales de la serie *Fantasy Island* [Isla de fantasía]: Tattoo, interpretado por Hervé Villechaize, y el Sr. Roarke, interpretado originalmente por Ricardo Montealbán. Pero, en esta versión, el Sr. Roarke había sido reemplazado por Joseph Goebbels, ministro de propaganda Nazi. Hay unas cuantas cosas que Goebbels y Villechaize tenían en común: ambos se suicidaron antes de cumplir cincuenta años y ambos estudiaron artes antes de desarrollar las carreras por las que hoy son conocidos. Goebbels tenía un

doctorado en teatro y Villechaize realizó estudios de pintura en la École des Beaux-Arts de París. Pese a ello, son sus papeles en la historia de los medios de comunicación lo que los hace anfitriones ideales para *Islas de tragedia y fantasía*.

Mundialmente reconocida, la serie *Fantasy Island* (1977-84) está fuertemente vinculada con formas de colonialismo tan antiguas como lo son Próspero y Calibán de Shakespeare. Los personajes de Tattoo y el Sr. Roarke presidieron un mundo imaginario de ocio y placer que de igual manera marcaba el inicio de la era neoliberal a la cual se asocia el fenómeno de las bienales de arte. Joseph Goebbels, por su parte, formó parte del proyecto a través de su papel como curador estrella —aunque el término, desde luego, no se utilizaba aún en ese tiempo— de la exposición *Entartete Kunst* [Arte degenerado] realizada en Alemania en 1937.[9] Mucha gente marca el comienzo del "fenómeno de las bienales" con La Biennale di Venezia. Sin embargo, muchos ignoran la importancia de la producción montada por Goebbels y Adolf Ziegler en la historia de las exposiciones de gran formato y su impacto a nivel internacional. Los más de dos millones de visitantes que atrajo la exposición hicieron que incluso La Biennale di Venezia de ese año pareciera una feria de pueblo. El rostro de Goebbels,

—

9 Entartete Kunst fue un término utilizado por el régimen Nazi para describir obras de arte modernistas y de vanguardia consideradas no-alemanas, subversivas o culturalmente corruptas. La infame exposición de Arte degenerado, realizada en Múnich en 1937, mostró obras de arte confiscadas de artistas como Kandinsky, Picasso o Klee, presentándolas de una manera que intentaba ridiculizar y desacreditar al arte moderno. Esta campaña fue parte de un esfuerzo mucho mayor por imponer una estética controlada por la ideología Nazi. Ver: *Degenerate Art: The Fate of the Avant-Garde in Nazi Germany* (cat. Exp.), curada por Stephanie Barron (Nueva York: Harry N. Abrams INC Publishers - Los Angeles County Museum of Art, 1991)

elevado sobre la arquitectura modernista del Pabellón Cuba, mantuvo esa historia en primer plano durante los talleres colectivos y las conversaciones sobre la realización de exposiciones, totalitarismos y otros desastres provocados por el hombre.

Una parte clave del proyecto se centró en la creación del Teatro de Operaciones Estadísticas, un grupo temporal de investigación que activó talleres e intercambios durante la Bienal. Esta reunión del grupo se llevaba a cabo en una galería interior independiente, donde se incluyó también una exhibición de grabados, mapas, diagramas de investigación, libros y otros materiales disponibles para consulta y uso durante los talleres. Dos producciones no realizadas por Lasch y el Teatro de Operaciones Estadísticas fueron la inserción de la serie de televisión estadounidense en el "paquete semanal", un compendio de contenidos digitales para mirarse sin conexión, y la contratación de dobles de Villechaize y Goebbels como anfitriones de las actividades en vivo de la Bienal en Cuba.

Pedro Lasch: en la intersección del arte, la política y el entretenimiento

Dannys Montes de Oca Moreda
21 de julio de 2022
[p. 105]

A Pedro Lasch le conocí en el 2012 cuando, como organizadora de los eventos teóricos de la Bienal de la Habana, invité al grupo Estéticas decoloniales, liderado por Walter Mignolo en Duke University,[10] a participar

—

10 El panel tuvo lugar en el Centro Teórico Cultural Criterios con la participación de Dalida María Benfield, Raúl Moarquech Ferrera Balanquet, Pedro Pablo Gómez Moreno, Pedro Lasch, Alanna Lockward y Miguel Rojas-Sotelo. Ver: *Onceana Bienal de la*

en su onceana edición. Tuve, así, la oportunidad de entrar en contacto con su obra y entender el desarrollo de su práctica como un camino imprescindible para pensar el arte contemporáneo en su empeño de transformación social. Sin embargo, lo que más me impresionó fueron sus aportes a esos mecanismos de artisticidad que no se ubican en la construcción formal de una poética dentro de la tradición estética occidental, sino que proponen la creación de una metodología alternativa y paralela, capaz de activarse como parte y complemento de nuestras vidas cotidianas.

No es casual, entonces, que Pedro Lasch fuera uno de mis invitados a *Entre, dentro, fuera* (2015), una exposición co-curada junto al académico Royce W. Smith para la 12 Bienal de La Habana. Ésta reunía a artistas cubanos y estadounidenses de diferentes orígenes, cuyas obras funcionaban como puentes de intermediación social dentro de la estrategia general a la que convocaba el evento.[11] El espacio seleccionado para la exposición fue el Pabellón Cuba, por ser un recinto bien ubicado en la trama urbana de la ciudad y de una amplia accesibilidad, que no se limitaba a exhibiciones de arte. Esto permitía acoger tanto el diálogo de obras y artistas, como las

—

Habana: Prácticas artísticas e imaginarios sociales (La Habana: Centro de Arte Contemporáneo Wilfredo Lam / Consejo Nacional de las Artes Plásticas, 2012).

11 *Entre, dentro, fuera. Entre la idea y la Experiencia. XII Bienal de la Habana*, curada por Dannys Montes de Oca Moreda y Royce W. Smith (La Habana: Centro de Arte Contemporáneo Wifredo Lam - Consejo Nacional de las Artes Plásticas, 22 de mayo de 2015 - 22 junio de 2015). Con la participación de: Agnes Chávez (Cuba-EE.UU.), Pedro Lasch (México-EE.UU.) Elizabeth Stevenson (Canadá-EE.UU.), Levente Sulyok (Bulgaria-EE.UU.), Stephanie Syjuco(Filipinas-EE. UU.), y los cubanos Susana Pilar Delahante Matienzo, Omar Estrada, Adonis Ferro, Levi Orta, Guillermo Ramírez Malberti, Glenda Salazar y Harold Vázquez.

prácticas que se desarrollaron dentro-fuera del propio campo artístico.

Su propuesta, *Islas de tragedia y fantasía: las bienales de arte y otros desastres globales*, debía entenderse desde el accionar de sus componentes estructurales y la manera poco común de articularlos; si tomamos en cuenta sus fricciones, giros inesperados y complejas intertextualidades. Se trataba de una propuesta híbrida y transdisciplinar que se componía de una instalación de banderas con nombres de bienales, fechas y/o ciudades protagonistas de desastres; un diagrama —de una simetría perfecta y proporciones justas— que organiza la estructura, los componentes y agentes implicados en las bienales de arte y en situaciones que pueden ser concebidos como desastres; una especie de biblioteca o sala de consulta de materiales bibliográficos y audiovisuales; la re-transmisión por televisión nacional de la serie estadounidenses *Fantasy Island* [La isla de la fantasía] (1977-1984),[12] así como su distribución en cassettes, discos y el "paquete semanal",[13] y la creación de un grupo de investigación denominado Teatro de Operaciones Estadísticas, con el objetivo de generar sesiones de debate.

La obra sintetizaba, por un lado, la experiencia personal del artista en la primera edición de la Ghetto Biennale en Puerto Príncipe, a fines del 2009. Un evento que no tuvo mucho impacto en los medios de comunicación, en contraste con la cobertura de los trágicos acontecimientos del terremoto que azotaría a esta ciudad en

—

12 Esta acción a pesar de ser planteada como parte del proyecto, no fue realizada en el marco de la bienal.

13 El "paquete semanal" es un sistema informal de recopilación de información, promoción, comunicación, conexiones y distribución alternativa que circula en toda Cuba y reúne material audiovisual de todo tipo (con excepción de la política y la pornografía), a partir de clasificaciones temáticas y de género.

enero de 2010. Por otro lado, Lasch se preguntaba sobre el crecimiento acelerado de las bienales de arte durante las últimas décadas, paralelo a los desastres mundiales (naturales o provocados por la acción humana). ¿Cómo el nombre de algunas ciudades, asociadas a catástrofes, servía como fachada para el mejoramiento de las condiciones económicas del lugar pese a no atender las condiciones estructurales en los períodos entre bienales? ¿Cómo, en nombre del arte, se realizaban proyectos que superaban y no respetaban las infraestructuras concebidas para la vida diaria de muchas ciudades?

Este desmontaje se cruzaba con la perspectiva crítica del libro de Naomi Klein, *La doctrina del shock. El auge del capitalismo del desastre*, presente en la sala de consulta junto a otras obras literarias o ensayísticas que, aunque le anteceden, documentan de manera irrefutable un maridaje entre desastres y colonialidad, modernidad y dominación, naturaleza y civilización. Se encontraban libros como *La tempestad* de William Shakespeare, *El corazón de las tinieblas* de Joseph Conrad, *Los jacobinos negros* de C. L. R. James, y *Calibán* de Roberto Fernández Retamar, que además permitían indagar la relación entre conceptos como utopía y espacios de control. Esta relación también era verificable en la serie *La isla de la fantasía*, donde los protagonistas eran invitados a satisfacer sus anhelos y ambiciones para luego acoger las vicisitudes más inesperadas.

Lasch cruzaba todas las variantes posibles de una situación contemporánea en la cual se interceptaban arte, cultura, política y entretenimiento. Desde la perspectiva de las bienales y los desastres, nos obligaba, por ejemplo, a recordar la operación simbólica montada por Joseph Goebbels, ministro de propaganda nazi, y Adolf Ziegler, curador del régimen, y su posible impacto en la historia de las megaexposiciones globales. El rostro de Goebbels, aparecía en el cartel que anunciaba la obra de Lasch, enlazando la mencionada serie televisiva con la exposición *Entartete Kunst* [Arte degenerado], realizada en la Alemania del 1937: una maniobra que demonizaba al arte vanguardista, apelando a los cánones de un arte alemán conservador. Al referir este programa propagandístico, Lasch insinuaba también la sorpresa que pudieran darnos muchas bienales y eventos internacionales, encubiertos bajo el aura de la contemporaneidad neoliberal.

A las preguntas generales que contempla el proyecto habría que añadir muchas otras que se basan en el contexto inmediato de La Habana y su historia de resistencia y producción cultural. Siguiendo ese hilo, el Teatro de Operaciones Estadísticas activado por Pedro propuso, por ejemplo, debatir sobre la historia de confrontaciones e intentos de "normalización" de las relaciones entre Cuba y los Estados Unidos bajo la perspectiva de un desastre histórico envuelto en intereses económicos y políticos; sobre la televisión como medio que vinculaba la vanguardia artística y cultural con la industria del entretenimiento; el "paquete semanal" como estrategia de resistencia cultural frente a los límites de circulación de la información; o los recursos y las estrategias implementados por la Defensa Civil cubana para la recuperación de un país permanentemente azotado por desastres naturales como los huracanes. También, se abordaron las estrategias económicas para la implementación de la enseñanza y hacer posible la vida artísticas en Cuba, condicionadas por las circunstancias arbitrarias del bloqueo, y consecuentemente todos los temas que pudieran derivarse.

Estos talleres, junto a los libros citados, los diagramas y las recontextualizaciones históricas de bienales y desastres, establecían nexos tangenciales entre los temas y subtemas propuestos por el artista. De alguna manera, su estrategia se conectaba con la experiencia del teatro post-dramático, entendido como una forma de entrecruzamiento entre la instalación, la performance, la deriva intelectual, e incluso un debate realizado como *happening*, desplazando la atención de la pieza hacia situaciones cotidianas y acontecimientos históricos otros que los participantes traían al espacio, del cual emergía como resultado un espacio de conciencia política.

El efecto de *shock* generado por los propios componentes interconectados de la obra nos llevaba a la necesidad de desentrañar tanto su tipología participativa como aquellos eventos, sucesos y situaciones de desastres que, o pretendían ocultarse, o nunca habíamos visto bajo este prisma. Como artista defensor de los posicionamientos promovidos por las estéticas decoloniales y activo en bienales y eventos periféricos sobre arte, Lasch establecía una conexión con el juego de afectos promovido por la exposición, aunque se trataba realmente de un juego de responsabilidades históricas, generacionales y globales. Visto en la distancia, Pedro Lasch ha sido, una y otra vez, coherente con su propia trayectoria, colmada de implicaciones geopolíticas y de miradas críticas, iniciadas con la experiencia colectiva 16 Beaver Group[14] y que complementa actualmente con su labor como profesor, teórico y colaborador de organizaciones de inmigrantes, grupos indígenas y trabajadores internacionales. Su calidad recala no tanto a través de un activismo que pudiera terminar encapsulado, sino de en un conjunto de herramientas que ha sabido colocar en las fronteras entre arte

—

14 Pedro Lasch fue miembro activo de 16 Beaver Group, espacio autogestionado por artistas desde 1999 en el 16 de Beaver Street, Nueva York. El colectivo ha funcionado como un lugar de encuentro para personas involucradas en el arte, la política y la educación, promoviendo el intercambio de investigaciones, preocupaciones y estrategias de acción colectiva.

y política, no sólo por su capacidad para generar narrativas, articulaciones simbólicas y eficacia sobre las audiencias, sino por su impulso a ensanchar y dilatar las prácticas del arte, que son, en definitiva, la atalaya desde donde nos envía sus luces.

Art World Disaster [Arte Mundo Desastre], Beirut, 2013

[p. 111]

Instalación de pancartas, exposición en galería y programa de talleres

Esta obra fue producida por la AUB Byblos Bank Art Gallery en Beirut, Líbano, en 2013. Las pancartas aparentemente celebratorias del corporativo fueron utilizadas para detonar diálogos con participantes locales por medio de una serie de talleres y conversatorios públicos. También, fungieron como ejes artísticos y conceptuales para una exposición y programa público que incluyó a artistas, estudiantes, curadores, activistas y académicos locales.

Arte y desastre
Octavian Esanu
Julio 9, 2022

[p. 115]

En 2013, las Galerías de Arte de la American University of Beirut (AUB) organizaron un proyecto de Pedro Lasch enfocado en investigación, pedagogía, activismo y arte para el cambio social. Lasch propuso una exposición-taller-curso titulada *Art World Disaster* [Arte Mundo Desastre], en colaboración con el profesor de arte de la AUB, Kasper Kovitz, y los alumnos del curso Concept 1. A lo largo del semestre —mucho antes de la adopción de la enseñanza en línea durante la pandemia—, Lasch impartió clases, condujo visitas de estudio y

sesiones de crítica a través de internet. Lasch y Kovitz trabajaron individualmente con los estudiantes para ayudarlos a mejorar metodológicamente sus proyectos, desde las ideas iniciales hasta la fase final de producción y exposición. La fase final del proyecto, que Lasch llevó a cabo en Beirut, involucró impartir las últimas sesiones en persona, organizar un taller y varios debates, así como ayudar a los estudiantes y a los artistas locales a instalar sus obras en sala.[15]

En el texto de la muestra, Lasch explica que la idea del proyecto surgió poco después de su participación en la Ghetto Biennale de Puerto Príncipe, en 2009. Lasch cuenta que aquella Bienal en Haití fue memorable en muchos sentidos, pero que, a pesar de los intentos de los organizadores y los artistas por atraer la atención del público internacional interesado en el arte y la cultura, apenas hubo interés por ese "evento marginal". Un mes después, una gran catástrofe azotó Haití. El terremoto de enero de 2010 no sólo trajo sufrimiento y muerte a la isla, sino también la atención de los medios de comunicación internacionales. De pronto, periodistas estadounidenses, expertos en gestión pública, amantes del arte y críticos culturales "descubrieron" el arte en la parte occidental de la isla La Española. A la luz de esta reveladora experiencia caribeña, Lasch también produjo una serie de mantas en las que juntaba los nombres de "zonas culturales" con "zonas de desastre" (por ejemplo, "Venecia/Chernóbil", "Sharjah/Kanungu" y "Kassel/Banqiao"). Al colgar estas mantas en la galería, entre las obras de los estudiantes y artistas locales, invitó al

—

15 Entre los artistas estaban Magali Claude, Dima Hajjar, Sandra Issa, Nayla Kronfol, Sana'a Mouhaidli, Edwina Nassar, Ghassan Nassar, Georges Rabbath, Christopher Rizkallah, Saba Seyedeh Sadr, Nataly Sarkis, Lara Tabet, Karen Zeidan. Como parte del programa de la exhibición, hubo una conversación pública entre Lasch y el artista Walid Sadek.

público a reflexionar sobre los controvertidos mecanismos de legitimación cultural de nuestra época.

Quienes se han comprometido con una historiografía materialista saben desde siempre que toda zona cultural es al mismo tiempo una zona de desastre. En la tesis VII de las "Tesis sobre la filosofía de la historia",[16] Walter Benjamin subraya el vínculo entre cultura y barbarie. Se podría interpretar su tesis diciendo que las obras de arte no sólo expresan, representan y transmiten lo armonioso, lo bello, lo majestuoso y lo sublime, sino que también —y al mismo tiempo— ocultan contradicciones y conflictos: la explotación laboral, el arduo trabajo del esclavo, el sudor del oprimido. Si se leen las mantas de Lasch a través de las tesis de Benjamin, se entiende cómo cada edición de La Biennale di Venezia, para mostrar lo más bello y lo más verdadero —o ambas cosas—, debe también ocultar lo más feo y lo más falso. El exquisito fruto del genio artístico es también el producto de quienes trabajan para limpiar, supervisar y darle mantenimiento a una cultura cuyos placeres de la representación no llegan a saborear, o por los que no se les reconoce más allá de ser mano de obra asalariada.

Y en Kassel, para que cada documenta muestre el triunfo de la democracia occidental mediante lo que se denomina "arte contemporáneo", también se debe ocultar la dudosa relación que esta democracia —y su arte— mantiene con las fuerzas del mercado y, en el mundo actual, con prácticas tiránicas y genocidas, así como con aparatos coercitivos que silencian a quienes aún creen en los valores que esta democracia sostienen sólo de manera formal.

—

16 Walter Benjamin, "On the Concept of History" en Marxist Internet Archive, trad. Dennis Redmond (1940). Consultado el 12 de mayo de 2025, en: https://www.marxists.org/reference/archive/benjamin/1940/history.htm.

Verdad y falsedad, democracia y mercado, libertad y represión, belleza y fealdad, educación e ignorancia, trabajo y capital, cultura y barbarie, arte y desastre: todo se entremezcla, todo constituye un rico tapiz cuyos esplendorosos pliegues revelan tanto como ocultan sus reversos.

En su serie de mantas, Lasch sitúa el arte y el desastre —o la cultura y la barbarie—, en un contexto global más amplio cuando asocia lugares de acumulación simbólica y material de capital (Kassel, Venecia, Sharjah) con lugares de devastación económica o política, constituidos históricamente por la expansión colonial, la esclavitud, la modernización competitiva y la globalización.

Otra cosa está implícita en la conceptualización de este evento: hoy en día nuestro sistema económico y cultural se inclina más hacia la barbarie o el desastre, si pensamos en los extremos de esta oposición. Sobre este asunto, Naomi Klein ha sugerido que el *shock*, el terror, la guerra y los desastres naturales se han convertido en el combustible preferido del capitalismo neoliberal. Desde el punto de vista económico, el desastre se ha utilizado como excusa, pretexto o remedio para lo que el discurso neoliberal presenta como el principal problema de nuestra época: la supuesta ineficiencia del mercado. Para resolverlo, el desastre se ofrece como justificación económica y estética, así se transfieren los recursos vitales de los pobres a los ricos y —en términos estéticos—, de los "feos" a la "gente bella", como se ha llamado históricamente a la clase media alta. Como demuestra el trabajo de Klein, esta transferencia estético-económica se probó por primera vez en América Latina y Europa del Este durante los años ochenta y noventa, antes de aplicarse a escala mundial. El desastre es el combustible que mantiene estable el reactor del capitalismo del espectáculo, y corresponde a los medios de comunicación corporativos seguir enriqueciendo este combustible y llevando la atención del mundo hacia los lugares de mayor devastación natural, cultural, política o económica, como lo ejemplifica el testimonio de Pedro Lasch sobre el terremoto de 2009, en Puerto Príncipe.

El arte y el sufrimiento (o la desgracia) siempre han sido cercanos. Lo que ha cambiado es la forma en que se manifiesta esa cercanía, de quién es el sufrimiento que el arte aborda. En la antigüedad, el sufrimiento, la pena, la desesperación, la locura y el dolor encontraban expresión, por ejemplo, en la tragedia griega. Sin embargo, en aquella época no todos eran bienvenidos a expresar el sufrimiento de una forma elevada. La tragedia tenía poder de convencimiento porque sólo unos pocos elegidos sabían cómo sufrir adecuadamente, por ello su fuerza para ofrecer alivio y distracción colectiva, o para educar a los jóvenes con las acciones ejemplarizantes de grandes personajes. Una cosa es que la desgracia le ocurra a un príncipe, un rey o un semidiós, otra muy distinta que le ocurra a un simple mortal. De acuerdo con las definiciones clásicas de la tragedia, aceptamos participar en el sufrimiento heroico de los primeros, pero no consentimos compartir la angustia de los segundos. Para el príncipe, el sufrimiento formaba parte del destino divino; para el trabajador libre o el esclavo, era simplemente la miseria de la vida cotidiana. En la era moderna, con la desaparición de reyes y príncipes, dioses y rituales, sacrificios y mitos, la tragedia —como forma ennoblecida y elevada del sufrimiento—, pasa a un segundo plano en la cultura de masas. Esta nueva realidad, marcada por valores pragmáticos, igualitarios, materialistas y realistas, se centra en los aspectos cotidianos de la vida y contrasta con el *ethos* de la tragedia clásica, muy lejano a las realidades diarias del vendedor, el abogado o el empleado. La tragedia, que durante siglos fue la forma superior y dominante de expresión humana del dolor, ha sido desplazada por los pensamientos y el lenguaje de la gente común. Lo que antes era trágico se ha convertido simplemente en miseria, desgracia y desastre.

El pecado original de la cultura del desastre no sólo está presente en sus temas y motivos, sino también en sus ubicaciones. Un desastre de gran magnitud se convierte en un escenario de cultura masiva: cuanto más atroz es el desastre, mayor es el escenario, más brillante es el foco de atención y mayor es la euforia competitiva. Esto es evidente en nuestro más reciente desastre: la guerra en Ucrania. Cuando apenas Rusia provocó la guerra, las celebridades de Hollywood y otras figuras políticas o culturales occidentales se apresuraron a ir a Ucrania para mostrar su apoyo, al mismo tiempo, aprovechaban la oportunidad para aumentar su visibilidad en la cobertura global del conflicto. Se precipitaron a Ucrania y a otras zonas de guerra para ponerse bajo los reflectores o situarse frente al telón de fondo del desastre, cosechando prestigio cultural y extrayendo capital simbólico al aprovechar la energía intensificada que se había acumulado a partir del duelo colectivo y la resiliencia de las comunidades afectadas. La situación no es muy diferente en el caso del "mundo del arte". Los escenarios más conocidos del arte contemporáneo son también zonas de grandes catástrofes históricas. La historia de La Biennale di Venezia está estrechamente ligada a la expansión colonial de Italia en el norte de África a finales del siglo XIX. En lo que respecta a Kassel, documenta se creó tras la Segunda Guerra Mundial como parte de la desnazificación y la autopurificación llevadas a cabo bajo la fría mirada de los victoriosos aliados. Esta conexión entre las zonas artísticas y las zonas de calamidades, entre la cultura y la barbarie, puede extenderse a muchas otras bienales y exposiciones que han proliferado en nuestro mundo del capitalismo del desastre.

Al igual que la economía, la cultura
y Hollywood, el arte contemporáneo
actual es consecuencia del desastre. Sin
embargo, el proceso funciona de manera
diferente en distintos lugares. En los países occidentales, la atención se centra en
desastres históricos lejanos (esclavitud,
colonialismo, racismo, fascismo, nazismo,
comunismo) que deben ser confrontados
sin cesar para que nuestro presente contemporáneo parezca más feliz, más libre o
más próspero. Por el contrario, los países
no-occidentales se ven obligados a explo-
tar sus propios desastres, con frecuen-
cia como resultado reciente de desastres
lejanos del primer mundo (como el colonialismo o la esclavitud). Para tener éxito
como artista del Sur Global, a veces es
necesario (por horrible que pueda sonar)
tener la "suerte" suficiente de haber formado parte de una desgracia que haya
tenido una importante repercusión global.
Los ejemplos abundan: desde el colapso
de la Unión Soviética hasta el genocidio en
Ruanda, la guerra civil libanesa, Chernóbil
y Fukushima; la lista de artistas asociados
con estos desastres es extensa.

En Líbano, donde se llevó a cabo el proyecto *Art World Disaster*, los críticos y
artistas locales suelen debatir la relación
entre los desastres locales y el éxito internacional de la escena artística beirutí.
Desde la guerra civil libanesa hasta el 11
de septiembre, y desde la invasión israelí
del Líbano hasta la explosión del puerto
de Beirut, esta serie de desastres ha
atraído una atención internacional significativa, generando espacios de exhibición
y visibilidad que tanto artistas y trabajadores culturales locales como extranje-
ros han utilizado como fuentes materiales
y de inspiración artística. Tras la invasión israelí de 2006, por ejemplo, numerosos museos occidentales, revistas de arte
estadounidenses, críticos metropolitanos,
curadores e instituciones aprovecharon la
oportunidad para presentar exposiciones,
números especiales de revistas de arte o
textos curatoriales y teóricos centrados en
el Líbano. Esta estrategia funcionó en el
largo plazo, atizando el papel continuo de
Beirut como un importante centro cultural en la región. En el pasado, durante la
llamada "edad de oro", fueron su locali-
zación geopolítica, el sector bancario y la
riqueza petrolera los que contribuyeron a
otorgarle este estatus; después de 1989, la
prolongada guerra civil se convirtió en la
principal fuente de energía cultural, con-
troversia, inspiración y material artístico.
Las comunidades artísticas que no han
sufrido un desastre reciente deben espe-
rar (como los artistas sirios, quienes sólo
recientemente han sido foco de atención).
Muchos otros, en el Sur Global, tendrán
que ser pacientes hasta que la próxima
invasión estadounidense, israelí, nazi o
rusa genere nuevas oportunidades para el
arte y el desastre.

Of Saadiyat's Rectangles & Curves or Santiago Sierra's One Sheikh, Two Museum Directors, Three Curators, One University President, Two Architects, and One Artist Remunerated to Sleep for 30 Days in 13 × 14 foot Windowless Room with Shared Bathroom and No Door [Sobre los rectángulos y curvas de Saadiyat o Un jeque, dos directores de museos, tres curadores, un presidente de universidad, dos arquitectos y un artista pagado para dormir por 30 días en una habitación sin ventanas de 4 m², baño

compartido y sin puertas de Santiago Sierra], 2013

[p. 121]

Póster de campaña digital, edición impresa ilimitada y juego de 6 pinturas sobre lienzo, 60 × 60 cm c/u

Esta obra fue la contribución de Pedro Lasch para la campaña internacional de justicia social llamada 52 Weeks of Gulf Labor [52 semanas de labor en el Golfo], cuyo diseño fue presentado en la semana 14 y fue incluido también en la publicación *The Gulf: High Culture/Hard Labor* [El Golfo: Alta cultura/ardua labor], editado por Andrew Ross.[17] El trabajo de Lasch, junto con otros 51 artistas de diferentes partes del mundo participantes en la campaña, buscó señalar las condiciones laborales inaceptables en la construcción de campus universitarios, museos de arte y sedes de bienales en la isla Saadiyat de los Emiratos Árabes Unidos. Dado que las instituciones participantes eran todas de carácter global y afirmaban representar los intereses del arte y del aprendizaje, una respuesta internacional parecía crucial. El póster muestra el nombre de cada edificio debajo de la imagen que lo representa en el conjunto de pinturas. Éstas sólo muestran el área del edificio de cada uno y sus nombres se muestran en cédulas de museo.

Semblanzas
(en orden de aparición)

Pedro Lasch es un artista visual, profesor de la Duke University, y director del Laboratorio de Práctica Social en el John Hope Franklin Humanities Institute.

Ha presentado exposiciones individuales y proyectos como *Open Routines* (Queens

—

Museum), *Black Mirror* (Nasher Museum), *Abstract Nationalism* (The Phillips Collection), *Art of the MOOC* (Creative Time), *Una propuesta escultórica para el Zócalo* (Casa Wabi) y *Politics of Fiction* (Espacio México Montreal); así como exposiciones grupales en MoMA PS1 (Nueva York), MASS MoCA (North Adams); The Royal College of Art (Londres), Hayward Gallery, Baltic Centre for Contemporary Art (Gateshead); Centro Nacional de las Artes, Museo Universitario Arte Contemporáneo MUAC, Galería Palacio Nacional (Ciudad de Mexico); Prospect.4: New Orleans (2017), Gwangju Biennale (2006), Bienal de La Habana (2015), dOCUMENTA (13) (AND AND AND, Kassel, 2012), documenta fifteen (Atis Rezistans/Ghetto Biennale, Kassel, 2022), y 56 La Biennale di Venezia (Creative Time Special Project, 2015).

Lasch es autor de seis libros y su obra ha aparecido en numerosos catálogos y revistas como *October*, *Saber Ver*, *Artforum*, *ARTnews*, *Cultural Studies*, *The New York Times* y *La Jornada*. Su obra pedagógica online *ART of the MOOC* ha tenido más de 78,000 participantes inscritos en 134 países desde su lanzamiento en 2015.

Cristina Paoli es maestra en Diseño gráfico por la London College of Communication y licenciada en Diseño gráfico por la Universidad Iberoamericana. Es autora del libro *Mexican Blackletter* (2006). Es fundadora de PERIFERIA (2011), un estudio de diseño y edición de libros de arte y comunicación gráfica cultural en la CDMX.

Ha diseñado libros y/o gráficos para instituciones como SITE SANTA FE, Museo Tamayo Arte Contemporáneo (México), Museo Universitario Arte Contemporáneo-MUAC (México), Centro de Arte 2 de Mayo (España), Pabellón de México en la 53 y 54 La Biennale di Venezia; el Pabellón de Chile en la 15 Biennale Architettura; editoriales como Alias (México), Arquine

17 *The Gulf: High Culture/Hard Labor*, Andrew Ross (ed.), (Nueva York: OR Books, 2015).

(México), Cosac Naify (Brasil), Hatje Cantz (Alemania), Electa (Italia), Editorial RM (México-España), Turner (México-España), Buchhandlung Walther König (Alemania); y artistas como Francis Alÿs, Teresa Margolles, Melanie Smith, entre otros.

En 2014 obtuvo la Mención Honorífica en la categoría de Colección del 1er Premio Latinoamericano al Diseño Editorial (Buenos Aires) por el diseño de la colección Folios MUAC, y el DAM Architectural Book Award otorgado por Deutsches Architekturmuseum y la Feria de Libro de Frankfurt por el libro *Talca: Cuestión de educación*.

André Eugène fue co-curador de la participación de Atis Rezistans/Ghetto Biennale en documenta fifteen, realizada en la Iglesia St. Kunigundis en Kassel junto con Leah Gordon. Nació en el centro de Puerto Príncipe en 1959 y es una figura clave del colectivo de artistas conocido como Atis Rezistans y del movimiento más amplio llamado los Escultores de Grand Rue.

En 2006, André Eugène participó en una gran obra escultórica colectiva que forma parte de la colección permanente del International Slavery Museum en Liverpool. Es co-director de la Ghetto Biennale, que tiene lugar en Puerto Príncipe desde 2009. Su obra ha sido expuesta en el Musée d'ethnographie de Genève; el Parc de la Villette y el Grand Palais (París), el Fowler Museum at UCLA (Los Ángeles); el Frost Science Museum (Miami), Pioneer Works (Nueva York) y el MOCA de North Miami; Nottingham Contemporary y la Triennale Milano. Su trabajo también formó parte del Pabellón de Haití en la 54 La Biennale di Venezia.

Leah Gordon fue co-curador de la participación de Atis Rezistans/Ghetto Biennale en documenta fifteen, realizada en la Iglesia St. Kunigundis en Kassel. Es artista, curadora y escritora. Su trabajo explora las historias interseccionales del sistema de plantaciones en el Caribe, los *Enclosure Acts* y la creación de la clase trabajadora británica.

La obra de Gordon ha sido exhibida internacionalmente en espacios como el Museum of Contemporary Art Australia (Sídney), the Dak'art Biennale (Dakar), the National Portrait Gallery (London), y el Norton Museum of Art West Palm Beach). Es co-directora de la Ghetto Biennale en Puerto Príncipe; fue co-curadora de *Kafou: Haiti, Art and Vodou* en Nottingham Contemporary, y de *PÒTO-PRENS: The Urban Artists of Port-au-Prince* en Pioneer Works (Nueva York).

Su libro *Kanaval* fue publicado en 2021, y en 2022 su aclamado y premiado largometraje documental *Kanaval: A People's History of Haiti in Six Chapters* fue proyectado en salas de cine y transmitido en el programa BBC Four's Arena. Su obra también ha sido presentada en el MOCA North Miami y en el Haus der Kulturen der Welt (Berlín).

Atis Rezistans realizaron las obras para la Iglesia St. Kunigundis en Kassel, en la documenta fifteen, junto con sus colaboradores internacionales del grupo Ghetto Biennale. Atis Rezistans es un grupo dinámico de artistas, en su mayoría provenientes de la clase trabajadora, que trabajan en el barrio de Grand Rue, en el centro de Puerto Príncipe, Haití, a menudo en condiciones adversas y difíciles.

Es una comunidad cambiante compuesta por artistas experimentados y maduros, así como por una variedad de artistas jóvenes emergentes. En 2009, Atis Rezistans organizó la primera Ghetto Biennale y, en los últimos doce años desde entonces, han recibido a más de trescientos artistas internacionales y formado numerosos lazos colaborativos sólidos. Los miembros participantes en documenta fifteen fueron Katelyn Alexis, Wesner Bazile, Adriana Benjamin,

Jerry Reginald Chery a.k.a. Twoket, Patrick Elie a.k.a. Kombatan, André Eugène, Londel Innocent, Louis Kervans a.k.a. Bakari, Jean Jonas Labaze, Michel Lafleur, Jean Muller Milord a.k.a. Soso, Jean Robert Palenquet, Herold Pierre-Louis, Mario Pierre-Louis a.k.a. Prela, Evel Romain, Jean-Claude Saintilus, Reginald Sénatus y Wilerme Tegenis, todos de Haití.

Ghetto Biennale realizó las obras para la Iglesia de St. Kunigundis en Kassel, Alemania, en documenta fifteen, junto con sus colaboradores del colectivo Atis Rezistans. Se trata de un grupo de artistas internacionales que surgió a lo largo de más de una década de producciones colaborativas con Atis Rezistans en Puerto Príncipe. Ghetto Biennale reúne a artistas de muchas generaciones, que trabajan en una amplia variedad de medios, todos comprometidos con el apoyo a los artistas haitianos y sus comunidades, y con la celebración de la importancia global de la historia y la cultura haitianas.

Los miembros participantes en documenta fifteen fueron Cat Barich (Alemania), Simon Benjamin (Jamaica/Estados Unidos), Tom Bogaert (Bélgica), Demar Brackenridge (Jamaica), Nanne Buurman (Alemania), Vivian Chan (Gran Bretaña), Camille Chedda (Jamaica), John Cussans (Gran Bretaña), Edouard Duval-Carrié (Haití/Estados Unidos), Leah Gordon (Gran Bretaña), Sheldon Green (Jamaica), Bastian Hagedorn (Alemania), Jean-Louis Huhta (Suecia), Laura Heyman (Estados Unidos), L (Estados Unidos), Pedro Lasch (México/Estados Unidos), Henrike Naumann (Alemania), Carima Neusser (Suecia), Roberto N Peyre (Suecia), Martina Vanin (Italia), Elizabeth Woodroffe (Barbados/Gran Bretaña).

Hoor Al-Qasimi es la presidenta, directora y fundadora de Sharjah Art Foundation (SAF), que funciona como una catalizadora y defensora de las artes en Sharjah, así como a nivel regional e internacional, fundada en 2009. Al-Qasimi ha ampliado continuamente el alcance de la Fundación a lo largo de sus más de diez años de historia realizando exposiciones de gran escala que han itinerado internacionalmente, residencias para artistas y curadores en artes visuales, cine y música, comisiones y becas de producción para artistas emergentes y una amplia gama de programas educativos.

En 2003, Al-Qasimi co-curó la Sharjah Biennial y desde entonces ha continuado como directora de la bienal. En 2017 fue elegida presidenta de la International Biennial Association (IBA), cargo que trasladó la sede de la IBA a Sharjah. También es presidenta de The Africa Institute y presidenta del consejo de la Sharjah Architecture Triennial. En 2020, Al-Qasimi fue curadora de la segunda Lahore Biennale en Pakistán.

Carolyn Christov-Bakargiev es la directora del Castello di Rivoli Museo d'Arte Contemporanea y de la Fondazione Francesco Federico Cerruti en Turín. Es la ganadora del Audrey Irmas Award for Curatorial Excellence en 2019. Fue Edith Kreeger Wolf Distinguished Visiting Professor en Teoría y práctica del arte en Northwestern University (2013–2019).

Christov-Bakargiev comenzó su carrera en el arte escribiendo reseñas para la revista *Reporter* y para el periódico *Il Sole 24 Ore*. Las amistades con artistas en Italia y a nivel internacional, como William Kentridge, Alighiero Boetti, Pierre Huyghe, Francis Alÿs, Mario y Marisa Merz y Jannis Kounellis, impulsaron su trabajo curatorial. Curó las exposiciones de verano en la Villa Medici (1998–2000), y fue curadora en jefe en MoMA PS1 en Nueva York. En 2008, curó Biennale of Sydney, seguida por dOCUMENTA (13) en 2012 y la 14 İstanbul Bienali en 2015. Entre sus numerosas publicaciones destaca la monografía *Arte Povera* (Londres, Phaidon Press, 1999).

Andrea Giunta es profesora en la Universidad de Buenos Aires. Fue directora fundadora del Center for Latin American Visual Studies en la University of Texas at Austin. Ha sido profesora visitante en Duke University, la École des hautes études en sciences sociales, Columbia University y Humboldt University; de igual manera ha recibido becas de la Guggenheim Foundation, Getty Museum, Rockefeller Foundation y Donald D. Harrington Fellows Program.

Fue curadora de la retrospectiva de León Ferrari en el Centro Cultural Recoleta (Buenos Aires), co-curadora de *Verboamérica* de la colección permanente de arte latinoamericano del Museo de Arte Latinoamericano de Buenos Aires (MALBA), y co-curadora de *Radical Women: Latin American Art, 1960–1985* en el Hammer Museum, el Brooklyn Museum y la Pinacoteca de São Paulo. Desde 2020 ha desarrollado diversos proyectos en respuesta al contexto de la pandemia de COVID-19, como curadora en jefe de la Bienal do Mercosul 12: Feminine(s): Visualities, Actions, and Affects en Porto Alegre, curadora de *Pensar todo de nuevo* en Les Rencontres d'Arles, así como de la exposición *Cuando cambia el mundo. Preguntas sobre arte y feminismos* en el Centro Cultural Kirchner.

Yuko Hasegawa es la Directora Artística del Museum of Contemporary Art Tokyo (2016–presente) y profesora en la Graduate School of Global Arts en Tokyo University of the Arts (2016–presente). También es directora del 21st Century Museum of Contemporary Art, Kanazawa y directora artística del Inujima Art House Project (2011–presente).

Ha trabajado en numerosos proyectos de bienales, entre ellos: la 7 Moscow International Biennale of Contemporary Art:

Clouds⇄Forests (2017–2018), 2 Beijing Photo Biennial: *Unfamiliar Asia* (2015), Sharjah Biennial 11: *Re:emerge, Towards a New Cultural Cartography* (2013), la 29 Bienal de São Paulo (2010), la 12 Biennale Architettura (2010), La Biennale di Venezia, Pabellón de Japón (2003), Shanghai Biennale (2002–2003) y la 7 İstanbul Bienali (2001).

Rujeko Hockley es curadora asistente en el Whitney Museum of American Art. Es la curadora de la retrospectiva de Julie Mehretu y co-curadora de la Whitney Biennial 2019. Otros proyectos en el Whitney incluyen *Toyin Ojih Odutola: To Wander Determined* (2017) y *An Incomplete History of Protest: Selections from the Whitney's Collection, 1940-2017* (2017).

Anteriormente fue curadora asistente de arte contemporáneo en el Brooklyn Museum, donde co-curó *Crossing Brooklyn: Art from Bushwick, Bed-Stuy, and Beyond* (2014) y participó en exposiciones de artistas como LaToya Ruby Frazier, Bruce High Quality Foundation, Kehinde Wiley, Tom Sachs, así como acerca de la colección permanente del museo. Es co-curadora de *We Wanted a Revolution: Black Radical Women, 1965-85* (2017), exposición originada en el Brooklyn Museum y que viajó a tres sedes en Estados Unidos entre 2017 y 2018. Forma parte del consejo de Art Matters y del consejo asesor de Recess.

Candice Hopkins es curadora y escritora de ascendencia tlingit. Es curadora principal de la Toronto Biennial of Art y co-curadora de la SITE SANTA FE Biennial 2018. Formó parte del equipo curatorial de documenta 14 en Atenas y Kassel, y co-curó importantes exposiciones como *Sakahàn: International Indigenous Art, Close Encounters: The Next 500 Years* y la bienal SITElines.14: Unsettled Landscapes en Santa Fe, Nuevo México. Sus escritos, ensayos y presentaciones incluyen "Outlawed Social

Life" en *South as a State of Mind* y "Sounding the Margins: A Choir of Minor Voices" en Small Projects, Tromsø, Noruega.

Ha impartido conferencias en FKA Witte de With, Tate Modern, Dak'Art, Artists Space, Tate Britain y University of British Columbia. Ha recibido premios como el Hnatyshyn Foundation Visual Arts Award for Curatorial Excellence y el Prize for a Critical Essay on Contemporary ArtPrix en 2016, otorgado por la Foundation Prince Pierre de Monaco. Es ciudadana de la Carcross/Tagish First Nation.

Miguel A. López es escritor, investigador y ex codirector y curador en jefe de TEOR/éTica en San José, Costa Rica. Ha publicado en revistas como *Afterall, ramona, Manifesta Journal, e-flux journal, Art in America, Art Journal* y *The Exhibitionist*, entre otras. Sus libros más recientes, como autor y editor, incluyen *Robar la historia. Contrarrelatos y prácticas artísticas de oposición; The Words of Others: León Ferrari and Rhetoric in Times of War; Agítese antes de usar. Desplazamientos educativos, sociales y artísticos en América Latina; Alianças de Corpos Vulneráveis; The Obscene Death: Drawings 1982–1987: Sergio Zevallos;* y *A Wandering Body. Sergio Zevallos in the Grupo Chaclacayo, 1982–1994.* También ha curado *Social Energies / Vital Forces: Natalia Iguiñiz: Art, Activism, Feminism; Balance and Collapse. Patricia Belli: Works 1986–2016; Teresa Burga. Estructuras de aire* (junto con Agustín Pérez Rubio); y *God is Queer* para la 31 Bienal de São Paulo (2014). López es cofundador del espacio de arte independiente Bisagra, en Lima, Perú.

Cuauhtémoc Medina es crítico, curador, historiador del arte e investigador en el Instituto de Investigaciones Estéticas de la Universidad Nacional Autónoma de México (UNAM). Es curador en jefe del Museo Universitario de Arte Contemporáneo (MUAC) de la UNAM, en la Ciudad de México. Fue el primer curador asociado de Arte Latinoamericano en la Tate Modern (2002–2008) y curador en jefe de la Manifesta 9.

También fue curador en jefe de la 12 Shanghai Biennale: *Proregress. Art in an Age of Historical Ambivalence.* En 2012 se convirtió en el sexto galardonado con el Walter Hopps Award for Curatorial Achievement, otorgado por la Menil Collection. Medina ha curado eventos y exposiciones como *Cuando la fe mueve montañas* de Francis Alÿs (Lima, 2001), *20 Million Mexicans Can't Be Wrong* (South London Gallery, 2002), y *La era de la discrepancia. Arte y Cultura Visual en México 1968–1997.* En 2009 curó el proyecto de Teresa Margolles presentado en el Pabellón de México en La Biennale di Venezia.

Gabi Ngcobo es artista, curadora y educadora. Entre sus proyectos curatoriales recientes se encuentran *All in a Day's Eye: The Politics of Innocence in the Javett Family Collection,* en el Javett Art Centre – University of Pretoria, *Mating Birds* en la KZNSA Gallery (Durban). En 2018 curó la Berlin Biennale: *We Don't Need Another Hero* y fue una de las co-curadoras de la 32 Bienal de São Paulo (2016).

Es miembro fundadora de la plataforma con sede en Johannesburgo NGO – Nothing Gets Organised (2016) y del Center for Historical Reenactments (2010–2014). Los textos de Ngcobo han sido publicados en diversas publicaciones, entre ellas *Uneven Bodies (Reader)* (Govett-Brewster Art Gallery, Aotearoa, 2021); *The Stronger We Become,* el catálogo del Pabellón Sudafricano en La Biennale di Venezia (2019); *Public Intimacy: Art and Other Ordinary Acts in South Africa* (Yerba Buena Center for the Arts/SFMOMA, 2014); *We Are Many: Art, the Political and Multiple Truths* (Verbier Art Summit, 2019); y *Texte zur Kunst* (septiembre, 2017). En noviembre de 2020, Ngcobo fue nombrada directora curatorial del Javett-UP.

Lucia Pietroiusti es curadora de General Ecology en las Serpentine Galleries, Londres, así como curadora de *Sun & Sea (Marina)* en el Pabellón de Lituania en la 58 La Biennale di Venezia. Es también curadora de POWER NIGHT en E-WERK Luckenwalde (2021) y co-curadora de la Shanghai Biennale 2020–2021.

Entre sus proyectos destacan el festival recurrente sobre la conciencia entre especies The Shape of a Circle in the Mind of a Fish, la publicación *More-than-Human* y el proyecto editorial y de investigación *Microhabitable*. En Serpentine, Pietroiusti fundó y dirige General Ecology, una iniciativa estratégica para incorporar temas y metodologías ambientales en todas las producciones y redes de las galerías, así como Back to Earth, que reúne más de 65 campañas artísticas a favor del medio ambiente. Actualmente en desarrollo, la General Ecology Network es una red que convoca a más de cien personas y organizaciones de distintas disciplinas para ensayar transformaciones sistémicas lideradas por artistas y orientadas al medio ambiente, así como para cerrar la brecha de conocimiento y traducción entre cultura, creatividad y ecología.

ruangrupa es un colectivo radicado en Yakarta, establecido en el año 2000, cuyos integrantes Ajeng Nurul Aini, farid rakun, Iswanto Hartono, Mirwan Andan, Indra Ameng, Ade Darmawan, Daniella Fitria Praptono, Julia Sarisetiati y Reza Afisina fueron los curadores de documenta fifteen. Como colectivo de artistas, ruangrupa ha estado involucrado en numerosos proyectos colaborativos e intercambios, incluyendo su participación en importantes exposiciones como la Gwangju Biennale (2002 y 2018), İstanbul Bienali (2005), Asia Pacific Triennial of Contemporary Art (Brisbane, 2012), Singapore Biennale (2011), Bienal de São Paulo (2014), Aichi Triennale (Nagoya, 2016) y *Cosmopolis* en el Centre Pompidou (París, 2017).

En 2016, ruangrupa curó *Sonsbeek '16: transACTION* en Arnhem, Países Bajos. Entre 2015 y 2018, ruangrupa co-desarrolló, junto con varios colectivos de artistas de Yakarta, la plataforma cultural Gudang Sarinah Ekosistem en el almacén Gudang Sarinah en Pancoran, al sur de Yakarta. En 2018, ruangrupa también co-inició Gudskul, un espacio público de aprendizaje creado para practicar un entendimiento expandido de los valores colectivos, tales como la igualdad, el compartir, la solidaridad, la amistad y la convivencia.

José Roca es curador y director artístico de la 23 Biennale of Sydney. Dirige FLORA ars+natura, un espacio independiente para el arte contemporáneo en Bogotá, y es curador de la colección LARA, en Singapur. Fue curador de Arte Latinoamericano en la Tate Britain (2012–2015) y durante una década estuvo a cargo del programa de artes del Banco de la República en Bogotá. Roca fue co-curador de la Trienal Poli/gráfica en San Juan, Puerto Rico (2004), de la 27 Bienal de São Paulo (2006), y del Encuentro Internacional Medellín MDE07 (2007). Fue director artístico de Philagrafika 2010 y formó parte del jurado de premios de la 52 La Biennale de Venezia (2007). También fue curador en jefe de la VIII Bienal do Mercosul. Es autor de *Transpolitical: Arte en Colombia 1992–2012* y *Waterweavers: A Chronicle of Rivers*, publicado en el marco de la exposición homónima. Roca fue Curatorial Fellow en el Whitney Independent Study Program, así como Whitney-Lauder Curatorial Fellow en el Institute of Contemporary Art en Filadelfia.

Ralph Rugoff fue director Artístico de La Biennale de Venezia 2019 y curador invitado de la 13 Biennale de Lyon. Desde 2006 es director de la Hayward Gallery en Londres, donde ha curado numerosas exposiciones colectivas, entre ellas *The Painting of Modern Life: Paris in the Art of Manet* *and His Followers* (2007), *Psycho Buildings: Artists Take On Architecture* (2008) y *The Infinite Mix: Contemporary Sound and Image* (2016), así como importantes retrospectivas y exposiciones individuales de artistas como Ed Ruscha, Jeremy Deller, Tracey Emin y George Condo. También fue director del California College of the Arts Wattis Institute en San Francisco.

Entre 1985 y 2002 escribió crítica de arte y cultural para numerosas publicaciones, colaborando ampliamente en revistas especializadas y periódicos como *Artforum*, *Artpresse*, *Flash Art*, *Frieze*, *Parkett*, *Grand Street*, *The Financial Times*, *The Los Angeles Times* y *The Los Angeles Weekly*. Su libro *Circus Americanus* (1995) es una colección de ensayos que exploran fenómenos culturales del oeste de Estados Unidos. Durante ese mismo periodo comenzó a trabajar como curador independiente, organizando exposiciones como *Just Pathetic* (1990) y *Scene of the Crime* (1997).

Trevor Schoonmaker es director del Nasher Museum of Art en Duke University. Fue contratado en 2006 como el primer curador de arte contemporáneo del museo, y desde entonces ha contribuido a definir la visión curatorial y la colección de arte contemporáneo de la institución. Bajo su liderazgo, el museo se ha enfocado en reconocer y apoyar a artistas diversos que han sido históricamente subrepresentados.

Entre las exposiciones destacadas en el Nasher se encuentran: *Naama Tsabar: Composition 21* (2019); *People Get Ready: Building a Contemporary Collection* (2018); *John Akomfrah: Precarity* (2018); *Southern Accent: Seeking the American South in Contemporary Art* (2016); *Wangechi Mutu: A Fantastic Journey* (2013); *The Record: Contemporary Art and Vinyl* (2010); *Barkley L. Hendricks: Birth of the Cool* (2008); y *Street Level: Mark Bradford, William Cordova and Robin Rhode* (2007). Curó la New Orleans Triennal, Prospect.4: *The Lotus in Spite of the Swamp* (2017) y *Black President: The Art and Legacy of Fela Anikulapo-Kuti* en el New Museum of Contemporary Art, Nueva York (2003). Schoonmaker fue miembro de la junta directiva de la Andy Warhol Foundation for the Visual Arts de 2010 a 2018.

Dannys Montes de Oca Moreda es investigadora, curadora y crítica de arte, con sede en La Habana. Ha sido directora general y curadora de la Bienal de La Habana, así como directora del Centro de Arte Contemporáneo Wifredo Lam, en La Habana. Es coordinadora principal del evento teórico de la Bienal. También fue curadora de la Bienal de Asunción, en Paraguay. También es co-autora del libro *Memoria: Cuban Art of the 20th Century*, así como co-curadora de *Doble Seducción* para la Sala Amadís, INJUVE, en Madrid.

Entre sus premios y residencias internacionales destacan el Premio Nacional de Crítica de Arte Guy Pérez Cisneros, otorgado por el Consejo de las Artes Plásticas (La Habana), investigadora en residencia en Hunter College (Nueva York), investigadora en residencia en el Ludwig Forum für Internationale Kunst (Aquisgrán), investigadora en residencia en el Digital Poetics and Politics Summer Institute en el Departamento de Cine y Medios de la Queen's University (Kingston, Ontario), curadora en residencia en el Grand Water Research Institute (Isla Hornby/ The Power Plant Contemporary Art Gallery, Toronto) e investigadora en residencia nuevamente en la Queen's University.

Octavian Esanu concibe la historia del arte, la crítica, la curaduría y la gestión de exposiciones como parte de su práctica artística. Fue director fundador y primer curador del Soros Center for Contemporary Art (Chisináu). Desde 2012, es director y curador fundador de las Galerías de Arte de la American University of Beirut (AUB), y es profesor asociado en el Departamento de Arte e Historia del arte, donde imparte cursos sobre historia del arte, historias de exposiciones, así como métodos, prácticas y teorías del arte y sus modos de exhibición.

Tiene estudios en Artes visuales, Agitprop del socialismo tardío y Representación realista socialista, Diseño capitalista y arquitectura de interiores, además de un doctorado en Historia del arte contemporáneo y estudios visuales por la Duke University. Su investigación, que combina trabajo teórico y práctico, gira en torno al estudio de las grandes transformaciones y transiciones del arte en el contexto de los procesos globales de modernización y neoliberalización. Desde 2011, forma parte del colectivo editorial internacional de *ARTMargins Print*, revista publicada por MIT Press.

Six Color Puzzle Variation (detail), 2021 from the series *20 22 Painting Cycle*, 2020-2022. Industrial enamel on interchangeable wood pieces, variable dimensions

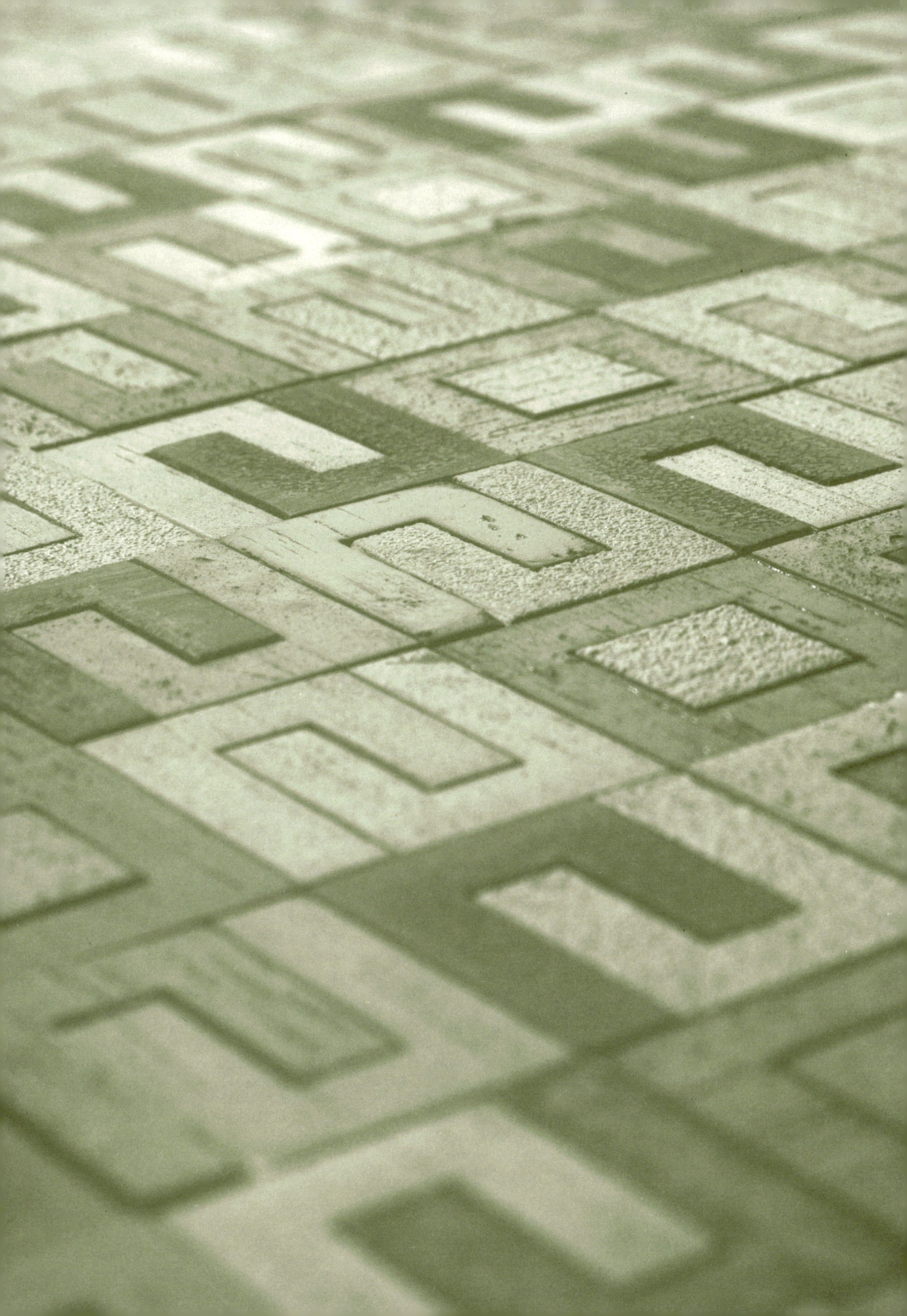

20 22: Art Biennials and Other Global Disasters

by Pedro Lasch

This publication is the concluding element of Pedro Lasch's contribution to Atis Rezistans and the Ghetto Biennale's participation in documenta fifteen. The project originated after the 1st Ghetto Biennale (2009) and has since taken shape through several iterations: *Art World Disaster* (2013) at AUB Byblos Bank Art Gallery; the contribution to *52 Weeks of Gulf Labor* (2013); *Islas de tragedia y fantasía* [Islands of Tragedy and Fantasy] (2015) at the Bienal de La Habana; *La plaga* (2021) at RƎEXISTENCIAS. Bienal de Arte y Descolonialidad; the *Painting Cycle* and online conversations *20 22 The Ongoing Biennial* (2021); and, finally, *20 22 The Common Wind* (2022), Lasch's intervention in documenta fifteen as part of the Atis Rezistans and Ghetto Biennale exhibition at St. Kunigundis Church in Kassel.

Esta publicación constituye el elemento final de la contribución de Pedro Lasch a la participación de Atis Rezistans y la Ghetto Biennale en documenta fifteen. El proyecto, iniciado después de la 1 Ghetto Biennale (2009), se ha desarrollado en distintas iteraciones: *Art World Disaster* [Arte Mundo Desastre] (2013) en AUB Byblos Bank Art Gallery; la contribución a *52 Weeks of Gulf Labor* [52 semanas de Gulf Labor] (2013); *Islas de tragedia y la fantasía* (2015) en la Bienal de La Habana; *La plaga* (2021) en RƎ-EXISTENCIAS. Bienal de Arte y Descolonialidad;

el Ciclo de pinturas y conversaciones en línea *20 22 The Ongoing Biennial* [20 22 La bienal en curso] (2021) y, finalmente, *20 22 The Common Wind* [20 22 El viento común] (2022), la intervención presentada en documenta fifteen en la iglesia de St. Kunigundis en Kassel.

Acknowledgements
Agradecimientos

This publication has been funded in part by Duke University's faculty research grants. The most recent collaborations with Atis Rezistans and Ghetto Biennale have been made possible by the generous support of the Mellon Foundation.

Esta publicación fue financiada en parte con fondos de investigación para profesores de Duke University. Las colaboraciones más recientes con Atis Rezistans y Ghetto Biennale fueron posibles gracias al generoso apoyo de la Mellon Foundation.

To all those who contributed to this publication, to the members of **Atis Rezistans**, **Ghetto Biennale**, **ruangrupa**, and to all participants in the works.

A todas las personas que contribuyeron a esta publicación, a los integrantes de Atis Rezistans, Ghetto Biennale, ruangrupa, y a todas y todos los participantes de las obras.

documenta fifteen: Cem A., Noor Abed, Lydia Antoniou, Sofia Asvestopoulos, Patrick Drücker, Thomas Engelbert, Gözde Filinta, Gertrude Flentge, Linda Gottwald, Ayşe Güleç, Frederikke Hansen, Feodora Heupel, Jonathan Hohmann, Roberta Huldisch, Chiara Ianaselli, Tyuki Imamura, Martin Jungermann, Lara Khaldi, Norgard Kröger, Olaf Lange, Jana Lepple, Andrea Linnenkohl, Nicola V. Manitta, Jasa McKenzie, Nancy Naser Al Deen, Baharak Omidfard, Marlies Peller, Torben Röse, Lea Sambale, Lisa-Maria Schaaf, Susanne Stein, Hito Steyerl, Jaroslava Tomanová, Robin Vehrs, Robert Hötzel and his students | y a sus estudiantes, RURU Kids & Sobat Sobat, who led the mirror mask workshops | quienes dirigieron los talleres de las máscaras de espejo.

Duke University & Ongoing Biennial Cycle: For its collaborations with Haiti in 2009 | Por sus colaboraciones con Haití en 2009; Michael Blair for their recording and video editing support | por la grabación y edición de video; Lou Bennett, Mingyong Cheng, Emma Geiger, Moriah LeFebvre, Emily MacDiarmid, Soozy Tierney for their production and research support | por su apoyo en producción e investigación; Anne Barlow, Laura Corey, Sylvie Fortin, Esther Gabara, Jon-Sesrie Goff, Valerie Hillings, Shambhavi Kaul, Ranjana Khanna, Miguel Rojas Sotelo, Pete Sigal, Nzinga Simmons, Gennifer Weisenfeld for their contributions to | por sus aportes a *The Ongoing Biennial Conversation Cycle*. Thanks also to Gracias también a Joaquín Barriendos, Fred Moten, Rafal Niemojewski &Virginia Roy.

Beirut & Gulf Labor: Amanda Abi Khalil, Haig Aivazian, Shaina Anand, Ayreen Anastas, Marwa Arsanios, Marco Baravalle, Scott Berzofsky, Doris Bittar, Paula Chakravarty, Nitasha Dhillon, Octavian Esanu, Noah Fisher, Rene Gabri, Mariam Ghani, Angela Harutyunyan, Amin Husain, Amal Issa, Emily Jacir, Cherine Karam, Collectif Kahraba, Kasper Kovitz, Naeem Mohaiemen, Walid Raad, Andrew Ross, Walid Sadek, Gregory Sholette, Ashok Sukumaran, Christine Tohme, Jalal Toufic, Anton Vidokle, Visualizing Palestine.

Bienal de La Habana: Tania Bruguera, Jorge Fernández, José Fernández, Dannys Montes de Oca Moreda, Raúl Moarquech Ferrera-Balanquet, Zusel Suárez Muñiz, Chemi Rosado-Seijo, Royce W. Smith, Andrea Valentina Bastidas.

RꓱEXISTENCIAS: Adolfo Albán Achinte, David Arteaga, Manuel Amaya, María Costanza Topica Clavijo, Jimena Guerrero Ramírez, Luis Felipe Palacio Guerrero and all performers | y a todos los performers.

Published by
Publicado por
Temblores Publicaciones on the occasion
of | con motivo de documenta fifteen

Edited by
Editado por
Jesús A. Villalobos Fuentes

Editorial design
Diseño editorial
Cristina Paoli · Periferia

Texts by
Textos de
Octavian Esanu
Pedro Lasch
Dannys Montes de Oca Moreda

Excerpts from conversations with
Fragmentos de conversaciones con
Hoor Al-Qasimi, Carolyn Christov-Bakargiev,
Andrea Giunta, Yuko Hasegawa, Rujeko
Hockley, Candice Hopkins, Miguel A. López,
Cuauhtémoc Medina, Gabi Ngcobo, Lucia
Pietroiusti, farid rakun (ruangrupa), José
Roca, Ralph Rugoff, Trevor Schoonmaker

Founder and Executive Director
Fundadora y directora ejecutiva
Dorothée Dupuis

Editorial Director
Director editorial
Jesús A. Villalobos Fuentes

Associate editor
Editora asociada
Vania Macias Osorno

Outreach Coordinator
Coordinadora de alcance
Camila Iriarte

Administration
Administración
Ana Rosella Arce

Editorial Team
Equipo editorial
Ana Isabel Garduño

English Translation
Traducción al inglés
Ellen Freeman

Spanish Translation
Traducción al español
Torrivilla / Ana Gabriela García /
Ricardo Malagón Borges

Copy Editing in Spanish
Corrección de estilo en español
Manuel Alejandro Ladino Rodríguez /
Giacomo Orozco

Copy Editing in English
Corrección de estilo en inglés
Ellen Freeman / Kimberly Kruge /
Tess Rankin

Interns
Pasantes
Andrés García Contreras / Mariel Atta
Delgado / Eduardo Cruz Ibarra / Diana
Hernández Estrada

All visual artwork, images, and photographic
records are authored and/or courtesy of the
artist unless otherwise indicated.
Todas las obras de arte visual, imágenes y reg-
istros fotográficos son autoría y/o cortesía de la
artista a menos de que se indique lo contrario.

ISBN: 978-607-26906-5-3

First edition, 2025
Primera edición, 2025

Printed and made in Mexico
Impreso y hecho en México

Distribution in Mexico and Latin America
Distribución en México y Latinoamérica
Temblores Publicaciones
info@temblores.mx
www.temblores.mx

**Distribution in the United States
of America and Canada**
Distribución en Estados Unidos
de América y Canadá
ARTBOOK I D.A.P.
75 Broad Street, Suite 630
New York, NY 10004
www.artbook.com

Distribution in Europe
Distribución en Europa
Les presses du réel
35 rue Colson, 21000 Dijon, France
info@lespressesdureel.com
www.lespressesdureel.com

Copyright © 2025 Temblores Publicaciones,
Dr. Rafael Lucio, 103-B12 2 Sagitario 1,
Colonia Doctores, Cuauhtémoc, 06720,
Mexico City | Ciudad de México, México
www.temblores.mx

Copyright © of the artworks |
de los trabajos artísticos
Pedro Lasch

Copyright © of texts | de los textos
The authors

Copyright © of translations |
de las traducciones
The translators

Copyright © of images | de las imágenes
The authors

Printed and bound in Mexico City in
December 2025, at the workshops of Artes
Gráficas Panorama. Typeset in Excelsior
and Sofia Pro, and it was printed on 120-
gram bond paper and 60-gram snow cream
paper. This edition is limited to 800 copies.
Impreso y encuadernado en la Ciudad de
México en diciembre de 2025, en los talleres
de Artes Gráficas Panorama. Se utilizaron las
tipografías Excelsior y Sofia Pro, se imprimió
sobre papel bond de 120 g y papel snow cream
de 60 g. Se tiraron 800 ejemplares.

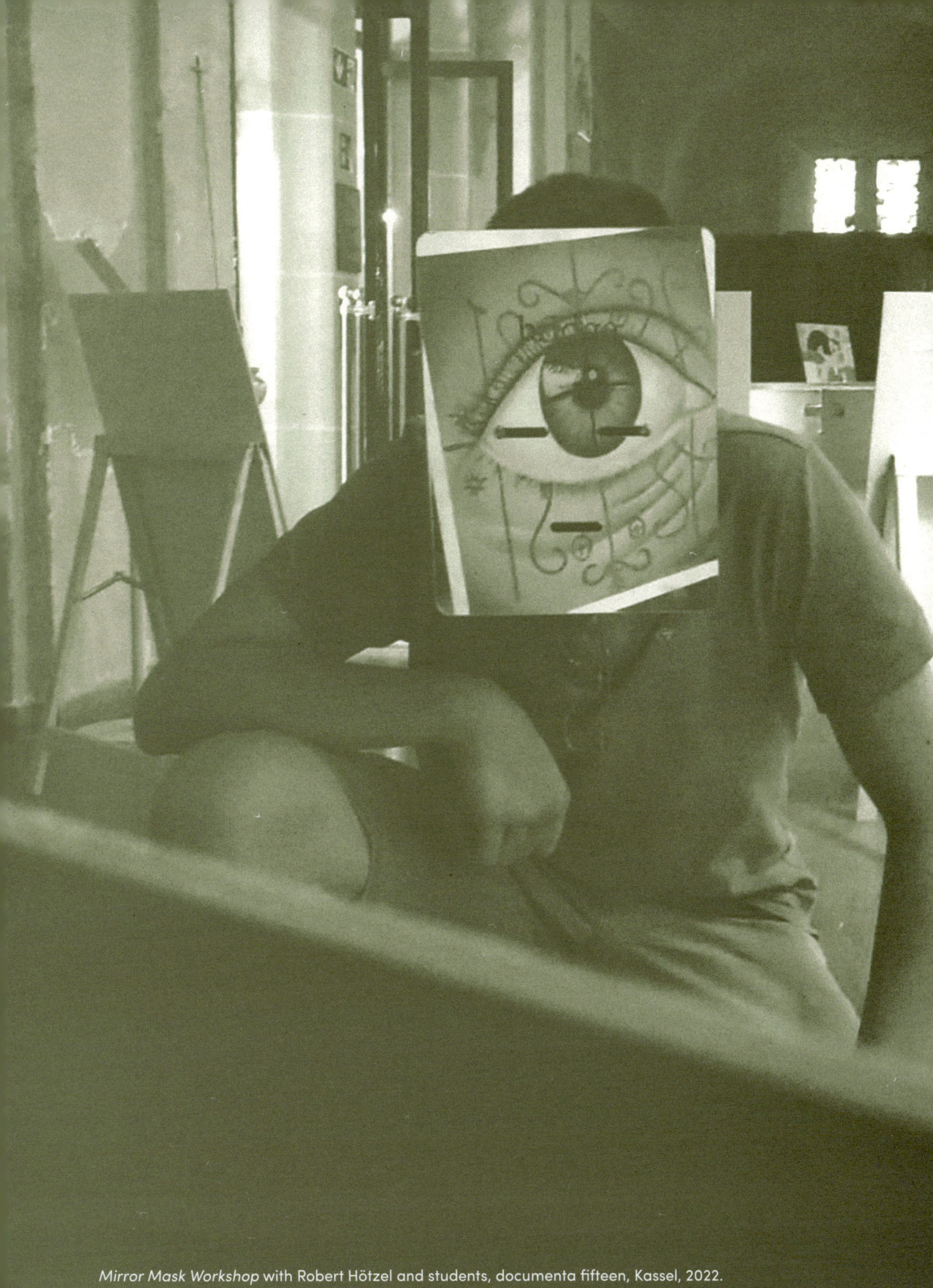

Mirror Mask Workshop with Robert Hötzel and students, documenta fifteen, Kassel, 2022.
Reflected in mask: Michel Lafleur, The Eye, 2000. Photography: Robin Lenartz

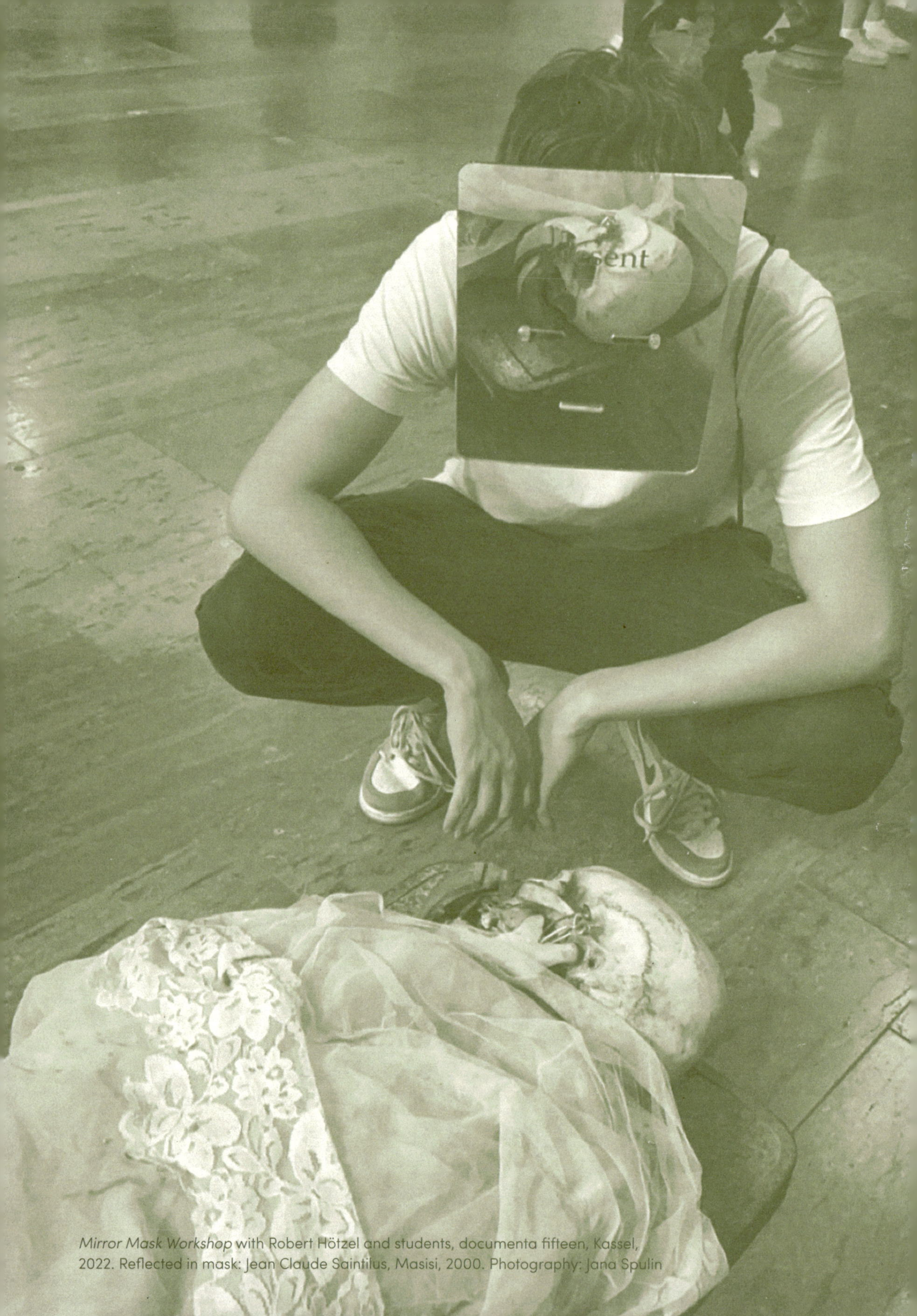

Mirror Mask Workshop with Robert Hötzel and students, documenta fifteen, Kassel, 2022. Reflected in mask: Jean Claude Saintilus, Masisi, 2000. Photography: Jana Spulin